Books by Dr. Robert R. Blake
and Dr. Jane Srygley Mouton:

CORPORATE EXCELLENCE THROUGH
GRID ORGANIZATION DEVELOPMENT

THE MANAGERIAL GRID

MANAGING INTERGROUP CONFLICT
IN INDUSTRY

CORPORATE DARWINISM

GROUP DYNAMICS—
KEY TO DECISION MAKING

A Systems Approach

*CORPORATE EXCELLENCE THROUGH
GRID ORGANIZATION DEVELOPMENT*

A Systems Approach

Corporate Excellence Through
GRID
ORGANIZATION
DEVELOPMENT

ROBERT R. BLAKE
President, Scientific Methods, Inc., Austin, Texas

JANE SRYGLEY MOUTON
Vice-President, Scientific Methods, Inc., Austin, Texas

GULF PUBLISHING COMPANY
HOUSTON, TEXAS

*CORPORATE EXCELLENCE THROUGH
GRID ORGANIZATION DEVELOPMENT*

*Copyright© 1968 by Gulf Publishing Company,
Houston, Texas*

Library of Congress Catalog Card Number 68-21510

Acknowledgments

Four kinds of contributions aided in writing this book. One has been by members of Scientific Methods, Inc., who have evaluated the book and made recommendations regarding its presentation. In addition to strengthening its technical content, R. Anthony Pearson and Barbara Peek Loftin have made important editorial contributions. Richard L. Sloma is responsible for certain case materials, particularly in Phases 2 and 3. Thomas V. Murto, Jr., Richard B. Palmer, O. Fred Peterson and J. Roy Richardson have tested the concepts against their field experiences with Grid Organization Development. Linda Green Bell was responsible for the quantitative research summarized here.

A second source of influence is from persons outside Scientific Methods, Inc. Either through their knowledge of Grid Organization Development from incompany applications or by studying the text, they have made important suggestions and recommendations. Included are: Zenas Block, Group Vice President, DCA Food Industries, Inc.; Richard T. Forrest, Director of Personnel, Lever Brothers Limited; John D. Gray, President, Omark Industries, Inc.; Chalmer K. Lyman, Director, Division of Personnel Management, United States Department of Agriculture, Forest Service; Herbert H. Meier, General Manager, Baytown Refinery, Humble Oil & Refining Company; G. Ross Murrell, Coordinator of Far East Refining, Esso Standard Eastern Inc.; Geoffrey R. Simmonds, President, Simmonds Precision; John R. Thamer, General Supervisor, Management Training & Development, The Bell Telephone Company of Canada; B. Frank White, Regional Commissioner, Internal Revenue Service; and A. T. Willis, Organization Development Coordinator, Lago Oil & Transport Company, Limited.

Clayton Umbach, Manager, Book Division, Gulf Publishing Company, has worked in the various stages of writing this book in ways that have significantly influenced its quality.

A third kind of contribution by individuals and by corporations is less direct but no less important. It is from experiments in

Grid Organization Development which have been conducted in many firms throughout the world. These experiments afforded an opportunity to evaluate strengths and limitations at various stages of evolution of the Grid Organization Development design and to weigh many issues that have emerged.

Testing the concepts and methods for their usefulness in international situations has been furthered through association with Eric Brightford, President, Scientific Methods (Australia) Pty. Ltd.; Jorge Chapiro, President, Chapiro y Asociados, Buenos Aires, Argentina; J. MacKenzie, Principal, Management Training Centre, and Anthony D. McCormick, Director, British-American Tobacco Company Limited, London, England; Allen Myra, President, PTStanvac (Indonesia); Toshio Tanaka, Manager, Public Activities Administration, and Ichiro Uyeno, Chairman of the Board, Institute of Business Administration and Management, Tokyo, Japan.

The references supplied are another source of contributions to the composition of the book. Those included are ones which assist the reader to examine documents that expand various facets of Grid Organization Development beyond the details provided in the text.

Robert R. Blake
Jane Srygley Mouton

Preface

The purpose of organization development is to achieve an excellent corporation. "Excellence" means the corporation is truly well managed and utilizes members most fully toward its productive aims.

Corporations and such other complex organizations as government agencies, educational institutions, and hospitals are the organisms of society. Through their activities, efforts are made to satisfy man's goals and aspirations. Operating an organization effectively to achieve corporate purpose of profit through the soundest utilization of human capacities is recognized as one of society's major problems. It is also one of society's great opportunities. Few organizations have as yet realized excellence. Most miss it by a wide margin. Many years of theory, development, research, and field experiments have culminated in this book, which describes a way to achieve excellence by changing a corporation from what it *is* to what it *should* be.

History provides many examples of ways managers have tried to improve organization effectiveness. Beginning with the industrial revolution, continuing with the emergence of scientific management, and up to today's application of sophisticated computer-based systems and simulation techniques, men have sought to control the operational variables thwarting success. On the dynamic side, the subject of human motivation has found fascination throughout recorded history, but with more real learning on this subject in the last fifty years than in the preceding 5,000. Until recently, however, these two areas of human exploration have not been integrated effectively. In fact, much of what has been developed down these two paths has produced conflict and often appears mutually exclusive. Grid Organization Development represents a unity of thought on which managers can find meaning, substance, and cohesiveness.

The roots of organization development lie in four major concepts. These are powerful ideas that are present in today's society. They already have had a great influence on the course of human affairs. They are discovery, education, correction, and prevention. *Discovery* is the first concept—that through the application of scientific methods, basic processes of nature can be brought under human control. *Education* is based on the idea that knowledge and skill can be acquired. One useful application is to increase mastery of the environment. *Correction* is one way of using knowledge to change or eliminate conditions that are barriers to effectiveness. *Prevention* is based on the concept that through the use of knowledge and skill, barriers which reduce effectiveness can be anticipated and avoided so that they do not become chronic. Organization development is not restricted to the use of any one of these concepts. It utilizes all in a planned and integrated manner in the pursuit of corporate excellence.

Most important, organization development utilizes *discovery* methods. Through use of critique, it provides for creativity, invention, and innovation, constantly searching its processes, performance, personnel, and products for relationships between cause and effect as a basis for new insight.

Heavy reliance is placed on *education*. Education can aid the organization's membership in learning about basic processes of motivation, communication, involvement, commitment, creativity, and confronting conflict. All of these are essential in enabling members of a corporation to concentrate their energies on fulfilling its objectives. Education also enables an organization's membership to investigate the business logic which is employed. Faulty or non-existent business logic can be replaced with sound strategies of business thinking for genuine financial accomplishment. Educational aspects aid those who run the business to utilize techniques of management science in effectively analyzing their existing problems and planning for the future.

Concepts of *correction* aid managers in diagnosing and curing maladies of attitude and performance. These can be eliminated only when their underlying causes are understood. Then conditions can be introduced that promote motivation.

Organization development provides the basis for valid communication and sound planning. Concepts of *prevention* are used to anticipate difficulties before they develop into chronic problems. When sound direction is achieved, opportunities can be created and seized as they emerge. This reduces the need for later correction of what otherwise would have been past mistakes. Management is the intelligent use of concepts of discovery, education, correction, and prevention in the pursuit of corporate excellence.

Because an organization is a complex organism of society, it is inevitable that organization development activities also will be complex. Grid Organization Development is a systems approach. It is multi-dimensional. Its unit of application is the corporate entity, not individuals. Many of the significant variables of organization are included, not just one or two. It deals with individual behavior, teamwork, intergroup relations in organization performance and functioning, and the organization's history, traditions, precedents, and past practices—the total corporate culture. It is multi-disciplinary. The knowledge and skills required have their origins in the disciplines of business logic and management science and in the behavioral sciences of psychology, sociology, cultural anthropology, institutional economics, and political science. It is multi-phasic. The massive effort essential for achieving corporate excellence cannot be made all at once. Specific steps toward excellence must be taken and consolidated before other steps can be taken. Being a systems approach, Grid Organization Development integrates the complex variables of organization with one another within the framework of the whole. This is in contrast with approaches that deal with subsystems as though they were mutually exclusive or deal with parts on a piecemeal basis. Fundamentals must be understood before advanced concepts are meaningful. Organization development is a step by step process and moves from one level of application and development up to another. It is neither static nor fixed in a series of prescribed mechanical steps. Because it is dynamic, education and application are followed by more education at a new and higher level and more complex opportunities of application. The order of phases also has the advantage of a cumulative impact. Achievements at one level open up new opportunities for application at another. If organization development is complex, it is also a total and inclusive strategy for achieving corporate excellence. The six-phase approach is designed to bring a corporation to the highest stage of excellence attainable in the light of today's knowledge. Activities of consolidation, strengthening, refinement, and putting new knowledge to work as it emerges continue thereafter, for development is a never ending affair.

Although organization development is complex in its entirety, the concepts at its foundation and the methods of its execution are not. They are simple because they are fundamental. The orderly arrangements that lead to excellence through the series of phases contribute further to its simplicity because one sequence of steps is taken and completed before another series is begun.

This description of organization development is based on many research and field experiments extending over the past 20 years. Five initial experiments were conducted, each in a different autonomous segment of one international company. From what was learned in the first experiment, the basic pattern of organization development was varied and enriched and in the second experiment was tested, evaluated, and corrected again. The third, fourth, and fifth applications provided a basis for strengthening and refinement. Once the pattern of organization development had been perfected, it was applied in a variety of corporations, government agencies, and other complex organizations. Thus, its usefulness in the achievement of corporate excellence by organizations of varying sizes and complexity and engaged in widely different pursuits has been evaluated. The next major step was its application in the development of business institutions operating in South America, Europe, Australia, and Asia. The insights gained are included in this book and offer much promise for the acceleration of corporate development in emerging nations.

The concepts on which organization development rests appear to be fundamental. They have relevance for integrating effectiveness wherever men are engaged in the organized pursuit of objectives.

This book is written for those actively engaged in pursuing corporate excellence through organization development. Its purpose is to provide background and a framework for understanding the rationale and methods of development, phase by phase. Case studies illustrating the kinds of situations encountered are provided for insight into the concepts, strategies, tactics, and consequences of each major aspect of organization development. This book also provides perspective for students of organizations, whether they are employed in business and industry or government or investigating problems of organization effectiveness in a college or graduate school.

Robert R. Blake
Jane Srygley Mouton

AUSTIN, TEXAS
FEBRUARY, 1968

Contents

CORPORATE EXCELLENCE THROUGH
GRID ORGANIZATION DEVELOPMENT

A Systems Approach

1

A MODEL FOR CORPORATE
EXCELLENCE

Corporations in a free enterprise business society face no choice but continually to increase their effectiveness. Only recently an executive vice president of a large corporation remarked, "The *pace* has changed. Things will never be like they were. The rate of acceleration has shifted. In today's market conditions, we figure our company has to grow at a rate of nine percent a year to avoid being overtaken, and we are not interested in just staying even. We intend to be livelier than that!"

Corporations that do not recognize this tend to stand still, to checkmate themselves, or even worse to fall farther behind. Over the long haul they are outstripped and toppled by those who have made themselves strong and energetic, capable of sustaining or increasing their competitive advantage. It becomes imperative for a corporation to retain its continuity and enlarge its capacity for business effectiveness as it moves into the future. Through achieving corporate excellence a company can do so.

Not all corporations are geared to excellence. A corporation usually approaches the future in one of three ways. One is to keep on with what it is doing in its characteristic manner. The assumption is that because it has performed fairly well or even very well in the past, it has not gone far wrong and the safest way to proceed is to keep on repeating the pattern. This way avoids possible pitfalls of experimentation. As long as competition is not keen, it promises progress. It could on the other hand

1

be an ostrich-like approach preventing perception of the future in a clear eyed way.

A second option is to embrace the idea of improving with an eclectic, short term, every-day-in-every-way-we-try-to-do-better approach. This attitude keeps corporation members searching for refinements. It can contribute much toward gradual improvement but always within the narrow limits of the *status quo*.

A third corridor into the future is to reach beyond the present by designing and implementing a strategic model for corporate excellence. The picture must be well conceived and valid when tested against the most rigorous criteria of business logic. When such a model is understood, agreed with, and embraced from top to bottom throughout an organization, its members can take action to overcome discrepancies that exist between how the enterprise *should be* managed to excel and how it *is* being operated.

Grid Organization Development is an approach to achieving an ideal of corporate excellence to strive toward and to perfecting a sound system of management which can convert striving into execution.

CORPORATE EXCELLENCE

What is meant by "corporate excellence"? Is there a giant yardstick to measure each corporation to determine whether or not it is "excellent"? Are there criteria to apply to the large and small, to the simple and complex?

An excellent corporation is able to achieve and sustain an outstandingly high return on investment over long periods of time.[1] Its managers have learned how to identify and create new opportunities while meeting present responsibilities. They plan for the future in the face of stiffening competition and rising costs. The excellent corporation unceasingly strives to increase the competence of its managers to manage and its employees to produce. There is upgrading in the sophistication of technological aspects of marketing, production, and research and development. The concept of synergy is understood and exploited. Excellence involves the enrichment of the capacities of members of the corporation for using facts and data as the basis for thinking and analyzing and for finding quick and valid solutions to the inevitable parade of problems of operational life.

The aim in an excellent corporation is to insure that its members apply their unbounded energies in a self-committed and enthusiastic way to contribute to reaching difficult but challenging corporate objectives.

BARRIERS TO CORPORATE EXCELLENCE

Many executives agree that top priority should be assigned to attaining corporate excellence. Yet they also acknowledge that their corporations have not come close to achieving it. Why has progress not been far more rapid in closing the gap? Only through a valid answer to this question is it likely that barriers to business effectiveness can be eliminated and excellence achieved. The common barriers to business effectiveness as identified by managers are shown in Box 1.

The foremost barrier to corporate excellence is communication, the next greatest is planning. This is true whether the company operates in the United States, Great Britain, Japan, or elsewhere.[2] While other problem areas vary in importance and reveal interesting differences between countries, none approach these two as such significant barriers to corporate effectiveness.

Communication

What is meant when communication is identified as the number one problem? Here are illustrations of what managers say.

"People work in their little niches as though they had blinders on. They don't talk with one another enough to see what needs to be connected."

"The word is so filtered by the time it gets up to me that I have no idea what's going on with the troops."

"If you really want to know what's going on in the company, ask your wife. Even better than that, the elevator operators man the real message center. It comes through them faster than it goes down the pipeline."

"Management thinks we are union baboons and are trying to steal the front gate."

"The union doesn't understand we have to make money to stay in business. They think the old man is Simon Legree with dollar signs etched on the gold buttons of his blazer."

"Don't ask me how the company is going. I've not been told."

Are these problems of communication? Absolutely. Achieving

Box 1
Communication and Planning Are the Two Foremost Barriers to Corporate Excellence

Barriers to Effectiveness	Percent of companies in which this is identified as one of seven key barriers		
	United States	Great Britain	Japan
1. Communication	74.24	63.63	84.84
2. Planning	62.12	63.63	65.15
3. Morale	45.45	45.45	46.96
4. Coordination	45.45	22.72	31.81
5. Critique	42.42	28.78	33.33
6. Commitment	39.39	45.45	21.21
7. Control	33.33	28.78	35.29
8. Profit consciousness	31.81	36.36	31.81
9. Creativity	25.75	45.45	48.48
10. Getting results	21.21	30.30	45.45

Managers from 198 companies, 66 each in the United States, Great Britain, and Japan representing a wide variety of businesses provided these data. Corporations from the three countries were matched with one another by nature of the business and corporate size. Managers were matched by responsibility and level in the firms. They identified corporate areas regarded as the most significant barriers to be overcome in achieving excellence in their own corporations. While barriers beyond the first two vary in importance, the first two are the same regardless of country, company, or characteristics of the managers reporting.

understanding and overcoming misunderstandings are widespread and pervasive difficulties of modern corporate life. But from another point of view, they are *not* communication problems. They are symptoms of a far deeper and more significant cause. The likelihood is that the effort to communicate could be doubled by spreading the word—out, up, down, and sideways.

The result very often is a multiplication of misunderstanding rather than an increase in understanding. If communication is not the obstacle, what is it?

The underlying causes of communication difficulties are to be found in the character of supervision. Effective management includes sound relationships between boss and subordinates, within work teams, and between divisions of the corporation. When these are carried out within a work-oriented culture which provides the basis for clear objectives that arouse full commitment, close cooperation, and quick response, it is unlikely that problems of communication would arise or keep recurring. The solution to the problem of communication is for men to manage by achieving production and excellence through sound utilization of people.

For a manager to manage himself as well as to supervise others in a sound way, he must make explicit use of theories of behavior. For example, imagine that one man, no matter how technically competent, is supervising another. If he has little knowledge of what really makes men tick, less than a precise sense of why men act as they do, only a vague awareness of what motivates others, will he be able to get excellent results? A chief executive who had climbed the technical ladder to the top position of corporate leadership once said, "The only thing wrong with people is that they don't have meters on their foreheads. I have no way of knowing how much steam is built up inside them. I can't see whether they are on or off, whether they feel any pressure at all or are about to blow up." Can such a man be expected to lead others by carrying complex deliberations to a sound conclusion, by gaining their involvement and commitment to corporate results, by developing others to take on heavier responsibilities?

Multiply this example by the variety of obstacles that exist in boss-subordinate teamwork and interdivisional coordination. The product is a small indication of the depth and severity of communication blockages existing throughout corporations today.

Use of behavior theory as a basis for integrating people into the productive and profit objectives of a firm is an essential in mobilizing human resources. Managers are not really managing behavior in most corporations today. They may be driving it, criticizing it, monitoring it, tolerating it, accepting it, or buying it. Only rarely are they really leading it. Many are going along

with mediocrity, not because they like it but because they cannot
see how to motivate others to thorough, problem-solving excellence. They concede to the unpleasant realities, not because they
like them, but because they fear the resistance to change and resulting criticism were they to try to alter them. They consent to
the idea of a half loaf in preference to none because a half loaf
is better than none, not because they prefer a half to a whole loaf.

Behavior theory has demonstrated its usefulness for solving
problems of communication. It provides a strong foundation
which makes possible sound human interaction in the pursuit
of organization goals. Use of behavior theory to achieve results in an excellent corporation can no longer be regarded as
a luxury. It is an urgent necessity. It is a key to the untapped
reservoir of human energy which must be utilized if a corporation is to increase its operational effectiveness.

Planning

The second most widespread barrier to business effectiveness, as reported in over 60 percent of companies in the United
States, Great Britain, and Japan, is planning. "Planning" means
designing and implementing programs of operational effort which
insure that anticipated results will be achieved. What do managers mean when they say planning is their number two problem? Here is what they say.

"How in the devil can you plan around here? You can't plan
crises. It's all I can do to put out the fires, the big ones, that is."

"What do you mean, a plan? We don't have plans. All we
have is pressure for results."

"Everything is planned, down to the smallest detail. We plan
to the point where flexibility is completely sacrificed. People
have learned — don't challenge it, just do it. As a result, we
turn out great reports, but profitability is on a gradually de-
clining slope."

As communication is seen as a symptom rather than the real
problem, planning also is seen as a symptom of a deeper
difficulty. Planning problems are but surface indications. They
reflect barriers to effectiveness rather than causing ineffectiveness. Just working harder at planning or being more precise
about it or taking more variables into consideration will no more
solve the planning problem than working diligently at spreading

the word will solve the problem of communication. The deeper cause of planning difficulties is an absence of business strategy or the use of a strategy which is based upon faulty business logic.

There are several orientations of business logic which are important to achieving corporate excellence. One is having clear financial objectives, preferably expressed in terms of return on investment. This involves a thoroughly thought-out minimum rate and amount of return on investment which is acceptable as a basis for continuing any line of business activity. It includes a definition of optimal rate and amount of return to be sought as the corporate objective. An ideal strategy contains clear-cut descriptions of the nature of the business or businesses that a company has committed itself to pursuing. The market it intends to penetrate is well defined and analyzed, not only for present customer potential but also for future prospects as well. A strategic model provides specifications for how the organization structure should be arranged for the soundest integration of effort. It contains a statement of twenty-five to thirty major policies which systematically express logical foundations that serve as guidelines for decision and action. Finally, the ideal strategic model identifies development requirements that those employed by the corporation can strive toward and that serve as the basis for corporate development.

Conditions for sound planning have been created when these properties of an ideal strategic model have been clearly thought out and concisely expressed and when they are understood throughout the organization. Corporate members know where the company is headed. Planning provides the maps showing the routes for getting there. This kind of fundamental solution to planning problems comes only when those who lead the firm have designed and implemented an ideal strategic model for corporate operations. An objective of Grid Organization Development is to solve problems of planning by implementing a strategic corporate model based on business logic.

Many if not all of the remaining problems shown in Box 1 appear to be consequences of difficulties stemming from faulty behavior theory or business logic.

Neither communication nor planning exist in isolation. Each contributes either to exaggerate or to reduce difficulties in the other. Effectiveness in work relationships contributes directly to strengthening the organization's capacity to design an ideal strategic model and to implement plans for achieving it. An ideal strategic model contributes directly to reducing problems of communication. The effect is not additive. It is synergistic; that is, members work together in a cooperative way so that the total effect is greater than the sum of the separate parts acting independently. Effective corporate members operating under sound corporate strategy may gain the strength essential for achieving a truly excellent corporation.

SIX PHASES OF GRID ORGANIZATION DEVELOPMENT

Barriers to corporate excellence are not difficult to identify. Doing something about them is another matter. The changes required are fundamental. Managers must perfect their ways of managing. The corporation has to perfect its strategies of doing business.[3]

The six phases of Grid Organization Development are designed to bring about fundamental changes, as shown in Box 2.

The first three phases are designed to solve problems of communication that are embedded in three vital elements of corporate culture: individuals, work teams, and intergroup relationships. Phase 1, the Grid Seminar, contributes to this objective through providing each member of the corporation with theories of management. These theories serve as a basis for sorting out causes of communication problems and designing individual corrective actions for them. Phase 2, Teamwork Development, extends the applications of the theories to solving communication problems embedded in the work team culture. Teamwork Development takes place among those members who work and interact daily and who must understand and agree with one another as to their purposes, objectives, and plans of action for achieving results. Phase 3, concerned with Intergroup Development, expands the application of these theories. They are used to increase the coordination of effort between organized units that have shared responsibility for achieving corporate goals. The first three phases of Grid Organization Development, which strengthen corporate culture in these ways, are designed primarily to remove obstacles to corporate effectiveness that are found in the processes of human communication. Even without moving into the last three phases of Grid Organization Development, a company can anticipate significant organization benefits.

Box 2
*How the Six Phases of Grid Organization
Development Contribute to Corporate Excellence*

Communication

1. *Grid Seminar*
Organization members learn theories of behavior on a one-by-one basis.

2. *Teamwork Development*
Work teams apply Grid theories to increase their effectiveness.

3. *Intergroup Development*
Organized units that must cooperate to achieve results apply Grid theories to increase effectiveness with which they coordinate effort.

Planning

4. *Developing an Ideal Strategic Model*
Executive leaders specify in terms of business logic the intellectual foundations of the firm.

5. *Planning and Implementation*
For each definable business segment, planning teams use management science and technology to design and the line organization to change its operations by implementing the operational specifications for each business segment.

6. *Systematic Critique*
The total effort is evaluated in order to review and consolidate progress made and to plan next steps of development.

The next two phases deal with problems of planning. In Phase 4, Ideal Strategic Model Development, a sound corporation based on pure business logic is contrasted with the strategies being applied in the conduct of the business. With the clear statement of an ideal strategic corporate model, it becomes possible in Phase 5 to plan against specified return on investment and dollar-volume objectives. Management science and technology are applied to design and execute the operational specifications of each definable business segment. These two phases make it possible for corporations to eliminate barriers which have their origins in faulty business practices. Phase 6, Systematic Critique, strengthens the corporate culture, refines the strategic model, sharpens the tactics by which the model is implemented, and identifies next steps of development.

While these six phases represent an orderly and logical sequence, they should not be regarded as mechanical. Dynamic organization development results when executive leadership completes Phases 1 and 2, then proceeds into Phase 4. The remainder of the organization moves through the phases according to the requirements of the total situation. All phases are indispensable to achieving corporate excellence, but rate, tempo, sequence, and specific points of application vary with the particular situation confronting the corporation. This order of phases is natural but not inevitable. It is natural in that the insight into personal behavior that a person gains in Phase 1 is a foundation for using it on the job or in Phase 2, Teamwork Development. Only when team effectiveness has been improved in Phase 2 is it logical to turn to Phase 3, Intergroup Development, to strengthen working relationships with other teams. Once the communication side of the problems of corporate excellence has been mastered, the planning side can be dealt with. The ideal strategic corporate model, Phase 4, comes before operational planning because it makes available a framework of business logic through which the vigorous planning and implementation activities of Phase 5 can take place. Systematic critique is a culminating step tying together and strengthening the whole as a unit and providing a basis for planning next steps. Any approach that treats development in a mechanical way can simply become another program. Approached in dynamic terms, Grid Organization Development provides a sound and fundamental way to achieve corporate excellence.[4]

SUMMARY

To achieve corporate excellence, the two critical barriers—communication and planning—most widely present in corporations must be constructively eliminated. When managers apply theories of behavior for sound communication among those who work to reach organization goals and when the business logic on which corporate effort rests is valid and clear, excellence is an almost inevitable result. Grid Organization Development, involving six phases of discovery, education, correction, and prevention, is designed to enable a corporation to strengthen its processes of communication and to increase its effectiveness in planning. It is a dynamic solution to dynamic problems of corporate life.

REFERENCES

1. As used throughout this book, "return on investment" conveys the concept of return on assets employed including outside financing. This concept of return on investment is an index of the effectiveness with which a corporation employs the assets available to it. The way in which this measurement is applied must be defined concretely to fit the requirement of a particular corporation. Service corporations and non-industrial organizations, such as government organizations, do not have such an index but often do have or can develop quantitative indexes that are equally useful for measuring organization achievement.

2. Data from these three countries are used for comparison purposes throughout the book. Data available from companies in other countries including Europe, Australia, the Middle East, and North and South America yield comparable findings. Except as otherwise indicated, all of the research data and field reports represent original work conducted in connection with Grid Organization Development activities and have not been published previously.

3. Grid Organization Development has also proved equally applicable for government agencies. Having as its major concern the problems of integrating people into production, Grid Organization Development has confronted many government agencies with thinking through more clearly what their production objectives are and the manner in which people are integrated into them. For this reason Grid Organization Development, with industrial instruments, has been applied in government agencies without modification.

4. *The Pyramid Theory for Achieving Corporate Excellence*, Chapter 14, amplifies general issues discussed in this chapter. The reader may wish to consult it as a next step.

2

THE GRID: BEHAVIORAL SCIENCE THEORIES FOR ACHIEVING PRODUCTION THROUGH PEOPLE

Agreement results when men reach a true meeting of minds. Then there are no communication problems. Misunderstandings and conflicting points of view no longer are barriers to communication. If agreements reached are valid in the light of known facts, actions taken will in all likelihood yield sound solutions. The human skills required for attaining such agreements are of a high order.

Problems of communication arise when for some reason agreement is not reached, as shown in Box 3. Loggerhead disagreement stands out as an extreme example of the breakdown of communication because it is so obvious. Disagreement may be present even though it is less visible when conditions of candor and forthright communication are absent. For example, agreement made with tongue in cheek is only disagreement disguised. Going along to avoid expressing differences in points of view is little more than a cover. Moving halfway by

Box 3

*Communication Problems Result from Lack of Skill
in Achieving a Meeting of Minds*

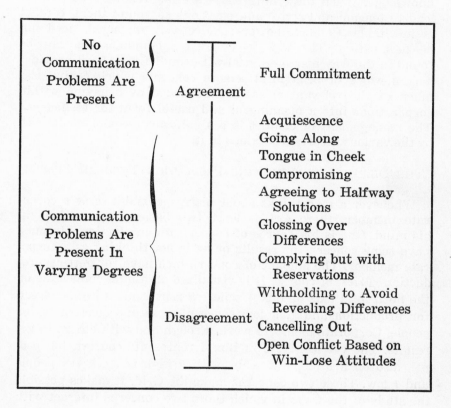

No
Communication
Problems Are
Present

Agreement

Full Commitment

Acquiescence
Going Along
Tongue in Cheek
Compromising
Agreeing to Halfway
    Solutions
Glossing Over
    Differences
Complying but with
    Reservations
Withholding to Avoid
    Revealing Differences

Communication
Problems Are
Present In
Varying Degrees

Disagreement

Cancelling Out
Open Conflict Based on
    Win-Lose Attitudes

finding a convenient compromise that permits differences to
be set aside is the same thing. Avoiding matters that would produce disagreement for the sake of harmony is a sham. Learning to achieve full, committed agreement—sound agreement
that is without reservation—is at the core of effective management.

What is the significance of face-to-face communication among
men as they talk with one another in conducting the business of
the corporation? Many opportunities for different points of view
arise when men debate possible solutions to their problems.

Disagreements can stem from differences in opinions, attitudes, apparent facts, views and perspectives, convictions, values, vested interests, background, experience, technological skill and knowledge. When these differences are not readily resolved but lead to tension and strife and emotions surround them, conflict is inevitable. Conflict, however, effectively managed, need not be destructive. The key to effective communication can be found in the way managers deal with conflict. The Grid provides a framework of behavioral science concepts which compresses much of the relevant scientific knowledge of behavior within corporations into a meaningful and useful form for managers.[1] The management of conflict is a significant element dealt with by the various theories contained in it.

The Dilemma of Achieving Production Through People

Whenever a man thinks about his responsibilities as a corporate member, there are at least two basic considerations in his mind. One is his degree of concern for production. He must have some concern for results or he is not thinking as a corporate member. The amount of concern men have for getting production varies, of course. It is visualized on a nine-point scale on the horizontal axis of Box 4, where *9* represents a high concern for production and *1*, a low concern. A second concern is for people. Corporate members work through and with others to get results. The vertical scale in Box 4 represents concern for people, also on a nine-point scale, with *9* high concern for people and *1* low. These two concerns make the Grid. It makes possible the study of the ways in which those two concerns interact with one another. The points of intersection represent theories— ways of thinking about resolving dilemmas of achieving production through people. Within the Grid framework, 81 different positions can be identified, but because of their importance, 13 different theories are emphasized. Five theories are clean-cut and straightforward. The remaining are combinations. Once the theories are identified and described, people recognize them. They can see the operation of these theories in the way their bosses, colleagues, subordinates, and they themselves think and act. These theories provide a solid basis for understanding the available alternatives.

Box 4

The Grid

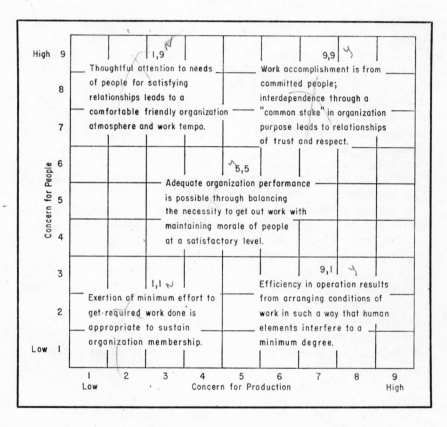

High 9   1,9

Thoughtful attention to needs of people for satisfying relationships leads to a comfortable friendly organization atmosphere and work tempo.

9,9

Work accomplishment is from committed people; interdependence through a "common stake" in organization purpose leads to relationships of trust and respect.

5,5

Adequate organization performance is possible through balancing the necessity to get out work with maintaining morale of people at a satisfactory level.

1,1

Exertion of minimum effort to get required work done is appropriate to sustain organization membership.

9,1

Efficiency in operation results from arranging conditions of work in such a way that human elements interfere to a minimum degree.

Concern for People

Low — Concern for Production — High

Whether or not he knows the Grid, a man applies one of these theories or combinations of them every time he speaks with his boss, his colleagues, or his subordinates—every time he acts as a corporate member. At the time he may, of course, be unaware of this; his actions may be so habitual that they have become "second nature" occurring without a moment's thought on his part. A major goal for a man in learning the Grid is to clarify for himself the theories he has been using as contrasted with other theories that might provide a sounder and stronger basis for his actions. This enables him to test his natural inclinations against behavioral science findings. He then has a solid foundation for revising the ways he learned in childhood, in academic life, and through his on-the-job learning experiences, or the attitudes he has accepted from the culture of the corporation. He can use this knowledge as the basis for increasing his strength as a man dealing with other men. He can use it to improve his effectiveness and achieve more positive results. He can use it to increase the personal gratification received by those with whom he works. When everyone in a corporation has an understanding of the behavioral science underpinnings of management, an organization has the foundation on which to build excellence.

Theories defined by the Grid encompass a wide range of managerial issues, such as the way in which a man goes about planning, directing, controlling, resolving conflict, releasing creativity, stimulating commitment, motivating teamwork, and so on. The effective management of conflict is one of the most significant issues in unleashing energies and establishing sound communication in an organization. The following synopsis touches on conflict, one of the issues of management that are treated fully in *The Managerial Grid* book. Since the Grid book is based upon the work of more than 500 behavioral science authors, the following synopsis provides a sample of the richness of available behavioral science findings as they relate to effectiveness.

There are many possible ways of discussing conflict and approaches to resolving it. One basic question is, "How can conflict be avoided?" A second is, "Once conflict is present, how can it be reduced or eliminated with the energy channeled into constructive problem solving?"

CONFLICT UNDER THE 9,1 THEORY

The 9,1 position on the Grid represents the thinking of a man who has a high concern for production and a low concern for people. Many operate with this theory at the core of their thinking. How would a man operating under a 9,1 style deal with the two questions?

Avoiding Conflict

A man thinking in a 9,1 way is intolerant of conflict. Through clear-cut strategies to prevent it, he tries to insure that it will not arise. His most characteristic approach is likely to be to give crystal clear instructions in an ironclad way so as to leave no room for misunderstandings, no loopholes. He tells his subordinate what he wants, repeats it, and then for good measure, nails it down again. If he asks, "Do you have a question?" he does not really expect an answer. His reason for asking it is to be able to say later to the subordinate, should he fail to deliver, "Look, I asked and you said you understood. What is your excuse for failing?"

The boss who thinks in a 9,1 way avoids conflict by telling and retelling at least twice. What the subordinate may think, whether he thinks what he has been told is the best way or whether he thinks at all, is beside the point. All his boss wants is that the subordinate do what he is told in the way he is told to do it. Understanding and agreement, he has been told, is irrelevant; compliance is what is expected. When the subordinate takes this, the boss thinks he has no communication problem. But he does!

Managing Conflict

In spite of the boss's efforts to avoid it in this directive manner, sometimes conflict does arise. For example, the boss calls in a subordinate and says, "Look, Joe, I have a problem here. I want you to get on it right away and do this. This is what you are to do. Got it? This way!" Joe says, "But look, boss, that is not the way to handle it. There is a better way, like this." Though perhaps irritated by this impertinence, the boss has been told that "good human relations" must be practiced around this organization, so he listens impatiently until he can stand it no longer, then says, "Yeah, Joe, but you do it the way I said." And Joe says, "But hell, boss, *that* will not give you what you want." Now the boss realizes he has a communication problem. How does he overcome it? He says, "Look, Joe, I told you what I want, and I want it, and I want it now. Go do it! And furthermore, when you get it done, I want you to go to the Training Department. Sign up for that course in listening. I'm going to follow your progress and you'd better make a good score. If you don't, either you go or we get rid of the Training Department." Joe knows to do it or else! He gives a mental salute.

There was disagreement and conflict in the situation. Now the conflict is gone. There is "agreement." That is managing conflict by the method of *suppression*. It is a direct use of power and authority to get a result. It is a fast way. Time? Not much wasted because it does not take much of it. But it does have limitations. One result that suppression produces is frustration, and frustration is a dangerous human emotion. It does not obey the laws of gravity. It does not roll off and disappear but has its own rules of discharge. The most primitive method of discharge is aggression. The straightest path of aggression is to eliminate the source of frustration. If the subordinate in the example were to "do what comes naturally," he would bang the boss in the head. The frustration would be gone. He would feel a sense of relief. For he "really gave it to him, but good!"

Aggression as a solution to frustration is not widely used in modern society. It is just not an available solution. But frustration *is* present, and it still must find avenues of release and does. For example, a person managed in this manner may begin to think creatively. His creativity is of an opposite kind than what organizations want, however. For the subordinate is asking himself, "How can I get him without being caught?" That is anti-organization creativity. The subordinate's goal is to foul up the operation by preventing it from working yet not to be observed doing so. He can "get" his boss this way, but the boss cannot get him. Under these circumstances, communication goes underground, and the boss only discovers the cause of problems after the fact if at all. Organizational cultures provide many examples of sabotage that arise from the tensions associated with 9,1 management.

Another consequence of suppression is its effect on commitment. Every company *wants* dedication and commitment from its members—executives, managers, supervisors, and workers alike. A 9,1 approach generates commitment, but too often in an anti-organizational direction. Frustrated men under these conditions turn to one another, saying, "Look, we haven't got any brains! If we did we wouldn't stand for this treatment! We should stand shoulder to shoulder and demand better treatment. We ought to join together and gain the strength to resist what is arbitrary and unfair!" By no means is frustration from 9,1 supervision the only reason men join unions, but it is certainly one important contributor. This reaction comes from technical personnel as well as hourly paid employees. It also is the reason that many a good, high ranking manager has either done a mental walkout, saying, "To hell with it," or a physical walkout, finding himself other employment.

These are some of the consequences of management of conflict by a 9,1 method.

CONFLICT UNDER THE 1,9 APPROACH

At the 1,9 position, there is a joining of low concern for production with a high concern for people. It is just the opposite in theory from 9,1. How might the 1,9 approach try to avoid conflict or when it does arise, try to make it go away?

Avoiding Conflict

The manager thinking in a 1,9 way says to himself, "I am the boss and he is the subordinate. But I want him to accept me. It makes me uneasy when I see others don't like me. The way to harmony is to keep him from being under pressure by encouraging him and letting him know he has my trust and confidence. Then we can feel friendly toward one another. I reassure myself that he is a good man. I know he wants to help and do what is best. So we talk. I ask him what he wants and what I can do for him that might be helpful."

This 1,9 attitude does avoid conflict. Unfortunately, the expense of this kind of harmony is loss of production, loss of "hard" thinking, and loss of real commitment to the job. It may promote boss-subordinate warmth, but neither customers nor stockholders nor corporate members themselves are prepared to buy warmth. For them, worth is more important!

Managing Conflict

Sometimes production pressure literally cannot be avoided. Then the manager who operates in a 1,9 way might invite his subordinate in and say, "Look, we have a little situation. The boss was by and I am embarrassed to have to interrupt you because I know you are busy. I'm afraid you are not going to like it too much, but I do think that we need to look at this . . ."

The subordinate might start to talk back a little, but he also might know that his boss becomes very anxious when someone disagrees with him. The boss might even start to smooth over differences in his attempt to make it appear that "everything is sweetness and light."

There are many ways to smooth over conflict. One is to get the subordinate to see how good things are as compared to how bad they might be. "It is a wonderful company! We have many fine things. We have an excellent retirement program, other benefits, and security. Let's not be unhappy with one another about this thing. It is not really very important. Every cloud has a silver lining. In every day in every way we *are* getting better and better, don't you think? So count your many blessings! Let us name them one by one, together! Things will work out." It is pretty hard for a man to be unpleasant when his boss smooths over the difference and invites him so earnestly to be nice. He accepts whatever the little pressure is and does the job, even though he may not agree with it, in the name of harmony with his boss and his own peace of mind. Under this approach a man doesn't feel suppressed, he feels smothered—with molasses. The cozy, calm, and caressing culture that results leads unfortunately to a state of peaceful coexistence. People get along, but without candor and with even less character. Because there are no sharp clashes, communication is smooth, but real problems that merit genuine discussion are not talked about.

This approach, of course, stifles creativity. Neither bosses nor subordinates can think in a sharp and clear way when they are being coddled and cajoled. Yet it is a theory that puts almost everyone in a comfortable state of mind and keeps alive a feeling of harmony. Yet the sacrifice in sound thinking and problem solving and in lost productivity can be unbelievable!

CONFLICT IN THE 1,1 CORNER

A low interest in production in the 1,1 approach is coupled with an equally low interest in people. How does a man who is thinking in a 1,1 way deal with the two problems introduced earlier—avoiding conflict, or when it is unavoidable, "managing" it?

Avoiding Conflict

A man operating with a 1,1 approach might say to himself, "The way to stay in this company and out of trouble is to be visible but not be seen. Retain neutrality in the face of conflict. To do that you've got to sacrifice the luxury of 'shooting off your mouth.' Listen, appear interested, but when you grunt, make the grunt neutral. Then those who look for your support in a positive direction will think you agree. Those wanting it in a negative direction will think you agree with them too. Or even better, in the loud clatter perhaps no one will even hear your grunt or notice that you are there! And as long as you are not noticed, you are not exposed to criticism or attack. Furthermore, if you aren't quoted because you haven't said anything, you can't be held accountable. There are many advantages to keeping silent."

That is the solution to the conflict problem under the 1,1 theory. Retaining neutrality is sometimes difficult for it is natural to think and to be involved, to have a stake in things, to make an investment of one's emotions and energies. Men are expected to have convictions, to stand for their beliefs, to contribute by disagreeing when they cannot genuinely agree. By the time a man has learned to act in a 1,1 way, he has learned a new set of skills to keep him out of trouble. He may not contribute, and the harm that he does not only to others but also to himself may not show up for years.

Managing Conflict

What does a man do when he is drawn in, when he cannot avoid conflict by staying out of the thick of things? The 1,1 orientation goes far beyond the passive "stay out" approach. That would be too obvious and others would catch on. A man can do it only up to a point. Beyond this, positive 1,1 actions become evident. There are several ways, depending on the specific problem, but they all share a common underlying quality.

One is to keep busy. What a man does is not important as long as he keeps busy—papers on the desk, papers in his hand when he goes down the hall. Then others do not want to interrupt him. Another way is to "study" problems. If asked for an answer by a subordinate, he delays. He requests a report so he can "really think about it." If asked by a boss, he tells him he is "studying it" or that someone else is or that he will "find out." (Usually the boss will forget to ask again!) Double-talk is another way to avoid saying anything while appearing to participate. "We could do X or we could do Y. And that may be good or bad." It is an answer, and by the time others have tried to understand what is said, somebody else will have gone ahead and diverted attention from this kind of 1,1 answer.

These and other ways help in the management of conflict by blunting an issue and taking the heat off long enough for attention to become riveted on a new issue that does not involve the man who is accommodating in a 1,1 way.

THE 5,5 OR MIDDLE POSITION

The 5,5 position describes another theory. "Push for production but don't go all out because you'll be known as hardnosed. On a nine-point scale, settle for five. And be interested in people, but don't go all out because you'll be known as soft. Find something in between hard and soft. On a nine-point scale, five is OK." This joining of five with five is "middle of the road."

Avoiding Conflict

How would a man operating in a 5,5 way approach his job? First, he would be likely to hold in highest esteem rules and regulations, habits and mores, traditions and rituals of the corporation. His approach would be, "Stay right in the center of things. The majority point of view has a lot to commend it. Do what others are doing. Say what others are saying. Think what others are thinking. Independence of thought and action is risky. Do not *try* to manage, just administer. Stay in the system, make progress in it, and help it move forward. The wheels of progress grind slowly, people move forward in small steps, not by turning things upside down. Only a few make dramatic contributions and they must be geniuses. By this approach you will never make dramatic blunders either." The man who acts according to this way of thinking is a member in good standing—acceptable but not exceptional. He makes steady progress in pay and promotion.

Managing Conflict

Under the 5,5 approach, when conflict cannot be avoided, the method of managing it is to "split the difference." There are many ways to split the difference. One is by compromise. For example, two men are at opposite poles on an issue and cannot get together. To demonstrate his flexibility and to show that he is a "reasonable" fellow, one proposes an intermediate position, a middle ground. By giving up something, he shows he is able to give and take. The suggested action may not solve the underlying problem, but it was not intended to do so. Yet it is workable. Compromise arrived at in this way gives each person something of what he suggested, even though not all of what he wants. The two in disagreement find a middle ground that both can live with and neither loses all. A contribution of a kind is made. Neither person is too deeply involved and neither is really committed to finding a genuinely sound outcome. Convenience replaces conviction as the criterion of decision. Both are "flexible."

Another way of splitting the difference is by voting or acting in the spirit of a committee man. Not many managers in companies today vote by raising their hands, but there is much poll taking, testing of the wind, and management by antenna. Many times the voting attitude is clearly evident, and decisions are made on the one-man-one-voice assumption of "majority rule." Then no one has more influence than anyone else. Everyone is fair and equal. For example, a group of seven men are in a meeting. It is five minutes to noon. The boss says, "Look, there are four of us who feel the better way to go is this way. Three of you think that way is better. In the interest of progress, which way should we go?" The three are not so obstinate as to hold out. They are in the minority position. They have presented their arguments but have not convinced the majority. Therefore they are expected to act according to Queensberry Rules of management to join the majority so that some action can be taken, progress can be achieved.

Communication under 5,5 is guardedly open as managers talk candidly about those matters that count little and carefully about those that are significant. The 5,5 approach is unlikely to result in dramatic bursts of creativity. It can promote small cat-steps of improvement that do not move far away from current practices and ways of operating. A reasonable degree of progress is to be expected. Excellence is sacrificed for expediency and eclecticism.

THE 9,9 THEORY OF TEAM EFFECTIVENESS

The 9,9 theory is a synergistic theory of behavior. A high concern for production is fused with a high concern for people. The way these two high concerns come together—the synergistic result of the two—brings about a different approach for getting results than does any one of those yet described.

Avoiding Conflict

A major strategy of the 9,9 approach to avoiding conflict is through the utilization of empirical data as the basis of problem solving and decision making. Faith is out, facts are in. Dogma is replaced by data, evasion by evidence. Trust and confidence are reinforced by tested competence. Respect for people is rooted in their fact-oriented thoroughness of knowledge on which their convictions are based. When managers are committed to thorough study, analysis, and logic, disagreements can take place that do not produce disruptive conflict. Decisions are based on the objective properties of the situation. Facts, not personalities, are the source of power and determine the course of action. Data have an authority difficult to describe. "Look, Joe, here is the problem. The background of it is this. Do you have any additional information about it? What facts are needed to find a solution for it?" Two men can be at different poles and with the introduction of new facts, either man can change his position. They can change their own minds, and they can do so without loss of face or without one's being "forced" into submitting to the other. In the context of new understanding, the problem itself has changed. Agreement can be reached on the basis of insight rather than through suppression, smoothing, seeking neutrality, or splitting the differences.

Managing Conflict

Sometimes facts are not enough because the problem is not one of fact. It may lie in the emotional attitudes of two persons toward one another which result in stereotypical thinking, persuasive argument, not listening, reacting defensively, closed mind attitudes, and so on. When barriers are present which prevent the use of fact to solve problems, the 9,9 approach is to get directly to the cause of the barriers. Then solution of the conflict is to face the emotions that are beneath the surface, examine them objectively, and probe for causes beneath them. In order to do this people must be committed to revealing their reactions of frustration, the reasons they feel misunderstood, and the ways in which their expectations or aspirations have been violated. Equally, they must be prepared to identify and to face up to the inherent limitations of competence which may be preventing them from making an effective contribution rather than to cover up or to pass the buck. When this kind of genuine behavior which can only be based upon open and unobstructed communication is achieved, the conditions are right for the surface problems causing disagreement to be resolved. When these highly personal attitudes can be forthrightly identified and discussed, presumed injustices and misunderstandings can be cleared up and genuine injustices and misunderstandings rectified. This way of confronting the emotions of disagreement and conflict provides a key for the creative resolution of conflict.

MODIFIED THEORIES

These five positions—in the four corner locations and in the 5,5 center—represent basic theories. Behavior can be characterized according to these positions or various other combinations as represented by eight additional possibilities.

One is 9,5, the *benevolent autocrat* approach in which strong production demands are modulated by the need to control without being arbitrary. The man whose behavior is based on 9,5 thinking would ask subordinates for their ideas and suggestions and whatever information they could contribute. Then he would tell them what his decision is. While such a decision can be excellent from an operational point of view, it is more than likely to result in people's saying what they think will be acceptable rather than what they think is right.

The *consultative* style is 5,9. It is a participative approach. Unlike 1,9, where discussion is predicated on the desire not to leave anyone out who might take offense, a man operating under 5,9 assumptions is truly interested in involving subordinates. His philosophy is that "people only support what they help create." The result is that he is reluctant to move until their support is assured and is eager to get it without examining areas of disagreement that are preventing support from developing.

Paternalism represents 9,1 control of work activities but care and warmth in a 1,9 way for welfare. Paternalism generates antagonisms toward the 9,1 control and dependency from the 1,9 attitudes toward caring. When persons feel dependent on others toward whom they feel aggressive, trouble is sure to exist beneath the surface. Aggression and feelings of dependency produce a volatile mixture. It is a situation in which subordinates at all levels from just beneath the top to the bottom rung on the ladder may turn in wrath against the hand that has fed them so well but also pushed them in such coercive and arbitrary ways. Hate is the offspring of paternalism. Rarely does it turn against the parent, but when it does, the wrath is great.

Another is the *wide-arc pendulum* theory. Here, as in paternalism, both 9,1 and 1,9 are at work, but under this theory they are never at work at the same time. The attitude swings from "tightening up" to "warming up" and back again. These swings tend to be tolerable as people learn to ride with them.

Under another mixture, *counterbalancing*, 9,1 and 1,9 are applied together, with a typical pattern being the line organization operating in a 9,1 manner and a 1,9 staff counterbalancing it. The "industrial chaplain," waiting for the "fed-up" employees who need a place to spill out their troubles, epitomizes this mixed theory.

The *two-hat* approach splits people and production, that is, management works on production problems in the morning and people problems in the afternoon. Once production problems have been dealt with, then morale is discussed.

Another mixed theory is the win-leave theory or the *9,1-1,1 cycle*. In a situation where a boss behaves in a 9,1 way and subordinate resists in a 9,1 way, one or the other eventually gives up and goes 1,1. Eventually the one who cannot win *leaves;* he does a "mental" walkout, often becoming the talented executive brought aboard by another company.

The *statistical 5,5* approach is illustrated by the manager who uses all five theories in his daily work, depending on the needs of the moment. He behaves inconsistently from one moment to the next but averages out to 5,5. His explanation is, "Everyone is different and so each requires a different kind of treatment." Everyone is, of course, different, but when it comes to a sound approach to dealing with conflict, these differences seem rapidly to disappear when persons are describing what they want in the way of a sound resolution of disagreement. This is pseudoflexibility in that a man is shifting with pressures in the situation and to adjust to others rather than exercising flexible leadership.

How other behavioral science formulations that apply to management relate to theories in the Grid is shown in Box 5.[2]

DOMINANT AND BACKUP THEORIES AND THE THIRD DIMENSION

Men act more or less consistently according to one or another of the theories that have been described. Whatever theory a man's way of behaving most resembles—9,9; 9,1; 5,5; 1,9; or 1,1—or a mixed theory—one represents his major or *dominant* approach, the one by which he customarily operates or acts. When things are not going well, a man may shed his characteristic way and turn to one or another of the alternative possibilities. The theory he typically turns to is his *backup*. The backup reflects a man's next most characteristic theory—the one he most consistently falls back on when his first theory does not work. It is a standby theory, available in reserve.

A third dimension, the thickness or depth of a man's theory, illustrates how he shifts from his dominant to backup. A man with a deep 9,9 would persist in searching for solutions to production-people dilemmas according to that way, whereas a man whose 9,9 theory is thin or shallow would abandon that approach to another at the first indication that things might not be going well. The same is true for any other theory which may be most characteristic of a manager—whether 9,1; 5,5; 1,9; or 1,1 or other theories.

A MODEL OF CORPORATE EXCELLENCE IN THE 9,9 THEORY

If a corporation is to achieve excellence, it is important that every man in the organization have a deep personal under-

Box 5

*Behavioral Science Formulations Applied
to Management*

Dynamic Administration by Follett is one of the classical treatments of problems of supervision. It deals with conflict from a 9,1; 5,5; and 9,9 point of view.

Motivation and Productivity by Gellerman presents developmental trends. This book traces threads of thought about factors in human effectiveness from the early 1920's up to the fairly recent past.

Interpersonal Competence and Organizational Effectiveness by Argyris presents the proposition that the way that organizations go about trying to get productivity is 9,1 and is inconsistent with the needs of those who manage and work in a corporation to be mature and healthy. The thesis is that 9,1 action produces 1,1 consequences. It also suggests ways for solving this problem, which appear to be a mixture of 5,5 and 9,9.

The Human Side of Enterprise by McGregor is a statement of two managerial philosophies, Theory X and Theory Y. These two views about the underlying assumptions of managing a business are sharply contrasted with the merits and limitations of each presented. Theory X appears to be pure "9,1" while Theory Y consists of an undifferentiated mixture of 1,9; 5,5; and 9,9.

The Human Organization by Likert presents four systems of management based upon studies of factors in supervisory behavior that are associated with varying degrees of productivity and morale. System 1 (Exploitive Authoritative) is in the 9,1 corner, System 2 (Benevolent Authoritative) is of a 9,5 character, System 3 (Consultation), 5,5, and System 4 (Participation Group), 5,9.

The Motivation to Work by Herzberg, Mausner, and Snyderman describes an investigation into ways of rewarding man. It shows that 1,9 types of reward systems have little effect upon productivity, as contrasted with other

Box 5 continued on next page

Box 5 (cont.)

ways which have strong production effects, and the motivators he designates are of 5,5 and 9,9 character.

The Managerial Grid by Blake and Mouton presents in a more complete way the different theories for solving the production-people problems and shows their applications for analyzing dilemmas of corporations.

Note—See Chapter References.

standing as well as a shared commitment to a model of an ideal manager and an ideal corporate culture. The two are inseparable. The Grid alternatives provide a rich variety of possibilities from which the surest path to excellence can be selected.

Many organization members after having studied the Grid have come to the conclusion that the 9,9 theory provides a model for reaching excellence. Through its use, communication can become clear and unobstructed, conflict resolved, commitment earned, and creativity contributed. The evidence of this is shown in Box 6, which demonstrates that when all of the complex aspects of managing are weighed and evaluated, the 9,9 way is selected as the preferable one. Though difficult to achieve, it is the one theory that makes the most productive use of an organization's members with the fewest undesirable side effects. Not only is it tough to achieve; it is the most demanding of personal effort. It is also the most personally rewarding of the possible ways to manage. Here are typical comments:

"9,9 is hard to accomplish. Yet there is no doubt in my mind that I have the courage of my convictions and I am really making the effort it demands. More important than me, 9,9 is putting this company into orbit."

"Two years ago, our company was shockingly 5,5 with a 1,9 backup. It had massive problems of 'me-tooism,' complacency, and tolerance of mediocrity. We have now been stirred out of our lethargy. It was almost too late, but we have finally begun to face up to operational realities. We've got a long way to go, but the corner has been turned. 9,9 is providing purpose and a

Box 6

Corporate Members in the United States, Great Britain, and Japan Conclude that 9,9 Is the Soundest Theory for Operating a Corporation

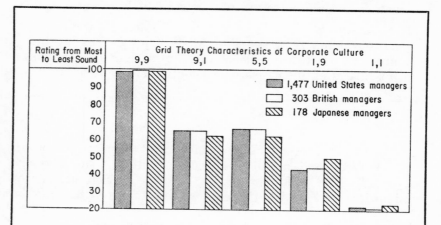

After studying Grid theory for a week, managers engaged in an experiment designed to answer the question, "What is the best way to operate a company?" Twenty questions about effective organization performance were discussed. Each question had five Grid alternatives to be ranked from "most sound" to "least sound" as the basis for operating a company. Thus these judgments relate to what people think would be sound, not necessarily to what does happen in companies. If any Grid alternative were chosen as "most sound" in all the 20 questions, the score would be 100 for the approach. If any Grid alternative were uniformly selected as "least sound" every time it appeared in the 20 questions, the score would be 20.

The graph shows that in the United States, Great Britain, and Japan there is almost uniform agreement that 9,9 is the soundest way to manage, the scores being 99.5, 99.9, and 99.2. 9,1 and 5,5 were selected as second best with about equal frequency. 1,9 was selected next and 1,1 was selected as the least sound approach to operating a company.

When this same experiment is completed after the Grid has been in use in a company over a period of two to three years, 9,9 retains the same strong first position, but 9,1 is selected over 5,5 as the second best approach.

sense of direction. Even though the task is Herculean, the risks involved in not making the effort are far more stark than not meeting the challenge."

"Basically, we were a 9,9 oriented company even before Grid OD. But getting into it provided the organization a lot more certainty. It has strengthened us. It increased our sense of urgency, heightened our tempo. We are moving in the same direction but we are more surefooted. We are outdistancing competition."

After several years of Grid Organization Development activity in one company, some corporate members met to identify what to them are the more important elements of 9,9. Their summary is shown in Box 7. Though it represents the thinking in one company, these managers said what has been expressed in different ways in many others.

SUMMARY *— Conclusion*

The Grid is a framework of behavioral science concepts which compresses much of the relevant scientific knowledge of behavior in corporations into a meaningful form. It provides insight into how to solve communication problems by increasing man-to-man effectiveness. Probably one of man's most challenging yet difficult assignments comes when he attempts to lead the efforts of others to achieve the purposes of the corporation. When a boss—regardless of his rank—thoroughly understands the Grid, he often sees his responsibilities in a new light. He comes to recognize that there are few things more significant in their human and personal implications than when one man is given the responsibility for the activities of others. Too often, those who have such responsibilities fail to pause and consider the direct influence, for better or worse, good or ill, that they have on those who report to them. They perhaps have taken little opportunity to consider that the quality of supervision a man receives often determines that man's destiny as well as the degree of gratification he experiences during a major portion of each day of each year for thirty years or more. The quality with which this is done—the character of the results achieved—the taste of the job each man has when he goes home to his family at the end of the day—all of these ought to be a central consideration to every executive, manager, or

Box 7

*What Organization Members Report To Be Important
Managerial Elements in a 9,9 Work Culture*

Managers:

—Have clear, forthright, and unobstructed communication with their bosses, colleagues, and subordinates

—Fully commit their energies to accomplishing that part of organization objectives for which they are responsible

—Confront disagreement and interpersonal conflict squarely, whether with another person or as a member of a work team

—Search for and find valid solutions to problems

—Experiment for innovative and creative solutions

—Accept nothing less than excellence of results

—Achieve effective coordination of effort through high quality teamwork

—Use critique of operational problems as the basis for learning

—Continuously revise the culture of the organization so its elements support problem solving instead of hampering it. (No practice is sacred just because it is old. No pronouncement is sacrosanct just because somebody spoke it.)

—Have a sense of personal purpose because the organization purposes and financial and program objectives are clear

—Expect thoroughness of study and preparation as the basis of participation

—Use knowledge and facts objectively as the basis for decision making

---

supervisor for the total length of his career. Managing according to a sound theory of behavior can contribute to the resolution of the foremost barrier faced by today's business society —getting genuine communication.

REFERENCES

1. Blake, R. R. & Mouton, J. S. *The Managerial Grid*. Houston: Gulf Publishing Co., 1964, p. 10.

2. Follett, M. P. *Dynamic Administration*. Metcalf, H. C. & Urwick, L. (Eds.), New York: Harper, 1940; Gellerman, S. W. *Motivation and Productivity*. New York: American Management Association, 1963, 151-159; Argyris, C. *Interpersonal Competence and Organizational Effectiveness*. Homewood, Ill.: Dorsey, 1962; McGregor, D. *The Human Side of Enterprise*. New York: McGraw-Hill Book Co., Inc., 1960; Likert, R. *The Human Organization*. New York: McGraw-Hill, 1967; Herzberg, F., Mausner, B., & Snyderman, B. B. *The Motivation to Work*. New York: Wiley, 1959; Blake, R. R. & Mouton, J. S. *Op. cit.*

3

LEARNING FUNDAMENTALS IN A GRID SEMINAR

While the Grid can be studied as an intellectual exercise to gain insight into its implications as the basis for sound inter-action, knowing and understanding it in a way that increases personal effectiveness is another and much more difficult matter. The first step to corporate excellence has been taken when a man has learned the Grid and can identify his own assumptions in relation to it. Then he is prepared to act in ac-cord with his insight. The seminar approach to studying the Grid has been found imperative in Phase 1 of Grid Organiza-tion Development. The more technical considerations that deal with rationale, design, and administration of a Grid Seminar on an incompany basis are discussed in Appendix I. The job of the Organization Development Coordinator, Appendix II, also might be examined at this time.

THE GRID SEMINAR

The Grid Seminar engages organization members in back-to-school learning. Learning the Grid is *not,* however, like other school-type teaching. The seminar is not conducted by expert teachers who have spent their lives in classrooms. It is conducted by managers who have dealt with the dilemmas of getting results through people. These are men with practical business acumen whose thoughts and energies have been focused on manufacturing, marketing, sales, engineering, or research and development. They are key men in the organization. They shoulder full responsibility for corporate effectiveness. These managers-instructors do little formal lecturing. Rather, they *manage* the learning process. It is their responsibility to:

—clarify goals and set standards of excellence for meeting them

—provide explanations to participants about what is to be done

—aid participants in figuring out for themselves the subtleties of Grid theories

—critique degree of success throughout the seminar and introduce corrective actions as necessary to insure high quality results.

In one way Grid learning is similar to school or college; there is homework based on the textbook, *The Managerial Grid*,[1] which participants study. They test themselves on it before the seminar begins. They also complete several other instruments, scales, and measures in advance. One instrument covers managerial values. Others are designed to help a man diagnose and analyze his theories. Another measures Grid properties that typify the culture of his corporation. These instruments are for a man's own use. They are not the usual "tests." They serve no purpose except to aid a man in seeing himself more objectively and in gaining a clearer understanding of the Grid characteristics of his own thinking. As shown in Box 8, participants learn that their conflict approach is less 9,9 and more 9,1 than they thought it was.[2] Many of the seminar activities provide participants opportunities to test the validity of their assessments of themselves and to correct them to the degree they are found invalid.

Homework is one similarity between a school situation and a Grid Seminar. But the Grid Seminar has no desks or big U-shaped tables like those often found in many rooms where courses take place. It has a general session room where participants meet around work tables for brief periods between teamwork sessions.

Box 8

Corporate Members See Their Approaches to Conflict as Less
9,9 and More 9,1 After a Grid Seminar than Before

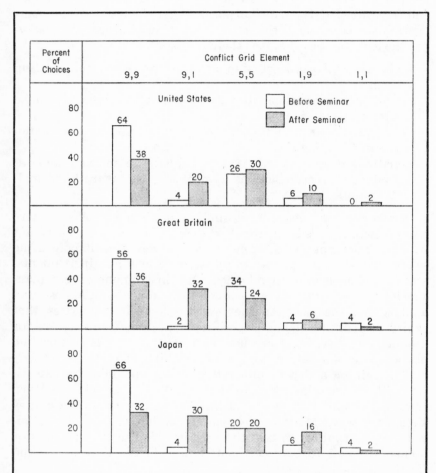

Personal reaction to conflict is one of several key elements
of human thought and action. Participants assess their own
typical ways of dealing with interpersonal conflict in homework
completed before the Grid Seminar. Each man selects the description which fits his approach to conflict from one of the
Phase 1 prework study instruments. He repeats this after he

Box 8 continued on next page

Box 8 (cont.)

has attended a Grid Seminar. He makes similar choices showing how he sees his decisions, convictions, emotions, humor, and effort. For the conflict element, he selects one of the following without its being identified with a particular theory:

9,9 When conflict arises, I try to identify reasons for it and to resolve it

9,1 When conflict arises, I try to cut it off or to win my position

5,5 When conflict arises, I try to be fair but firm and to get an equitable solution

1,9 I try to avoid generating conflict, but when it does appear, I try to soothe feelings and to keep people together

1,1 When conflict arises, I try to remain neutral or stay out of it

These data are for 150 managers, including 50 each from the United States, Great Britain, and Japan, matched with one another by size and kind of company, managerial level, job description, and age. This kind of matching permits comparisons across countries for managers' self-perceptions of theories.

Each man is a member of a study team of from five to nine members. Team members study in the same team for an entire week. Teams are composed of a diagonal slice of the company —persons from various levels of the corporation and various departments and divisions. A seminar is a replica in miniature of an entire company. When a team begins to operate, it is self-responsible. That is, it has no trainer sitting in as in sensitivity or T-Group training, no case leader as in the case method approach. Nor does an instructor appoint a member to be the leader, as one might in a conference leadership course.

Members work at perfecting their own solutions to problems of team effectiveness. The aim is to gain insight into issues of team organization and direction, of communication and commitment, of strategy and planning, of decision making and control. An example of kinds of issues explored is the character and quality of communication as given in Box 9. Data show that can-

Box 9

Participants Talk with More Candor and Sound Understanding of One Another by the End of a Grid Seminar

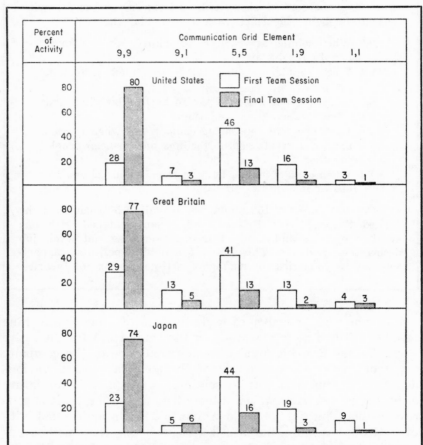

Upon completion of each problem-solving session, team members evaluate their effectiveness according to five major considerations. One is the character and quality of communication. Agreement is reached on how communication took place through use of the following five sentences:

> 9,9 Ideas and convictions were expressed with candor; differences were thrashed through to sound understanding

Box 9 continued on next page

BOX 9 (cont.)

9,1 Discussions were on a "win own points" basis; people steadfastly held their points of view

5,5 Although different opinions and ideas were expressed, reasonably acceptable positions were reached; people moved off their positions to make progress

1,9 Polite give-and-take resulted in a friendly session

1,1 Ideas and opinions were expressed with little conviction

Data are from 50 United States teams, 13 British teams, and 15 Japanese teams.

---

did communication with sound mutual understanding increases from the first to the last team session.

During the week, each study team engages in a series of team performance experiments. Team effectiveness in solving problems is measured against objective standards. These team achievement activities are designed to aid participants in learning the Grid as the basis for diagnosing people-production problems. The scoring is in the general session room. All Grid teams are assembled there, so comparisons can be made of the effectiveness of each in solving the problem, not only against objective criteria but in contrast with other teams. Typical results of these experiments are shown in Box 10, which demonstrates that teams can reach a higher standard of excellence than can individuals, working alone.

After scoring is completed and teams know where they stand, they return to their study rooms to critique operating effectiveness. Several hours may be spent in identifying obstacles that were present that must be eliminated or corrected for better team action in the next achievement experiment. Examples of typical barriers are shown in Box 11. Critique used to evaluate teamwork might be likened to a medical checkup. Facets of problem definition and analysis are examined, communication knots are untied, impasses producing unresolved disagreement are analyzed. The "body" of team action is thumped on, listened to, stethoscoped, peered into, and measured against standards of

Box 10

*Team Achievement Can Reach a Higher Standard of Excellence
Than Individuals Working Alone*

Results from Team Performance	Percent of Experiments
Yield better results than the average of individual scores	97
Yield synergistic results—that is, better than those of highest scoring individual	41
Yield worse results than the average of individual scores	2
Yield worse results than the lowest scoring individual	0

After the members of the Grid study team have come to agreement on their best solution to a complex problem, results of the team performance are scored against objective standards. The team result is compared with scores made by members when they were working alone as individuals before team discussions took place. Comparison of team scores with average individual scores of team members shows that teams almost always do better than the average individual and often better than the highest scoring individual on the team. Data are from 150 teams in United States seminars.

excellence. The basis for learning lies in seeing the gap between the character of team effectiveness possible and what is being achieved, and identifying causes of the gap and cures to correct them. Being specific about those aspects of team action that have resulted in effectiveness is equally important. When clearly understood, they can be further strengthened for use in future problem-solving activities.

After barriers to effectiveness have been analyzed and plans set for reducing them, another achievement experiment is introduced. Each of these measured effectiveness projects involves team members in meeting new challenges. Each scoring of team performance is followed by critique sessions to identify and

Box 11
Barriers to Team Achievement and Steps to Improve Problem Solving Are Identified During Critique Sessions

Barriers	Steps for Improvement
1. Failure to critique effectively "failure to critique sufficiently particularly in areas of unanimity" "failure to provide ongoing critique" "lack of sufficient challenge to individual positions taken"	1. Effective ongoing critique "timely critique-ongoing; devil's advocate" "strives for ability to conduct critique concurrently with individual participation" "self-critique of own contributions to team action"
2. Insufficient preparation "lack of awareness of facts" "lack of knowledge and information" "lack of proper preparation"	2. Better individual preparation before discussion "start with a thorough understanding of the facts" "review Grid materials and develop individual competence"
3. Poor planning—particularly regarding time management "no time budgeting" "inadequate control of available time" "wasting time" "inadequate planning and allocation of time"	3. Careful time management "allocate our time more effectively" "have time budget" "shut off extraneous conversation"
4. Ineffective communication "failure to draw all members into discussion" "extraneous information" "repetition of the same point"	4. More effective expression of ideas "each individual express his facts—no one interrupt" "commitment to make each member a contributing member" "more probing" "speak objectively and to the point (think)"
5. Too much compromise "insufficient challenge of position taken" "compromise is key to decision" "move off position to make progress"	5. More careful examination of minority views "abandon the concept of votes in favor of weight of data" "have strongly convinced member present his position; evaluate"

Box II Continued on next page

Box 11 (cont.)

"tendency to reach agreement rather than best solution"
"majority position not explained by its supporters"

6. Poor listening ability
"no effective system of listening and understanding of other's points of view"
"too many people talking at once"
"failure to listen"

7. Poor team goal setting
"lack of direction and goal definition"
"no planning, schedule, or guide for action"
"inadequate definition of objective and problem"
"insufficient definition of target and method"

8. Lack of candor
"we were not probing and being candid"
"candor is thin"
"not enough honesty"
"not enough interplay"

Data are from 19 study teams.

"carefully explore all individual contributions"
"debate and explore thoroughly even unanimous and minority opinions"

6. Attentive listening
"assure each team member is listened to"
"a dedication to one speaker at a time"
"attention on communication: tune receivers"
"listen constructively—recognize presence of pre-conceived ideas"

7. Define goals clearly
"take time to define problem so that each member of team understands"
"establish performance standards"
"define and analyze problem: examine alternate methods of solution"

8. Greater individual candor
"encourage confrontation"
"increase amount and depth of probing"
"resolve to have more open conflict"
"reach best solution through having conflict arise and not suppressed"

correct weaknesses as well as to reinforce strengths. This pattern occurs repeatedly during a Grid Seminar so that particular emphasis is placed on the use of critique as a learning method.

Box 12

*Far Greater Use Is Made of the 9,9 Approach to Critique by the
End of a Grid Seminar*

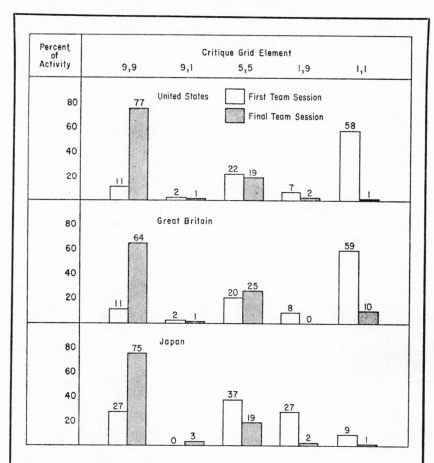

Team members evaluate the character of critique as applied
during problem-solving sessions using the following sentences:

    9,9 Ongoing critique of teamwork, both for improving
        action and for learning from it

    9,1 Faultfinding; unconstructive criticism

    5,5 Suggestions of how to do differently or better

    1,9 Compliments were given but any faults were not
        examined

    1,1 Little or no attention was given to discussing team
        action during the session

Data are from 50 study teams in the United States, 13 in
Great Britain, and 15 in Japan.

Corporate members come to appreciate the importance of using critique in daily operational activities to increase company effectiveness. Box 12 shows a sharp increase in the use of 9,9 critique by study teams at the end of a Grid Seminar in comparison with the beginning. As will be seen in later chapters of the book, this emphasis on the use of critique that is begun in Phase 1 is one of the most significant factors in organization development. In later phases, extensive use is made of 9,9 approaches to critique.

In another seminar activity team members identify for each man the Grid theories most typical of his thinking. This "reading back" is based on what members of his team have observed about him during team achievement experiments and critique sessions. It provides him with a mirror with which to examine his thinking. What a man learns about his thinking as revealed through the reactions of others is often different from what he had believed about himself. He either becomes convinced that the approach he has been using in daily work is soundest for achieving high quality results or he sees other approaches which, if applied, would make him more effective. He is free to accept or reject what he has been told, but the evidence provided is highly specific and concrete and reinforced by many examples. Most men react to what they are told with utmost seriousness, finding it a valuable source of insight into their own thinking and action.

As shown in Box 13, the reactions provided are not in Grid numbers but in tailor-made paragraph descriptions that describe the person's quality of thinking. Since a man rarely participates in discussion of his own paragraph but has the opportunity to hear points about himself unfold, as much learning is gained through listening to the writing of this paragraph as from the final product. Yet the final product is a capsule description which many keep with them back on the job to test what they have been told against their usual ways of operating.

GRID SEMINAR LEARNING OBJECTIVES

Another way to gain understanding of a Grid Seminar as Phase 1 of Grid Organization Development is to review its learning objectives.

Box 13
Grid Descriptions of Individual Managers Aid Them to Recognize Personal Characteristics of Their Thoughts

---

9,9

United States

His decisions are made by an intense search for facts coupled with a demanding and creative approach. He evidences strong, sincere convictions that can only be changed by sound and persuasive facts. When conflict arises, he moves quickly into a strong, searching position to resolve the conflict into a learning process. He reacts to tense situations by swift, affirmative action and counterarguments with visible effort to control his temper. He has a warm sense of humor that becomes rather pointed under pressure. He exerts strong effort and expects others to. Personal Grid theory sequence: 9,9; 9,1; 5,5; 1,9; 1,1.

British

He uses a mathematical approach to arrive rapidly at sound decisions after assembling and analyzing the facts. He has a tremendous confidence in his abilities and his decisions. He reviews his decisions and alters them in the face of new evidence. He responds to challenge and conflict effectively as an individual and as a team member, with a strong inclination to leadership. He retains balance and a sense of humor under tension. He is ambitious and committed to progress and will make the minimum number of compromises. His efforts and involvement do not allow him to tolerate incompetence. Personal Grid theory sequence: 9,9; 9,1; 5,5; 1,9; 1,1.

Japanese

He places high value on exploring for right decisions toward which he spares no personal effort and is willing to listen to others' opinions well. He is strong at heart but soft in approach. He is careful as well as highly willing to conduct fact-finding and research activities. Attending conferences, he correctly states his own opinions, but would not argue with other views or put others in his shoes. He is fairly conservative in expressing his own views, but tends to listen well to other opinions. In making decisions, his thought is that, rather than pushing his own ideas too hard, he should make sound decisions

Box 13 continued on next page

Box 13 (cont.)

that would bring about understanding and agreement by all. While he tends to take a rather neutral position in a conflict situation, he spares no effort in finding conflict causes and solving the underlying causes. His emotions are very stable and he can control himself even though he gets irritated in an urgent situation. He rarely shows a sense of humor, but it is not that he is short of humor and, in rare instances, his sense of humor is hard hitting. He gets the job done energetically and spares no minute effort, and also possesses a high level of guiding ability. He is well skilled in incorporating issues.
Personal Grid theory sequence: 9,9; 5,5; 9,1; 1,9; 1,1.

9,1

United States

He stands up for his ideas, opinions and attitudes even if it results in stepping on toes. When conflict arises, he tries to win his own position. He sometimes fails to listen and evaluate other ideas being presented. He holds up well under pressure even though his impatience is visible. When things are not going right, he defends and comes back with hard hitting humor and needling. He exerts vigorous effort. He takes pride in making ample preparation and making decisions to which he is highly committed. He will therefore defend his position vigorously and change his decision only when faced with convincing facts or logic.
Personal Grid theory sequence: 9,1; 9,9; 5,5; 1,9; 1,1.

British

He has strong convictions which are forcefully expressed but is willing to change quickly, provided sound alternatives are offered. He values creative reasoning, provided that it is concisely expressed. His pace is aggressive but directed toward perfection in decision making. This is shown by his critical reappraisal attitude. When conflict arises, he tends to cut it off as a first reaction, quickly becomes impatient and unsure, but contains his temper in order to maintain progress toward the target. His humor is used to achieve his goal, with a secondary aim of maintaining friendly relations.
Personal Grid theory sequence: 9,1; 9,9; 1,9; 5,5; 1,1.

Box 13 continued on next page

Box 13 (cont.)

Japanese

His thinking is "speedy" and he acts aggressively in a logical way to be sure that nothing has been left off the discussion. His eyes are the ones of an eagle, his tenacity is like a serpent, and his behavior reminds one of a squirrel. His posture is of a smart and polite gentleman, as he intends to be. But nobody will ever be able to penetrate his mind to touch his real self. He is greedy about seeking personal learning, Ah!! Once he is chosen as chairman, he glares at those "lazy" members who failed in completing the prework and never forgets their names till the end of the Seminar week: there is no other good word than "driver" to describe him appropriately. His opinions are always expressed in the name of justice and are listened to by others with awe and "stiff shoulders." What an indecisive attitude he reveals when he has to change his opinion very reluctantly! He sounds pathetic with his heart torn to pieces. Behold the man . . . the veins stand out on his pale forehead, his face is reddened, and his gazing eyes are fixed on one page of the text.

Personal Grid theory sequence: 9,1; 9,9; 5,5; 1,9; 1,1.

5,5

United States

He desires ideal decisions but accepts workable solutions the majority supports. He seeks to understand the convictions of others and to test them against his own. He examines conflict but often stays out of it. He usually maintains an even temper during periods of stress. He makes a sincere and continuous effort to contribute to team objectives, especially in helping improve team effectiveness.

Personal Grid theory sequence: 5,5; 9,9; 1,9; 9,1; 1,1.

British

He is a team man and he finds difficulty in maintaining his own convictions against stronger personalities. He is willing to yield. While generally accepting the majority decision, he will occasionally take a stubborn stand. He finds difficulty in expressing his thoughts and arguments clearly. He dislikes conflict and

Box 13 continued on next page

Box 13 (cont.)

has a high regard for good relations. He always seeks to help but prefers others to lead. He has an even-tempered, humorous personality.

Personal Grid theory sequence: 5,5; 9,1; 9,9; 1,9; 1,1.

Japanese

His expression of ideas is cautious. His attitude is mild and seldom discloses his real sentiments. But under high tension he often starts with a sudden momentum, insisting upon his own views. Under normal situations, he waits for ideas expressed by other people. When he finds his idea belonging to a minority, he is not so tenacious to push it through. Conversely, if he finds his opinion being agreed upon by a majority, or when the direction of the majority opinion becomes clear, he gains aggressively in his expression of ideas. All these traits are derived from his wishing to see a decision that can be agreed upon by all on the one hand, and from his fear of failure on the other.

Personal Grid theory sequence: 5,5; 1,1; 9,1; 1,9; 9,9.

1,9

United States

He strives for workable solutions by calmly sifting facts and may allow others to influence decisions. He prefers to seek ideas and opinions of others rather than initiating his own. He can become quite firm in his convictions. He is difficult to involve in a conflict but when aroused, he tries to get an equitable solution. He reacts in a warm and friendly manner but at times shows evidence of hesitation under tension. His humor is aimed at friendly relations. His effort is influenced by team activity, but he maintains a good, steady pace.

Personal Grid theory sequence: 1,9; 5,5; 9,1; 9,9; 1,1.

British

He places value on maintaining good relations and getting workable decisions but tends to accept majority decisions. He is a good listener and does not jump to conclusions. He is willing to accept new evidence rather than push his own minority views.

Box 13 continued on next page

Box 13 (cont.)

He is reluctant to put forth his ideas. He shows genuine friendliness. In the face of conflict, he withdraws rather than compromises. He shows self-control sometimes to excess. He does not get stirred up. He has controlled commitment. He retains his humor under pressure and shows unostentatious, steady effort. Personal Grid theory sequence: 1,9; 9,9; 5,5; 1,1; 9,1.

Japanese

He makes it a rule, as much as possible, not to use provocative words and actions. If you resort to self-assertion and make loud voices, you would get in trouble. Therefore, he listens well to opinions of other persons, and always acts mildly and gentlemanly. That is why he is called "very courteous" or "modestly polite." When he really wants something from somebody, he first makes sure what their positions are, and then starts getting what he wants bit by bit. When he assumes the responsibility for something, he works very hard in getting it done but on some occasions feels the pressure of that responsibility and becomes anxious about "the quality of results." Rarely does he feel that nothing more needs to be added for him to be satisfied with what he has accomplished through all-out effort. In actually doing things, careful doing is placed above all, and he gets it started after he has seen how the wind has been blowing. Thus, he hardly ever takes the position of the "first batter." When making important decisions, he gives a good depth of thought while he waits for his turn as the "last batter." Personal Grid theory sequence: 1,9; 5,5; 9,9; 9,1; 1,1.

Personal Grid theory sequence shown is from participants' self-rankings from most to least typical of their thinking at the end of the seminar.

1. *Learning the Grid*

The Grid is first and foremost a framework for identifying, analyzing, and solving production-people problems. It provides a way for a man to analyze his thinking—whether he has a

closed mind, for example, or whether he leans so strongly on
custom and tradition that he rarely thinks for himself. A person may see himself as having strong convictions but an open
mind and eager to examine new possibilities. The Grid deals
with communication, commitment, creativity, conflict, and a
wide range of other aspects of behavior which a man must
understand if he is to manage his effort effectively and release
the constructive capacities of others.

The Grid also creates a useful kind of shorthand or code language for discussing production-people problems in the endless
variety of ways that arise in any corporation. One manager remarked, "The Grid has given me a code to describe management actions. I can say, 'That's a 9,1 action' and others who
have been to a Grid Seminar understand immediately what I
mean. I can say, 'That's a 1,9 attitude' and we're all tuned in
to the same wavelength."

Others' comments made in describing the Grid are similar.

"The dimensions help a great deal. I can now see the obvious
connections between matters like commitment and convictions
on the one hand and production results on the other."

"I used to think that you could assume that you told people
what you wanted and they would want it too. I now realize that
the situation is one hell of a lot more complicated than that."

"I never really dreamed how important this business of conflict is. My approach when things got rough was to let people
alone and hope they'd simmer down. But now that I'm tackling
the issues face on, I feel a lot cleaner."

A young manager who had just stepped into line responsibility from a trainee assignment in his company put it this way:
"I was a brand new supervisor, and I had never realized that a
person could make choices about how to do it. At first I couldn't
figure it out, but once I learned the Grid, I realized that there
are many different ways of dealing with a situation, or of not
dealing with one and making it appear that you are. I see
I can make my brain do my thinking and not just let my mouth
go ahead and give the orders. A blunder it can help me avoid is
that I don't have to do the thinking for others. They've got
brains too."

The general trend of reaction is summed up in Box 14
which shows that participants have a much better understanding

Box 14

Participants Gain a Clearer Understanding of Production-People Problems from Attending a Grid Seminar

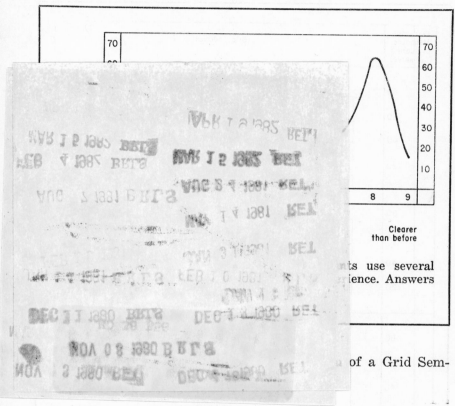

Clearer
than before

...ts use several
...ience. Answers

...of a Grid Sem-

2. *Increasing Personal Objectivity*

A condition for achieving personal effectiveness is that a man be objective in appraising himself, both in evaluating accurately his skills and strengths and in identifying obstacles that prevent him from achieving sound performance. Gaining this kind of personal objectivity is difficult. Persons naturally give themselves the benefit of the doubt. While it is easy to see the weaknesses and limitations of others, it is less easy to find and face up to weaknesses and limitations in one's self. Even though

BOX 15

Self-Ranking by Grid Theories Changes After Grid Seminar Attendance

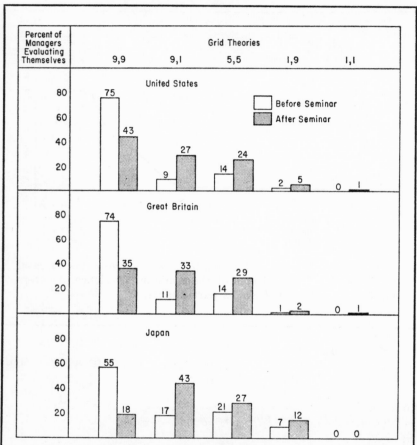

Data are from homework completed before a seminar compared with self-judgments made at the end of the seminar. The degree of change in self-perception of Grid theory is striking. Participants include 1,450 United States managers, 300 British, and 60 Japanese. Attention is drawn to differences between Japanese managers on the one hand and managers from the United States and Great Britain. At the outset, Japanese managers see themselves as less 9,9 and the same

Box 15 continued on next page

Box 15 (cont.)

> trend holds upon completion of the Grid Seminar. These differ-
> ences, which are statistically significant, are interpreted as point-
> ing to a genuine difference between oriental and occidental man-
> agement orientations.

difficult, attainment of this kind of objectivity is a prime
objective of Grid Seminar learning. A person must recognize
what needs to be changed before he can see possibilities for
change and implement steps for bringing it about. As shown
in Box 15, important progress in achieving this objective is
made in the Grid Seminar. Corporate members move away
from seeing themselves as 9,9 and move toward seeing themselves as 5,5 and 9,1. Corporate members report this shift
away from self-deception and toward self-appraisal based on
greater objectivity, as shown in Box 16. The significant point
here is that when a person can see himself as he actually is,
he has taken a major step toward real change. Now he is in a
position to do something about his behavior. To solve a problem,
one must be able to recognize that it exists and identify the
conditions that cause it. When a man gains personal insight—
a more objective awareness of himself—he has made an initial
move along the path that can lead eventually to increasing his
organizational competence.

It seems generally true that personally useful insights are
acquired from Grid Seminar attendance. However, it would be
incorrect to leave the impression that all change to the same
degree or to imply that every participant changes. A few benefit little or not at all, finding little or nothing in the learning
that is relevant. For whatever the reasons, the Grid Seminar
is insufficient to bring about the kinds of changes that would
result in constructive improvement. Furthermore, it should be
clear that some people already have achieved an outstanding
degree of organization competence. For them, the objective of
learning about themselves as individuals has little operational
implication except for reinforcing already present convictions
that they are on a sound path.

Box 16

The Shift Is Away from Self-Deception and Toward Objectivity
in Analysis of Personal Behavior After a Grid Seminar

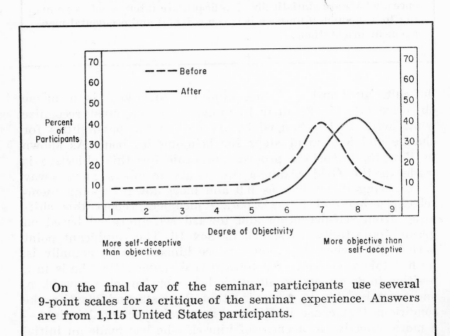

On the final day of the seminar, participants use several
9-point scales for a critique of the seminar experience. Answers
are from 1,115 United States participants.

3. *Achieving Clear and Candid Communication*

Unobstructed, candid, fact-based communication already has
been identified as one of the most pressing problems to be
solved in pursuit of corporate excellence. Corrections for communication difficulties take place throughout the phases of Grid
Organization Development, but the foundations are established
in the personal and team learning of the Grid Seminar. What
does unobstructed communication mean? It means presenting
one's own thoughts, feelings, and intentions clearly; revealing
reservations, doubts, and uncertainties; speaking with the degree of conviction that one truly has, neither dampening expression to imply low conviction when it is strong nor expressing a

degree of certainty as a bluff when convictions are low. There are other aspects, but this is the essence.

Unobstructed communication is a two-way street, however. On one side is accurate and full expression. On the other is accurate and unfiltered listening. To get clarity into communication, one must listen for understanding to the thoughts and feelings expressed. This means having the ability to hear what is being said. It means not being locked out because of a closed mind or a mind distorted by defensiveness. Equally, it means acceptance or rejection of what is said on the basis of the facts supporting it. It does not mean acceptance on faith or fellowship, nor does it mean rejection because of a feud. Other obstacles to sound listening include tender feelings, listening with bias, and prejudging. Removal of these constraints can result in listening and appreciating others' feelings, seeking to understand their expectations, aspirations, and values. Neither aspect—neither listening nor expression—is more important than the other. Both are essential as undergirding for a sound relationship between two persons conducting business. Participants learn these facts of communication in the Grid Seminar. Box 17 shows that after a Grid Seminar greater importance is attached to open minded listening and speaking forthrightly as the basis of sound communication.

While reviewing his reactions to the Grid Seminar, a manager commented, "I certainly saw the point that when people genuinely are committed to achieving a purpose, they can be frank and forthright without taking remarks as personal affronts. I saw the relevance of listening without preconception and came to value that others were listening to me, even when I was wrong, to understand what I was attempting to say."

"I just about had to conclude that I'd never listened to anybody. When my hearing aid got turned on, I could recognize that others besides me have ideas. Once I got the notion that a critical factor to being influential in a positive way is to really hear people, then they were able to hear me too."

"Listening for reservations and doubts and being listened to in the same way sure is awfully important if you're going to have effective communication. However, I've also found out it's one thing to see it in a classroom situation and another thing to do something about it in the heat of action."

Box 17

Participants Have a Greater Understanding of the Importance of Listening More Fully and Talking More Clearly After a Grid Seminar

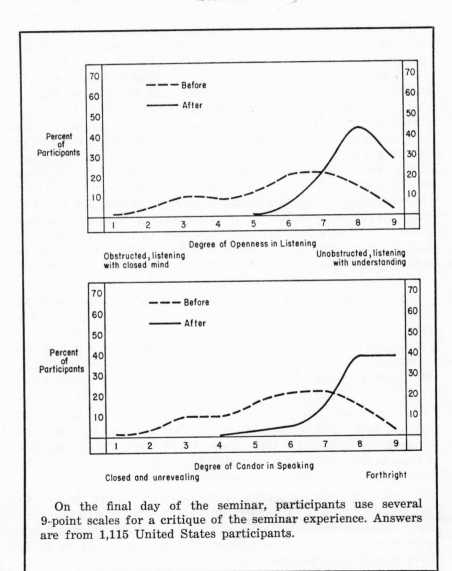

On the final day of the seminar, participants use several 9-point scales for a critique of the seminar experience. Answers are from 1,115 United States participants.

4. *Developing a Personal Philosophy of Corporate Values*

Some men have not had an opportunity to come to grips with what they believe is a sound approach to dealing with others in a corporate environment. Some have been too busy to think out and develop a philosophy which can direct their actions. Others have not thought it important to do so. Most have not been stimulated to do so. Yet real reward may only be possible when a man can say to himself, "I'm doing what I'm doing because I believe in it." In a Grid Seminar a man can meet himself in a face-to-face way and decide the kind of performance to which he could commit himself according to his basic values.

"I've come to think of work not as a means to an end, but an end in itself—as a rewarding and meaningful activity. It permits you to engage with others in a challenging use of the mind."

"The concept of synergy has resulted in an entirely different outlook on my part. I am constantly on the lookout for the creative clue and can see how the clashing of ideas can ignite the spark of innovation that even the most dogged, detailed individual thinking might not be able to reach."

"Corporate life is a vast human experiment. Cultivating its culture to make it more productive is possibly the most difficult task that society can ask of anyone."

5. *Getting Effective Teamwork*

When each of several men has a perspective on a complex problem but no one is in a position to see the whole situation, there is a requirement to think the problem through to an agreed upon best answer or action. The jobs of corporate members sometimes are interdependent in this way. The ability of one man to achieve something is hinged upon the contribution of another. The convenient assumption that each person will do the right thing in the right amount at the right time in the right order, without deliberate planning and without each knowing what the others are intending, is an act of faith that often has proved catastrophic. Similarly, making the assumption that several well written job descriptions will generate teamwork through each person's fulfilling his job description and knowing what to do also leads to gray areas of confused responsibilities, mutual misunderstandings, and contradictory actions. Hallmarks of sound interdependent action are well defined and understood objectives, clear knowledge by each of what he is to do, and opportunities for each to anticipate and therefore be able to predict how others will contribute their efforts. Getting this kind of high quality team action focused on problems that can be solved only by flexible access across divisional lines is a much needed contribution to corporate excellence. A Grid Seminar provides the opportunity to learn about matters of effective teamwork, as shown in Box 18.

"The Grid Seminar provided a demonstration that team effort should be increased in my company. We are not getting that extra punch, that final mile. Without well integrated teamwork, we are forced to move too slowly. We're pussycats when we could be tigers."

"I thought teamwork meant committees and meetings, so I was cynical about it. How wrong I was! The obvious conclusion from the Grid was that when team members had really captured the secret of thinking through, digging in, and separating wheat from chaff, they then were able to come up with a team answer that was objectively more valid than the best thinking on the same problem from any individual considered alone."

Clear comprehension of teamwork as a critical part of effective corporate performance is an objective in a Grid Seminar. Corporate members apply this knowledge to their own work teams in an organized way during Phase 2 to solve actual work problems they must cope with if they are to achieve excellence.

6. *Using Critique for Personal, Team, and Organization Learning*

Critique methods of learning, as contrasted with 9,1 criticism, 5,5 indirect suggestion and innuendo, 1,9 compliments, and 1,1 disregard, can increase excellence in performance, whether of an individual, a team, or a corporation. Critique is a significant aspect of the scientific method of learning in a Grid Seminar. As shown in Box 19, after a Grid Seminar, participants indicate that they have a better grasp of how to use critique as a basis for improving personal effectiveness.

Box 18

Participants Gain a Clearer Understanding of Effective Team-work After Grid Seminar Learning

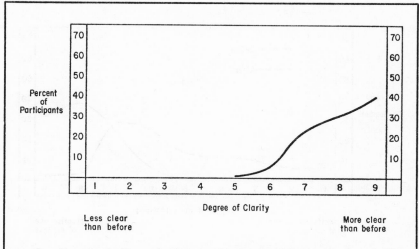

Degree of Clarity

Less clear
than before

More clear
than before

On the final day of the seminar, participants use several 9-point scales for a critique of the seminar experience. Answers are from 1,115 United States participants.

Using critique to review and learn about job-related problems, as well as to evaluate alternatives and possibilities of programs of action before launching them, is at the very heart of effective performance. It is probably the part of the learning where the greatest insight is gained about requirements for attaining true corporate competence. A manager recently explained, "I grasped another meaning for learning from experience. Indeed, deep down I've always felt that the school of hard knocks is what life really is. And I still think that is at least partly true. A lot can be taught by a hard knock. But when you stop and think about it, it is obvious that people can take some bad knocks and learn nothing from them. They may even learn the wrong thing. In fact, some get worse because they get 'gun shy.' By sitting down and discovering some-

Box 19

*Participants Have a Greater Understanding of Use of Critique
for Improving Personal Effectiveness After a Grid Seminar*

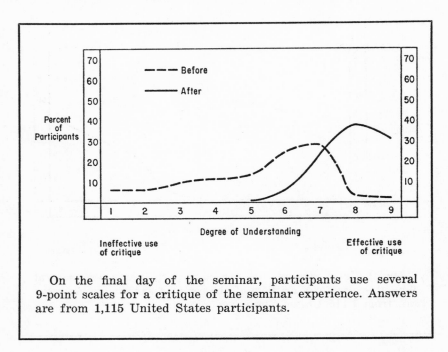

Percent
of
Participants

Degree of Understanding

Ineffective use
of critique

Effective use
of critique

On the final day of the seminar, participants use several
9-point scales for a critique of the seminar experience. Answers
are from 1,115 United States participants.

thing yourself, reviewing and evaluating and coming to a conclusion about an experience, you can form explanations that
aid you to do differently."

Another said, "The powerful thing is you can take a company and get everybody involved in a critique of it. Then, based
upon greater understanding, you can change the parts of the
company you are responsible for and recommend changes in
those you are not. What's fascinating to me is to see how much
savvy we have around here. Up and down the line people know
what they are doing, but even more important, they also know
what we should be doing. But the meat of the coconut is how
much everyone seems to be interested in working better. Critique sessions bring that out loud and clear. I'm struck by the
eagerness for change."

7. *Learning to Manage Intergroup Conflict*

Intergroup conflict is a condition that any company seeking corporate excellence must deal with. This is conflict between organization components—sales and manufacturing, union and management, headquarters and plant, and a variety of others.

A major experiment in the Grid Seminar calls for solving problems of implicit disagreement between Grid teams which are created to study strategies for creating constructive and cooperative relationships. The learning objective is to understand the conditions in the relationships between organization groups that can cause antagonisms and tensions which culminate in win-lose fights, compromise, peaceful coexistence, or isolation at the expense of problem solving. These are unconstructive relationships which often have a cancelling-out effect on whatever constructive problem-solving efforts may exist in either of the two groups. The learning in the seminar, as shown in Box 20, provides an orientation for seeing how to eliminate intergroup blockages in the work situation.

Many aggravating intergroup problems can be corrected when men think through and sort out their attitudes of vested interests. This often results in a person's recognizing that he has been unwittingly, sometimes out of blind loyalty, expressing attitudes and taking actions which promote frustration, antagonisms, and enmities. With such recognition, managers from contending departments or divisions have met informally— under their own steam—and talked out constructive approaches that resolved problems. Phase 3, Intergroup Development, is a deliberate effort to concentrate upon the resolution of intergroup cleavages.

8. *Applying the Grid Framework to Evaluating the Corporate Work Culture*

A distinguishing feature of an excellently managed organization is its ability to control and develop its culture rather than being entrapped by it—ensnared by its "requirements," entangled in its assumptions. Few organizations have learned to master their own work cultures.[3]

Box 20

Participants Have a Greater Understanding of Dynamics of Intergroup Conflict After a Grid Seminar

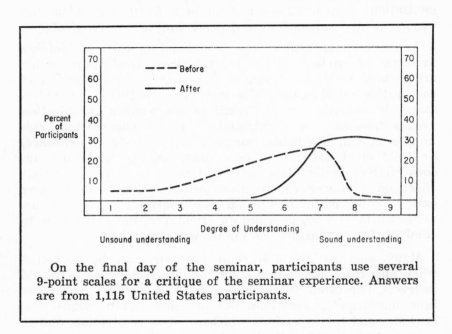

On the final day of the seminar, participants use several 9-point scales for a critique of the seminar experience. Answers are from 1,115 United States participants.

When managers use the Grid framework to analyze corporate culture, they see which Grid theories dominate the underlying actions and attitudes of their organizations. They come to recognize the extent to which modest attitudes toward corporate achievement may have crept into everyday crevices of corporate thought. In evaluating the cultural aspects of a corporation, Grid study teams first achieve agreement on what would be an *ideal* work culture. The discrepancies shown in the contrast between what an ideal work-oriented culture *would be* and what the actual work culture *is* appears in Box 21. Managers agree on what constitutes a sound corporate culture. Actual culture is far different from what is agreed to be most sound in all cases. It is less 9,9 than would be truly sound and less 9,1; a little more 5,5; more 1,9; and more 1,1 than it should be. These kinds of data cause managers to consider what must be

Box 21

Significant Differences Exist Between What Managers from the United States, Great Britain, and Japan View as an Ideal Corporate Culture and What Is True for Their Companies

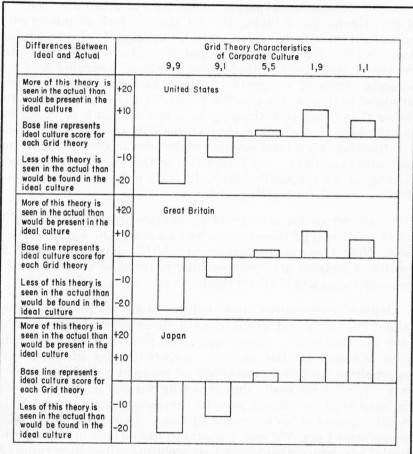

Data are from 1,477 United States managers, 303 British managers, and 178 Japanese managers. The range of scores possible for any Grid theory is 80 points. Box 6 (Chapter 2) presents the same data for the ideal culture choices where comparisons can be made among Grid theories and by country.

done to strengthen their own performance and that of the corporation if excellent results are to be achieved.

This activity demonstrates vividly how many firms are operating according to cultural attitudes which foster complacency and mediocrity rather than corporate achievement based on standards of excellence. This study in the Grid Seminar identifies a major element in corporate competence and arouses concern of participants for thinking about ways in which corporate culture might be brought under control. Participants also recognize through this activity the depth and pervasiveness of corporate culture in their own attitudes and thinking. Learning how to recognize cultural contamination and to provide constructive antidotes to it makes it possible to master the corporate culture rather than being restrained by it. When the kinds of attitudes and thinking that would be characteristic of a person's attitudes and thinking in an ideal culture can be seen in contrast to those that exist, conditions are favorable for the mastery of change. Coming to see corporate culture in one's own thinking and attitudes, though essential, is but a first step.

A manager on the last day of a seminar explained, "I thought I was doing what *I* thought was best according to *my* best judgment. Now I realize the extent to which I have fallen into a routine of judging almost everything in terms of previous practices and 'what would others think?' "

Another, commenting upon culture study of his own firm, said, "The open and down-to-earth discussions made possible have resulted in our examining sacred cows and rituals which were ordained by the founder, perpetuated by his son, and paternalized by three generations of reverent repetition. As an example, once we really dug into why we are doing things as we have been, we found reports righteously written and religiously filed—but no use made of them. As a result they have been chopped out. We now have three technicians in the experimental laboratory working on real problems rather than running useless checks and transmitting meaningless reports. We've gained the time the secretary wasted on keeping up the files and twenty square feet of file space. The important thing is that the seminar set a norm which made it a legitimate and responsible thing to do. When we critiqued corporate culture, we began to look at things that were wrong without feeling disloyal."

Another told a similar story. "It got built into the system years ago that no one ever talked to the union about a problem until he had cleared his pitch with Industrial Relations. It grew like Topsy. Industrial Relations coordinators got added and added and then one coordinator was assigned to coordinate every eight coordinators! Why? God only knows. By squeezing this juicy little piece of our culture, we found it was a bitter tasting lemon. Finally it was decided that dealing with the union in day-by-day matters is a line manager's job. Our line organization knows how to do it, maybe even better than those Industrial Relations 'Statesmen'—you know, corporate politicians, mahogony-desk lawyers. Problems are solved these days better and faster and with far less maneuvering than under the old system. We're running the business stronger than we were and the union is running a better union. The relationship is now one of mutual respect."

In dealing with culture, the goal is to increase objectivity in examining and evaluating the way the company operates, to set goals of cultural excellence, and to place in motion actions for correcting weaknesses and increasing strengths.

9. *Gaining Perspective and Orientation of the Phases of Grid Organization Development*

Corporate development does not continue simply because members of an organization participate in a Grid Seminar. Steps of followup application are essential to insure that change that promotes corporate excellence will occur. There are six phases of Grid Organization Development, of which Grid Seminar attendance is but the first. During the Grid Seminar, however, participants explore objectives of the remaining five phases and what activities members of the organization participate in. Reviewing Grid Organization Development in the seminar provides a basis for understanding throughout the organization of this approach for achieving corporate excellence and what will be expected. Organization members then have a basis for seeing the full implications. They can anticipate next steps and see what they will be called upon to contribute.

SUMMARY

Participating in a week-long Grid Seminar—studying the Grid as a framework for thought—enables corporate members to learn many important behavioral science concepts. It provides a foundation for increasing personal contributions to corporate effectiveness. But other issues are of concern, particularly the way in which a Grid Organization Development effort is launched. When this subject is not given careful attention, the strength of the Grid Organization Development effort can be reduced. The reason is that people have to be personally committed to contributing their energies toward corporate excellence, and this kind of personal commitment has to be earned. It has to develop in each person out of a sense of readiness to dedicate his energy and effort. It can only be earned through conditions that compel a person through his own convictions to want to strive for excellence. This most important aspect of Grid Organization Development will be considered next.

REFERENCES

1. Blake, R. R. & Mouton, J. S. *The Managerial Grid.* Houston: Gulf, 1964.

2. Throughout this chapter, data presented are from managers attending public Grid Seminars. They represent many companies rather than one or a few and thus constitute a cross-section of corporate membership. The descriptions of a Grid Seminar provided in this chapter show how seminars are conducted incompany as Phase 1 of Grid Organization Development.

3. When the phrase *work culture* is used, it denotes the culture throughout the organization—from the top to the bottom—and is not limited to the base of the pyramid where physical work is carried out.

4

GETTING STARTED
IN GRID ORGANIZATION
DEVELOPMENT

Coming to the decision to use Grid Organization Development to increase corporate effectiveness presents complex issues. It also involves a seeming contradiction. On the one hand, Grid Organization Development rests on self-motivated involvement and commitment of the organization's members to change the way the corporation is designed and the manner in which it functions. The soundest change comes about when the members want it because of their own insight and conviction that it is imperative.

Yet how is it possible for organization members to commit themselves to a program of change when they have no experience by which to judge the wisdom of such a decision? Can a manager be told that he is about to embark "voluntarily" on a journey of self-development and organization development —that he is going to want to be involved personally in developing his effectiveness and that of the corporation? The concept of voluntarism presumes that a person is free to choose from among alternatives. But how can men choose if they are unaware of the alternatives available to them? And, if unaware, how can they be forced to become aware "voluntarily"? Grid Organization Development is not something that can be done *to* a corporation. It goes against the underlying premise of the program to start it with an edict from the top.[1] Equally unattractive is endorsement based on faith. Since faith lacks fact to sustain it, it is unlikely to arouse clarity of conviction. Insight and understanding are stronger foundations.

TOP LED, TOTAL INVOLVEMENT

There are sound ways for a company to move into a fully operational Grid Organization Development project despite this apparent dilemma. These are tested ways, based on commitment, not on persuasion or edicts. Effective Grid Organization Development efforts are top led, they include *all* corporate members, and they involve them in a self-motivated way.

Grid Organization Development Must Be Led From the Top

If members of the top team in the organization are actively and spontaneously dedicating themselves to the development of the firm—not just running it, they are not asking others to do anything different from what they themselves are doing. Conversely, if those at lower levels of management are called upon to manage differently and better while those at the top of the corporation persist in their typical ways of managing, the gap between the top and lower echelons only grows larger. The lower levels are not being led, they are being told. The message is clearly, "Do as I say, not as I do!" This kind of activity only perpetuates the communication gap. What people are being told and what they know is true are two different things and they do not jibe. The falseness becomes plain, as pictured in Box 22.

A significant aspect of involving the top man in the organization development effort can be seen in Box 23. These data show that top men are likely to see fewer problems in their companies than do those whom they lead. When such corporate complacency is present, top men are less ready to exert the effort required to bring about change.

Furthermore, the designing of an ideal strategic model for the corporation in Phase 4 can only be done by the top team.

Box 22

Grid Organization Development Is Best Led When It's Top Led

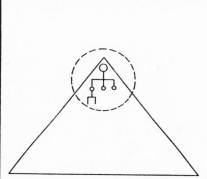 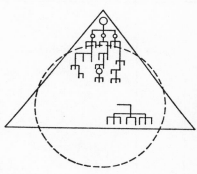

When only the top is involved in Grid OD, a sense of urgency and forward thrust is created in them, but the rest of the organization is unprepared to respond.

When Grid OD is initiated and led from the middle and involves those lower in the corporation, those ultimately responsible for the development of the corporation are not engaged in the thinking and analysis that creates a sense of urgency and provides forward thrust.

When Grid OD is led from the pinnacle, those ultimately responsible for the development of the corporation gain insight into the dynamics of change essential for providing forward thrust. A sense of urgency is widespread. The organization as a whole is prepared to respond.

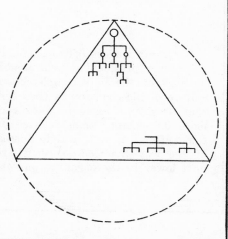

Box 23

*Grid Seminar Attendance Reduces Corporate Complacency
Through Removal of the Presidential Blindspot*

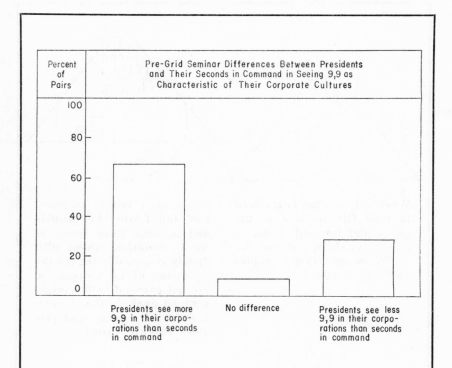

Corporate leaders often attend Presidential Grid Seminars in pairs, each president with a number two man. In prework, each member of the pair completes an instrument to describe the culture of his company in Grid terms. Data from 40 pairs show that presidents evaluate their corporations as being run in a more 9,9 manner than do vice presidents. This may indicate that before attending a Grid Seminar, presidents are less critical of the way their corporations are managed than are persons next lower in the organization—the seconds in command.

Box 23 continued on next page

Box 23 (cont.)

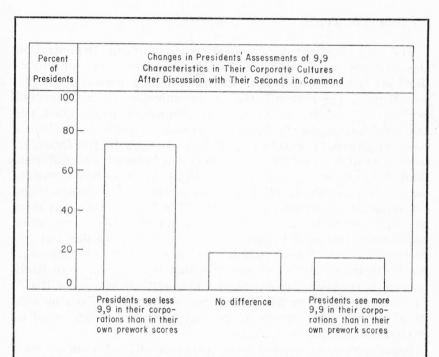

Percent of Presidents	Changes in Presidents' Assessments of 9,9 Characteristics in Their Corporate Cultures After Discussion with Their Seconds in Command

Presidents see less 9,9 in their corporations than in their own prework scores	No difference	Presidents see more 9,9 in their corporations than in their own prework scores

Toward the end of a Presidential Grid Seminar, each president and his vice president discuss the culture of their corporation and reach agreement on its Grid characteristics. The typical assessment is less 9,9 than the prework assessment of either pair member. Presidents, however, are more influenced in their thinking than number two men during the joint assessment of the corporation. Twice as many presidents see less 9,9 than they had reported in prework scores. The conclusion is that presidential self-deception regarding the effectiveness of their own corporations seems to be reduced. Becoming dissatisfied in this way is one key for getting action on organization development.

If the top team tries to superimpose a corporate model on its own unexamined behavior or on the powerful, deeply entrenched but silent culture of the corporation, it will produce but a modicum of change. The result can be a sham. Little energy is likely to be unleashed.

What Is "The Top"?

The organization development part of Grid Organization Development means *organization* development. The "organization" is the unit of development rather than a person or a component part. The reason is that an organization is an integrated business entity. Its members and component parts must act not only independently but also interdependently to realize a state approaching excellence. This statement is fundamental. Once it is understood that the whole can be more and different than the sum of its parts, possibilities for synergistic operations are recognized. With this recognition, the consequences for development efforts are great. This line of thinking does not lead automatically to the conclusion that the corporation is the organization development unit. It may mean this but not necessarily. An "organization" in the context of "development" means a whole—an entity which is sufficient unto itself in that it contains the essential autonomy for changing itself, as illustrated in Box 24. It requires no approval from outside itself to shift key aspects of its business which might need to be changed to achieve excellence.

Some companies are led from corporate offices in such a way that the corporate office is closely involved in the management of the business that the component is engaged in, the character of the market, the structural alignments of segments, and the policies that guide action. The whole must then be recognized as including the corporate office as well as subordinate components. Other companies are so structured that subsidiary segments or regional divisions or plants, under a concept of decentralization, have sufficient autonomy and freedom to change the basic character of their operations in those matters that need changing. They are free to improve their return on investment. By recommendation and approval they can exert strong weight on decisions that affect the nature of their business. They can define the market within which they intend to concentrate business activity. They can reformulate the structural relations among segments and components and interpret the major policies which govern their business decisions. Though

Box 24

The Organization Development Unit Is Any Component Which Is a Whole

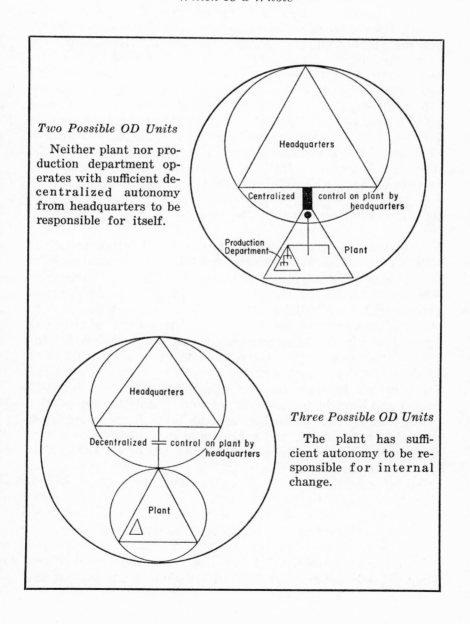

Two Possible OD Units

Neither plant nor production department operates with sufficient decentralized autonomy from headquarters to be responsible for itself.

Headquarters

Centralized   control on plant by headquarters

Production Department   Plant

Headquarters

Decentralized ‡ control on plant by headquarters

Plant

Three Possible OD Units

The plant has sufficient autonomy to be responsible for internal change.

capital expenditures undoubtedly are subject to higher level approval, the way that they are approved is the same as for any business transaction.

A subsidiary segment or a division or plant which acts under such autonomy is, from the perspective of development, a whole. The degree of autonomy is such that decisions for change are the responsibility of those who lead the operations. The corporate office's involvement in Grid Organization Development might be little more than consultative in this case. This issue defines perhaps the most fundamental organization development decision that can be made. It should not be glossed over or treated casually. Units that do not constitute sound development units are a work team, a section, department, or division within a plant or region. The unit is generally only a piece of a larger organizational culture in which it is embedded and of which it is a part. It is not the whole, only a slice.

All Corporate Members Must Be Involved

Leadership by the top is necessary. But it is not sufficient. Grid Organization Development must be based on the active and concentrated effort of *all* the organization's membership.[2] The top of the corporation may engage in its own development project with no parallel effort at lower levels, and this may be of significant value to the company. But if lower levels of management and supervision particularly are not included, the impact of the project at the top upon them is greatly lessened. If they are not drawn in, their creativity remains untapped, their interest in excellence and efforts toward it are not challenged and brought to fullest expression. If only the top participates, the gap that exists between the top and operating levels may only be widened, and such a gap may already be a barrier to corporate excellence. One of the goals of Grid Organization Development is to eliminate this gap by building a strong sense of organization identification throughout the corporation.

CREATING CONDITIONS FOR COMMITMENT

Men become committed to results from their own efforts. They not only become identified with their own success but also

Box 25

Steps for Getting into Organization-wide Grid Development

Background Reading	Gives an orientation as to how applied behavioral science is being used to strengthen organizations
Seeding	Provides a few organization members depth insight into Phase 1 and the Grid without the organization's being committed to doing more
Grid Organization Development Seminar	Gives a few managers a breadth and depth of insight into the whole of Grid Organization Development as the basis for evaluation and possible recommendations for next steps
Pilot Grid Seminar	Provides the organization a test tube trial of what would be involved were the organization to engage in Phase 1
Pilot Teamwork Development	Affords the top team direct understanding of how the Grid is applied to strengthening not only its team effectiveness, but also the effectiveness of individuals as the basis for assessing probable impact of Phase 2 applied on an organization-wide basis

come to identify their success with the success of the corporation. This identification of personal success with corporate success provides the added ingredient indispensable to corporate excellence.

How Grid Organization Development gets introduced is a major factor in its success. Finding a way to achieve an organization-wide awareness and conviction about the importance of Grid Organization Development among all members without demanding participation is the dilemma. The best approach lies in a series of preliminary steps that are exploratory and are designed to orient members to Grid Organization Development's possibilities, as suggested in Box 25. These steps permit the organization to test the implications of Grid Organization De-

Box 26

*Increased Productivity and Decreased Costs Are Related to Grid
Organization Development*

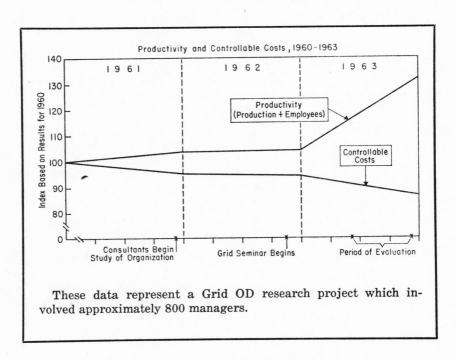

These data represent a Grid OD research project which involved approximately 800 managers.

velopment in a step-wise way without its obligation to become
deeply involved in it. If these steps are taken in a planned way,
organization members have the opportunity of developing their
own commitments through a series of self-convincing experiences. Orientation without obligation—the opportunity to test
the temperature before plunging in—produces awareness of possibilities from which a conviction-based decision can be made.

Background Reading

Several different kinds of background reading are available
to managers. Statistical studies have been conducted as one
way of evaluating the impact and results of Grid Organization
Development. Though they have proved exceedingly difficult

BOX 27

Interpersonal Misunderstandings Related to Poorly Managed Conflict Are Reduced and Unthinking Acceptance of Traditions Is Decreased After Grid Seminar Participation

Reduction in Interpersonal Misunderstandings		
Interpersonal Misunderstandings Were Increased	There Were No Significant Misunderstandings that Had To Be Explored	Interpersonal Misunderstandings Were Reduced
Percent Reporting 0	33	67

Reexamination of Culture		
Less Ready than Formerly to Take Another Look at Traditions and Past Practices	No Change One Way or the Other	More Ready to Reexamine and to Take Another Look at Traditions and Past Practices
Percent Reporting 0	14	86

to design and execute, such studies can be significant because they can be arranged to answer systematic questions in an orderly way. Control units can be contrasted with experimental ones and measurements can be taken repeatedly throughout several phases of Grid Organization Development. Findings from available studies have sought to assess development in this way. An example is shown in Box 26.[3]

Some studies have been based upon planned observations of corporations, as shown in Box 27.[4] Observational approaches usually involve keeping diaries or logs of observed changes in behavior, conducting interviews, or collecting tape recordings to be studied for cause and effect relationships and evaluation of how Grid Organization Development is affecting organization performance.[5, 6, 7] Since observational studies are preplanned, the investigator can determine on which aspects of the situation he wants to concentrate his observations. This method has the special advantage that a disciplined observer can often see more of the complexities of actual events than can be gained from quantitative measurement. Of course, this advantage carries with it the limitation that a human observation may result in a distorted picture because of the observer's emphasis.

Studies by corporate executives in firms where Grid Organization Development has taken place have been published.[8, 9, 10, 11, 12] Top man reports have a unique advantage. They provide interpretation of the impact of Grid Organization Development by those most responsible for the corporation and its effectiveness. Top man reports capture in words the subtlety and variety of change taking place in a company in a way that systematic research finds difficult to parallel, as shown in Box 28.[13, 14] Since these articles are written by executives, they portray conclusions reached and expressed from a corporate point of view. They answer the question, "What did Grid Organization Development accomplish for us and what are its limitations?" One disadvantage of top key executives' evaluations is that the authors do not have access to the controlled experiment type of systematic observation. They have given their commitment to the effort, and their conclusions should be interpreted on the basis of this fact. Conclusions reached, therefore, cannot be accorded the finality of proof but are open to interpretations as to "what really caused what?"

Articles that describe specific applications of Grid Organization Development can be found in such areas as the petrochemical industry,[15, 16, 17] banking,[18] merchandising,[19] tobacco,[20] railroading,[21] and others,[22] in the United States, Canada, Great Britain, Japan, and other countries.[23] For purposes of comparison, literature on development which is not Grid oriented is recommended. Several outstanding authors have commented upon the use of behavioral science methods for the induction of change and outlined approaches which are not Grid related.[24] Study of these published documents is an excellent step of orientation.

BOX 28

Conclusions Drawn by Key Executives from Different Companies About How Grid Organization Development Affected Attitudes Toward the Management of Conflict, Communication, Planning, and Production

President of a Medium Sized Electronics Firm	*Vice President, Marketing, Large Prepared Foods Firm*
We learned that conflict between individuals or within a group should not be suppressed, smoothed over, buried, or avoided.	Conflicts were apparent, but we were dealing with them in a new manner that was more constructive and creative. We were now becoming more concerned about the solution to the task or problem rather than fighting the person with the idea. We created the desire to foster productive solutions to our problems.
Bosses and subordinates increasingly recognize that when opinions are wrapped in hierarchy, too often they are accepted as fact. Subordinates must learn to challenge such opinions.	Before these sessions we had had a conflict between a marketing group and a production group. Marketing felt they were not getting sufficient support from production. And production felt out in left field—uninformed, uninvolved, and more-or-less second class citizens. These different points of view are classic in organizations. Both groups got together at the labs and began to understand and work on their problems. The different points of view were examined. Plans for improving the situation were developed. So, an interdepartmental problem was solved.
My work team decided that the greatest barrier to our im-	We see the need for listening to the soft voices and encour-

Box 28 continued on next page

BOX 28 (cont.)

proved effectiveness was the lack of candor. In our work team and within the company there were certain subjects that were considered too delicate or sensitive to be discussed between us. We defined these as the "sacred cows" of the organization. During our 3-day seminar, the environment was created in which all of these sacred cows were flushed out. As a result, action decisions were made to deal with the sacred cows, whose demise will save the company nearly $1 million in operating costs in the next 12 months.

We have a better understanding of the importance of planning. We see that lack of time becomes an excuse that can be eliminated through better planning.

The organization development program to us, and I believe to many other companies as well, is turning out to be a very valuable method for harnessing the latent resources of many minds in the corporation. People are learning to think and behave differently and in so doing are achieving things they never believed possible either for themselves or for their companies.

By integrating concern for production and concern for people

aging them to speak up. We recognize more dramatically our interdependence on each other and our need to work together.

We now do a better job of planning—because we have a better flow of data upon which to base our decisions.

I feel we also see job performance as more important. We understand the need to set tougher goals for ourselves. More people are now P & L conscious. We know we have to be experimental and innovative.

What we have learned has helped us immensely in improv-

Box 28 continued on next page

Box 28 (cont.)

in the right way, industry will be able to reach new heights of productivity and profitability. Even more important, individuals will obtain rewarding satisfaction and a sense of involvement and accomplishment in the production purpose not previously thought attainable in the traditional concepts of human endeavor in industry.

ing the overall performance of the organization and developing greater skills and competence on the part of our managers. As a result, our decision making people are able to operate effectively under the heavy pressures involved in the running of a thriving, growing business today.

"Seeding"

"Seeding" is another step. The idea is that a few members of the organization attend one-week Grid Seminars. The "public" Grid Seminars are held for attendees representing many companies.[25] The advantage of taking this step is that it provides organization members a firsthand basis for making an assessment without requiring any commitments beyond "taking a look" either from the organization represented or from the participants. The public Grid Seminar is a fact-finding way for those who have heard of the Grid to learn more about it. Then if the organization decides to take another step, the decision to move toward Grid Organization Development is based on recommendations from those who have directly examined it. Should their recommendations be to go further, several more steps are important, of course, before a final decision to launch a full scale Grid Organization Development effort is reached.

Who should be invited to attend a Grid Seminar to evaluate it? One consideration is the man's level. A higher level manager is likely to have a broad, overall perspective of his organization and therefore a firmer basis for drawing conclusions and seeing implications about how Grid Organization Development might contribute to strengthening business effectiveness. After higher level managers have convinced themselves that a next step should be considered, they may decide to invite others at lower levels. Then they may gauge the implications of Grid Organization Development from the perspective of corporate members at all levels.

A second consideration is that managers be tough minded but respected. Managers who have hardheaded views about how to achieve a sound business result and whose knowledge and opinions are respected by others are excellent for seeding. Their reactions carry weight. Even though tough minded, men who do not have the respect of their colleagues make poor evaluators since their conclusions probably would be questioned. Participation in a Grid Seminar nevertheless may prove valuable in aiding them to increase their personal business effectiveness.

Line managers are ideal "seeds." It is their lives and ways of working that will be affected most by a Grid Organization Development effort. The recommendations that the company engage in Grid Organization Development should be made on the basis of the line managers' understanding of it and not be merely a matter of line manager approval of recommendations by personnel or training staff members. The latter should, of course, be among the first to attend Grid Seminars because they will be actively involved in administering the organization development effort, but it is better to have line managers participate directly to grasp the implications of Grid Organization Development and to become solidly committed to its effectiveness.

Another consideration is the top man. He is the person who shoulders ultimate responsibility for the effectiveness of the corporation. More than any other, he should have firsthand knowledge and understanding of what Grid Organization Development is, what it would entail were it to be used to achieve excellence, what it asks of him, and what results might be expected from it.

Participants who attend a Grid Seminar as seeds should be clear about why they are doing so. It will be self-evident that although what they learn has personal relevance, their reasons for attending have nothing to do with their managerial competence. Equally they should realize that they are not being asked to attend as observers. Their objective is to participate in the learning experience in a natural way and take full advantage of the personal learning situation so as to be in a position to assess its usefulness to managers in their own corporations. If those who participate are unaware of these reasons for their participation, they are less likely to see the implications of what they are being asked to do.

With a sound seeding program, an important and valuable orientation step toward the Go-No-Go Grid Organization Development startup decision has been taken. If a decision is reached to pursue another route toward excellence, management will have made the decision on the basis of a knowledgeable and thoughtful weighing of firsthand evidence.

Understanding and Evaluating the Whole of Grid Organization Development

Only the first of the six phases of a total Grid Organization Development activity can be evaluated through Grid Seminar attendance. The decision to engage in Grid Organization Development should be based upon an evaluation of the whole. Positive evaluation of the Grid Seminar through a seeding program is necessary for such a decision but is by no means enough. Much deeper and fuller preliminary understanding of the implications and limitations of the whole is essential for a wise decision to engage in such an effort.

Brief Orientation. One way of providing such orientation is to arrange for a Grid Organization Development specialist to provide a one-day orientation to key organization members, describing the phases of Grid Organization Development from internal Grid Seminars in Phase 1 through systematic critique in Phase 6. Though this is no substitute for the depth of understanding gained through the fuller study made possible by the Grid Organization Development Seminar described below, it has one advantage. It is that many organization members may grasp the whole even though none is in a position to comprehend the depth of the major phases with any degree of technical understanding.

Intensive Study. Among advanced programs are Grid *Organization* Development Seminars. Grid Organization Development

Seminars provide thorough phase-by-phase examination of the entire scope of development activities. In the Grid Organization Development Seminar, minimum emphasis is given the Grid Seminar learning of Phase 1, since Grid Organization Development Seminar participants already have completed this step. Detailed examination is made of Phases 2 through 6. Each of these phases is studied in breadth and depth so that Grid Organization Development Seminar participants can grasp the nature of the activities involved, their probable implications, and their impact on an organization. This study provides further background for representatives of the firm to use in evaluating the possibility of implementing the whole of Grid Organization Development on an incompany basis.

Those who attend should have taken part in the seeding program. One should be a line manager, preferably the top man, while the second might be another line manager or a key manager in personnel or training. Such a pair constitutes an ideal selection. By attending the same seminar, the two can study together and evaluate each phase in the context of possible application in their own firm. The importance of this step is that it provides the organization with information about the entire effort. The kind of understanding that can be gained through attendance at a Grid Organization Development Seminar is a critical step in testing the fundamental decision to engage in a full Grid Organization Development effort.

Pilot Seminar

On completion of these appraisal steps, the evaluation may be further deepened through a pilot seminar. The pilot seminar becomes a test sample of the kinds of reactions to be expected from Phase 1 if a decision to move forward is made. In effect, it is a proving ground which permits an examination of any reservations and doubts about the soundness of conducting Grid Seminars on an incompany basis. Since those who study together in the same seminar teams are members of the same firm, whether or not this factor reduces or increases the learning or whether it makes no difference can be tested. The pilot seminar also permits an evaluation of reactions that arise when the instructors are line managers.

Box 29

The Pilot Seminar Is a Miniature of the Organization as a Whole

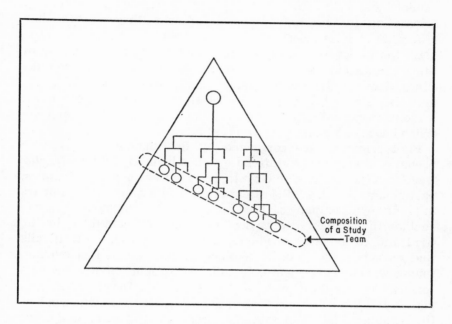

Composition
of a Study
Team

Those invited to attend the pilot seminar are a planned yet
random sample of the membership of the corporation, as shown
in Box 29. The corporation is described according to number of
levels, distribution of ages, formal education, and so on. Managers invited to attend the pilot seminar are selected according
to this plan but the specific individuals invited are identified
on a random basis. Only two of ten department managers might
be invited to attend, but precisely which two is determined by
lot. Three out of thirty divisional managers and thirty of 300
foremen would be selected in the same manner.

Persons selected are *asked* to attend, not *told* to do so. They
are provided full information about how they were selected.
They are led to realize that they are neither "crown princes,"
chosen for special grooming for the future, nor "problems,"
selected because of a lack or limitation, ineptness, or need for
coaching or "improvement" of some kind. Ideally, those
selected are convened and provided the background of steps

which the company has taken in evaluating Grid Organization Development as a potential corporate-wide endeavor. The criteria used in selecting them so as to provide a planned yet random sample of the company are presented. This kind of orientation insures understanding of why they, rather than others, have been selected. It provides an excellent way to explain the importance of reactions from this test-tube sample of the organization as a whole. If for any reason a person declines, another also selected on a random basis is invited to attend. In this way, it is possible for the organization to prevent persons from feeling coerced as it moves toward a binding decision based on results of the pilot seminar.

Pilot seminars are conducted by line managers who have prepared themselves by attending an advanced Grid *Instructor* Development Seminar. In Grid Instructor Development Seminars, participants acquire skills essential for conducting Grid Seminars in their own companies. The Instructor Development Seminar enables the manager to review the concepts contained in the Grid and to examine, evaluate, and work through the details that must be understood to conduct a high quality, fast moving, sound, learning experience. Installation support of line instructors can be provided by a Grid Organization Development specialist. His job is to consult with the line instructors who conduct the seminars. His assistance concerns their becoming specific and concrete on what to do and how to do it. After each sequence of the Grid Seminar, he and the line instructors "debrief" by identifying those aspects of the learning that went well and the difficulties that arose during the activity to find out how to avoid such problems the next time.

When the leadership of the organization has fully communicated that an approach to organization excellence, Grid Organization Development, is being considered, usually the entire organization membership grasps the character of the effort. Even more than that, they are likely to appreciate that company leaders have under way an explicit effort to assess the degree to which the company is ready to engage in the organization development program. Organization members up and down the corporate line who have not been involved directly in participation recognize that through their colleagues, they are being offered an opportunity to express their readiness to undertake the program—to commit their energies to bringing about corporate excellence.

A Pilot Test of Teamwork Development

The four steps of investigation already described place a corporation in an excellent position to make a firm decision about Grid Organization Development. Another step is possible which increases the thoroughness and depth of understanding of what Grid Organization Development involves and the demands that it places upon those who manage the firm. It is a pilot run of the second phase of Grid Organization Development. It is well worthwhile to take this step. In Phase 2 the concepts learned in Phase 1 are applied by the actual work teams of the firm to study how to increase work team effectiveness. This is Teamwork Development. It starts at the top of the organization.

In a situation where the top man and a few other managers have attended a public Grid Seminar and the other top team men have participated in an incompany pilot seminar, the whole top management team has had a direct learning experience with the Grid way of managing. Conditions are now ideal for the top team to evaluate Phase 2 on a "real life" basis, and this also provides a pilot project examination of it for organization-wide application. When the top team completes Phase 2, it is ready to make a penetrating evaluation of this significant aspect of Grid Organization Development.

TWO RESERVATIONS ABOUT GOING FORWARD

Two considerations are important to whether the corporation should move into Grid Organization Development even after the preliminary evaluation steps have been favorably completed. One concerns the organization's current problems, the other, the role of the top man.

Are There Problems To Be Settled First?

Managers in many corporations, through the testing process described, have recognized important problems needing solution. Some, for example, have recognized a need to face up to manpower reduction; others, that a fundamental organizational restructuring is imperative. They ask, "Should Grid Organization Development be launched and these matters be dealt with as part of the development effort, or should the development effort be deferred until such major actions have been completed?"

The resolution of this dilemma is clear. Such actions should not be postponed but should be taken when the urgency for doing so is recognized. The first and obvious reason is that problems should not be put aside when they need solution. The second is that solving major problems of the kind being discussed may be disruptive. It has proved far better to get them out of the way and then be in a position to use the organization development effort to knit the organization together in a sounder and more fundamental way. A third reason is that many significant issues are identified to be dealt with during the organization development effort itself. Many times these are of such magnitude that intense organization effort is needed to solve them, and if outstanding problems have been resolved before the development effort begins, corporate energies can be concentrated upon the new opportunities that the effort reveals.

Is the Top Man Ready?

Should a development effort be launched without the involvement of the top man? It can happen that all of the testing steps have been taken or Grid Organization Development has had a positive reception but without the top man's having become directly involved or demonstrated an intention of doing so. The top man may, indeed, be constructive in his support of the effort and eager to see it go far. Then the question is whether or not Grid Organization Development should be implemented.

How this dilemma is resolved has many implications for the success of the development effort. The most conspicuous is that without the involvement of the top man, it becomes impractical to engage in the design of an ideal strategic model of the corporation as the Phase 4 activity and so to proceed into implementation in Phase 5. Even without his participation, important positive results can accrue to the organization through the development steps of Phases 1 to 3, with all the advantages that come from improved communication. However, the company cannot realize the even more important improvements in corporate effectiveness that could be achieved through the solution of fundamental problems of planning and implementation. Without top man commitment, it would seem prudent to postpone launching a Grid Organization Development effort until key executives, through their own participation and insight, have fully committed themselves through their readiness to lead it.

SUMMARY

When all of these steps are complete—background reading, engaging in public seminars through a seeding program, further understanding through attendance at a Grid Organization Development Seminar, conducting a pilot Grid, engaging in instructor development, and the top team's engaging in a pilot run of Teamwork Development, the corporation has an excellent background for making a fundamental decision. The facts are in. The company is ready to decide whether or not to proceed into Grid Organization Development on an organization-wide basis.

These steps are calculated to resolve the dilemma that Grid Organization Development is strongest and has the greatest likelihood of leading to corporate excellence when persons engage in it because they are convinced of its importance, yet without a basis of understanding and insight, they cannot be expected to have convictions. The steps of investigation and evaluation described provide an organization with a foundation for representative members to experience directly significant aspects of Grid Organization Development and to make recommendations as a result of their learning experiences. This approach is the basis for fundamental decision making about an organization-wide effort and resolves this important dilemma. With these kinds of steps, problems of communicating throughout the organization about the significance to be attached to a major development effort have been automatically eliminated. Through this example, a key step has been taken toward reducing communication barriers to commitment to corporate excellence.

Once the decision has been made, participation in Grid Organization Development becomes a matter of normal expectation. Having reached this point, managers are expected to participate, and while they are provided the opportunity to disqualify themselves, the rule of the game is that it is a part of a man's corporate responsibility to prepare himself to further the capacity of the organization to achieve excellence.

REFERENCES

1. Blake, R. R. & Mouton, J. S. Initiating Organization Development. *Training Directors Journal,* 1965, *19,* 25-41.
2. Many corporations have started Grid Organization Delevolpment within the managerial, technical, and supervisory systems, including all personnel from the executive level through the first line of supervision. Significant advantages can be gained through this narrower concept of organization development. A next step in some companies has been to concentrate on the wage and hourly system. The fullest potential of Grid Organization Development is realized when it can be inclusive of the entire corporate membership.
3. For a full report of this study see: Blake, R. R., Mouton, J. S., Barnes, L. B. & Greiner, L. E. Breakthrough in Organization Development, *Harvard Business Review,* 1964, *42,* 133-155.
4. Blake, R. R. & Mouton, J. S. Improving Organizational Problem Solving Through Increasing the Flow and Utilization of New Ideas. *Training Directors Journal,* 1963, *17,* 48-57.
5. *Ibid.*
6. Malouf, L. G. Managerial Grid Evaluated. *Training Directors Journal,* 1966, *20,* 6-15.
7. Blake, R. R. & Mouton, J. S. Organization Development and Performance. Chapter 13, *The Managerial Grid.* Houston: Gulf, 1964.
8. Simmonds, G. R. Organization Development: A Key to Future Growth. *Personnel Administration,* 1967, *30,* 19-24.
9. Clasen, E. A. Blake in the Corporate Bloodstream. *NAWGA Conference,* New York: National-American Wholesale Grocers' Assoc., September, 1966, 37-39.
10. White, B. F. A Higher Dimension for Management Development. Paper prepared at the request of the Presidential Task Force on Career Advancement. Dallas, Texas: Internal Revenue Service, November, 1966.
11. National Foremen's Institute. The Managerial Grid. (Olin) *Executive's Bulletin,* 269, January 15, 1967.
12. National Foremen's Institute. The Managerial Grid Goes into Action. (Enjay) *Employee Relations Bulletin,* 1034, January 25, 1967.
13. Simmonds, *Op. Cit.*
14. Clasen, *Op. Cit.*
15. Blake, R. R., Mouton, J. S., Barnes, L. B. & Greiner, L. E., *Op. Cit.*
16. Blake, R. R. & Mouton, J. S. Managerial Grid Organization Development. *Petroleum Management,* 1965, *37,* 96-99.
17. Merck & Company. The Managerial Grid. *Merck Review,* 1967, *23,* 16-23.

18. Blake, R. R., Mouton, J. S. & Wallace, E. Use of the Managerial Grid to Increase Bank Management Effectiveness. *The Bankers Magazine*, 1966, *149*, 9-14.

19. Foster, G. The Managerial Grid in Action at Ward's. *Stores*, 1966, *48*, 42-44.

20. McCormick, A. D. Management Development at British-American Tobacco. *Management Today*, June, 1967, 126-128.

21. Robertson, W. The Managerial Grid in Action. *Monetary Times*, 1965, *5*, 39-45.

22. Portis, B. Management Training for Organization Development. *The Business Quarterly*, 1965, *39*, 44-54.

23. Foster, G. Making Managers-Executives on the Grid. *Management Today*, April, 1966, 33-38.

24. Bennis, W. G. *Changing Organizations.* New York: McGraw-Hill, 1966; Bennis, W. G., Benne, K. D. & Chin, R. (Eds). *The Planning of Change.* New York: Holt, Reinhart & Winston, 1961; Bradford, L. P., et. al. *Explorations in Human Relations Training.* Washington, D. C.: National Training Laboratories, National Education Association, 1953; Bradford, L. P., Gibb, J. R. & Benne, K. D. *T-Group Theory and Laboratory Method.* New York: Wiley, 1964; Ginzberg, E. & Reilley, E. W. *Effecting Change in Large Organizations.* New York: Columbia University Press, 1957; Jacques, E. *The Changing Culture of a Factory.* London: Tavistock, 1951; Lippitt, R., Watson, J. & Westley, B. *The Dynamics of Planned Change.* New York: Harcourt, Brace, 1958; Sofer, C. *The Organization from Within.* London: Tavistock, 1961; Thelen, H. *The Dynamics of Groups at Work.* Chicago: University of Chicago, 1954; Walker, C. *Modern Technology and Civilization.* New York: McGraw-Hill, 1962.

25. Grid Seminars are conducted regularly throughout the world. Further information is available from Scientific Methods, Inc., Box 195, Austin, Texas 78767.

5

INCREASING TEAMWORK

IN THE WORK TEAM

Operational improvements come about when Grid theory is injected into the bloodstream of an organization as the foundation for solving problems of communication and planning. Yet, a single week of studying human problems of integrating people into production does not begin to bring about fundamental corporate change. It is only a point of beginning. A person forty-five years old, for example, has spent his lifetime developing patterns of thinking and ways of interacting that are typical of him. These patterns tend to become fixed, so deeply embedded that they might be called his "second nature." Ways of acting and interacting come naturally, without a moment's thought. After patterns of thinking and ways of interacting have been repeated, rehearsed, and reinforced through life's experiences, they are in a man's bloodstream, in his muscles, bones, tendons, and joints. Such deep patterns do not change readily. Even the suggestion of change may arouse resistance if not soundly introduced. This is why so little change comes from short courses on behavior.

To continue the example, let us say the forty-five-year-old man has worked for the same company for twenty years. It too has become fixed in its traditional ways. Its organization culture has also become so deeply locked in the minds of its members that it is taken for granted. The company also has a "second nature." There is a company way which has come to be widely accepted.[1]

For improvements in effectiveness to take place, change must occur in these two factors—men with years of personal experience who are operating with fixed habit patterns and corporate cultures which have become so much a part of them that it is difficult for them to understand either themselves or the cultural properties of the company. This fusion of personal thought with the company way can be so strong that a man's thinking is locked in. Unlocking cannot be expected to occur after one week's Grid learning. Even two weeks' learning would do little to alter such embedded patterns of behavior and performance. Any short period of education, whether Grid learning or other, is likely to be of little value in causing fundamental change to take place when it is pitted against the combination of personal habits plus the traditions of organization culture.

It is not very useful to talk about an individual or an organization's culture in abstract terms. The performance of the man and the culture of the company come together. They intersect and interact in specific ways. These influences can best be observed in the work teams of an organization.[2] Work teams are organized clusters within which objectives exist even though they may be unclear, problems are solved or dealt with somehow, authority is exercised by one Grid approach or another, results are achieved to some degree. The work team, in other words, is the focal unit of interaction in the corporation. Eliminating or overcoming barriers to effectiveness that exist as individuals operate within these work teams is a first step of application in pursuit of corporate excellence.

Box 30 presents data from Teamwork Development sessions which identify in order of importance the actual problems of work teams that constitute barriers to their effectiveness. Many of the problems shown here are the same ones corporate members selected before they attended Grid Seminars to describe problems of their organizations. Communication and planning again are shown to be assigned very high priority but an important shift becomes evident when Box 30 is compared with Box 1 of Chapter 1. The use of critique has lower priority before Grid Seminar attendance. Having experienced

Box 30

Failure to Use Critique Is the Most Significant Barrier to Team Effectiveness with Communication and Planning in Second and Third Places

Barrier	Typical Comments	Percent
Critique:	"unwillingness to face facts" "proneness to 'gripe' rather than evaluate" "wait for leader to initiate critique" "inadequate inquiry and feedback"	80
Communication:	"we don't exchange fully and freely on matters of concern" "lack of receptivity" "lack of candor submerges conflict"	76
Planning:	"lack of realism" "inadequate follow-through" "no long range planning"	68
Creativity:	"we are afraid of failure when utilizing creative ideas" "conflict is not used to promote creativity"	52
Meetings:	"inadequate preparation" "lack of participation" "lack of direction"	40
Conflict:	"lack of experience in dealing with conflict" "stubbornness has prolonged conflict unnecessarily" "our convictions are expressed to a point of conflict and then we back off"	40
Tradition and Culture:	"plod along with established practice" "we seek the shelter of tried ways" "work by tradition and precedent without examining logic"	36

Box 30 continued on next page

Box 30 (cont.)

Coordination :	"each operates in his own little area"	36
	"insufficient exchange between divisions on progress"	
Control :	"confusion between meaning of control and direction"	30
	"absence of penetrating performance reviews"	
	"lack of yardstick to measure progress"	
Expression of Ideas :	"individuals hold own position after validity is negated"	26
	"quality of presentation suffers from insufficient preparation"	
	"politics dictate protocol"	

Members of the work teams in different corporations were asked to select seven key barriers to teamwork effectiveness. These problem areas can be compared with items selected as *barriers* to organization effectiveness in Box 1. Data were provided by 50 work teams, each representing a different organization in the United States.

the significance of critique for learning in a Grid Seminar, corporate members view their failure to use critique as the highest priority teamwork barrier. Thus, critique has come to be recognized as the key for getting at problems of communication and planning.

One goal of Phase 2 is for each manager to discover, not only through his own efforts but also through the eyes of his associates, his Grid theory, or the style he uses most on the job. When he has gained this insight, there is a possibility that change that has direct implications for improving his organizational competence can take place. A second goal is for each work team to investigate its manner of working by examining its own traditions, precedents, and past practices, its characteristic ways of doing things, its culture. When these two application steps have been taken, a basis has been created for each man to see more clearly how to operate in his job assignment. Members can identify barriers to achievement found in the practices of the team. Then the likelihood is increased that they can plan and carry out actions that result in more effective behavior of both team members and the team as a unit. There are many useful operational problem-solving approaches in addition to Teamwork Development. The strategy of problem solution through organization development application projects is presented in Appendix IV.

WHAT TEAMWORK DEVELOPMENT IS

Corporate members from all levels engage in Teamwork Development. But it starts at the top. In a typical top team experience, the man at the head of the autonomous development unit (the company president, a vice president, a plant manager, for example) and those who report to him (whether three, five, or fifteen) gather at a location away from the job. The place is one where team members are not harassed by problems of daily operations—the pink slip passed through a crack in the door.

As they did before a Grid Seminar, all have done preparatory homework. It is different from the homework of the Grid Seminar, however. Phase 2 homework uses Grid concepts for study of activities of the team whose members are present. Each man analyzes the culture of the work team as one part of the homework. Members also identify the most critical problems confronting the team and propose solutions which they believe can significantly increase effectiveness. In another part of the homework, team members write descriptions of their own execution of their responsibilities and their views of the other members as well.

Organization learning takes place when those who face the same problems diagnose them and develop solutions for them with little or no outside aid or intervention. The strategy of development uses team discussion. Each organization member, except the top man and those at the bottom level, engages in Teamwork Development at least twice and sometimes more. The first time is with the team in which the man is a subordinate and someone else is his boss. The second is when he is the boss and others are subordinates. This second application aids the closest possible linking between organization layers of teams. Done effectively, it bridges the communication gap between levels. The more technical considerations of rationale, design, and administration of Teamwork Development are discussed in Appendix III.

GOALS OF TEAMWORK DEVELOPMENT

Teamwork Development is designed to achieve six major objectives.

1. *Replacing Outmoded Traditions and Practices With a Problem-Solving Culture*

The way a team works often is influenced more by routines, rituals, and long established practices, by unfounded beliefs and party line attitudes, than by what actually needs to be done to solve problems. Team members may realize all is not going well but be unable to identify reasons why. In Phase 2, work team members examine customary ways of working and test the possibility that outmoded habits need replacing with stronger problem solving. A thorough look is taken at factors influencing the way the team operates. To make possible the development of common understanding and agreement on the facts and attitudes prevailing within the team, a first step is to get out into the open the attitudes about the team that members hold privately—their unexpressed feelings about it. These are probed, examined, discussed, and evaluated for implications for change and improvement.

A difficulty is commonly encountered in this activity. Team members tend to base their perceptions of their team on what they would like to believe, often seeing it as operating better than it actually does. To work toward eliminating this kind of bias, members agree on an *ideal* model of team problem solving. By reaching agreement on a model of excellence first, they have a basis of comparison to use for testing for objectivity when they attempt to agree on the characteristics of their own team culture. When this activity is completed, team members have agreed on how they *should be* working. With the exchange of facts and attitudes as seen from the experience of each team member, they have produced an image of the way

Box 31

When Team Members Agree on the Properties of an Ideal Team Culture, They Are More Self-Critical of their Actual Team Culture

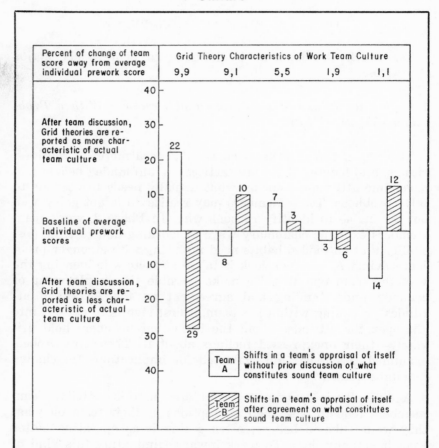

Members of both Team A and Team B completed individual prework describing Grid theory characteristics of their actual team cultures. Both teams spent several hours reaching agreement on their actual team cultures, but Team B's discussion of the *actual* culture was preceded by a discussion of what would

Box 31 continued on next page

Box 31 (cont.)

constitute an *ideal* team culture. The average prework scores for these two teams were essentially the same. The differences in the two teams' conclusions, as shown by their actual team culture scores, show the contribution of the discussion of the characteristics of an ideal team culture. Team A, which had no discussion of ideal team culture, shifted away from their prework scores toward reporting more 9,9, less 9,1, and less 1,1 in this actual team culture. Team B shifted away from their prework scores in an almost opposite direction, reporting less 9,9, more 9,1, and more 1,1 in this actual team culture. The consequence was that members of Team B set for themselves more challenging objectives for future performance than did members of Team A. The conclusions from this experiment have been verified many times. Thinking through what constitutes ideal specifications as a preliminary to evaluating the present situation and as a prelude to setting objectives for future performance is a general strategy for bringing about change which is used throughout the various phases of Grid Organization Development.

the team *has been* operating. Discrepancies, sometimes very important ones, between actual operations and sound teamwork become evident. With this accomplished, team members are in a position to deal with problems which may have been known about but ignored or which may not even have been recognized. The significance of this sequence of steps is illustrated in Box 31, which shows that after agreement has been reached on an ideal work team culture, the work team is seen far differently than when this first step of defining "what should be" is not taken. The conclusion is that once people who work together have committed themselves to a standard of excellence, they more clearly recognize the extent to which their performance falls below that standard. With this recognition, a work team has moved into a stronger position for shifting its performance from where it *is* to where it *should be* in order to achieve the maximum results within its reach.

Box 32

Improvement in Objectivity Results from Phase 2 Teamwork Development

Before Phase 2	Examination of Team Performance	After Phase 2
	Objective and valid; negative features confronted rather than ignored or justified	
	Almost totally objective	
	Moderately objective	
	Somewhat more objective than self-deceptive	
	About equally as objective as self-deceptive	
	Somewhat more self-deceptive than objective	
	Moderately self-deceptive	
	Almost completely self-deceptive	
	Self-deceptive and unrealistic	

Data presented in Boxes 32, 33, 35, 36, 39, 41, and 42 are from one top team of nine members. The data are provided as an example of typical findings since averaging data from many top teams obscures the individuality of the problems requiring solution. Data from the seven scales also point to another issue of the dynamics of change as brought about by Grid Organization Development. Before Teamwork Development, little agreement is seen among team members in their assessment of team characteristics. After Phase 2 discussions, a higher degree of agreement is present. This means that not only are the bases of judgment of team performance made more explicit, but also the standards of excellence upon which those judgments rest are of a higher order.

Box 32 shows changes in objectivity resulting from Phase 2 for one top team. Through Teamwork Development, this team improved greatly in objectivity in evaluating its team performance. Achieving objectivity in the appraisal of the team is of utmost importance. Only in this way does it become possible to plan and implement programs of action which provide a sound basis for teamwork excellence. The shift in thinking about the impact of traditions upon effectiveness is shown in Box 33. The conclusion is that Teamwork Development contributes significantly to bringing traditions under managerial control, shifting them toward contributing to a sound work-oriented culture.

Comments from managers about analysis of team culture give further evidence of the character of learning that results from it.

"When I rated our actual team culture, I thought we were pretty darn good. After debating through the ideal team culture and the implications of it, I realized what a big difference there was between where we were and where we ought to be going."

"If our work team had not gone through that ideal culture activity, I am sure we would still think we were pretty much 9,9."

"This learning forced us to take time to do things we should have been doing for years—defining our problems. This sounds kind of absurd, but we'd never all sat down at one time to examine where we stood and what our difficulties were."

2. *Increasing Personal Objectivity in Self-Assessment of Work Behavior*

This objective is to provide each member with accurate insights about his personal work behavior. Again the Grid is used as a framework of analysis. Insight is provided to each member in turn by his associates—those who have worked with him on the job day after day over an extended period of time. These are the persons within the company who know him best. They know what he is doing and how he is doing it. The man described may not like all he hears but he can listen without

Box 33

Those Traditions Which Have a Positive Impact on Team
Performance Will Be Carried into the Future After Phase 2
Teamwork Development

Before Phase 2	Impact of Team Culture	After Phase 2
	A positive impact on effectiveness; team culture supports effective team performance	
	Almost completely positive impact on effectiveness	
	A moderately positive impact	
	A somewhat more positive than negative impact on team effectiveness	
	An impact intermediate between positive and negative	
	A somewhat more negative impact on team effectiveness	
	A moderately negative impact	
	An almost completely negative impact	
	Negative impact on our effectiveness; team culture fully detrimental to effective team performance	

See Footnote, Box 32

defensiveness, that is, without rationalizing, justifying, denying, or explaining away what others are saying about his performance and behavior. The reason is that he is not listening to the opinions of one man who might be prejudiced but to a concerted view of all. A Grid picture of how each man has been performing his work is constructed. His work performance—the way he has operated within the dimensions of his job—is evaluated but only as a point of departure. The insights made available to him are about his approach to decisions, convictions, conflict, and so on. These are behavioral dimensions that are beneath the surface and which often are the reasons that work performance does not reach a peak of excellence. Typical descriptions are shown in Box 34. For a man to see accurately how he carries out his job is one thing but to be clear about the specific steps by which he might improve his performance is another. The team talks through with each member the actual steps he might consider for increasing the effectiveness of his contribution, not only as an individual but also as a team member. When this objective has been realized, the value from its impact for the pursuit of personal excellence is hard to match with any other method of critique or appraisal.

Corporate members widely agree that open and candid face-to-face communication is essential to sound supervision. Against the background of Grid Seminar learning during Phase 1, it is possible for the difficult barrier to corporate excellence, lack of such communication, to be reduced and in some cases eliminated. This activity of personal review of each team member is the turning point for the resolution of the communication problem. Box 35 shows the degree of shift in openness and candor achieved by one team. The communication culture of this top team before Grid Organization Development was described by one of its members. "There is mutual suspicion and distrust among members of the top team. Wholesale 'politicking' takes place in the halls, the men's rooms, and the executive dining room. The game is played in a series of subtle power moves. Departmental membranes are no longer permeable but hardened and non-porous. Horizontal communications are practically non-existent. Team members wear a mask of bland tolerance while suppressing feelings of resentment and distrust. Candor and openness of thought and feeling is almost totally absent. Minor day-to-day problems are discussed with some openness; the critical issues ferment between the communication crevices among team members."

Commenting on the breakthrough in the communication problem, a manager remarked on this activity of Phase 2. "There's a big value in looking at yourself through the eyes of your teammates. The men you work with don't seem to mind telling you. Furthermore, they can quote line and verse because you and they have been working together day in and day out, sometimes

Box 34

Personal Grid Descriptions Written by Work Team Members During Phase 2 Provide a Realistic Appraisal of a Man's Work Behavior

TOM GRAY

My ability to produce sound decisions is reduced because of a combination of late starting and too much concern for detail. I back down because of pressure from above and because I try to maintain good relations.

I have a good grasp of detail and I use opinions of others to develop firm convictions which I often defend regardless of opposing views. I communicate my position poorly. When my convictions are not strong, I tend to accept the opinions and attitudes of others without probing in depth.

I avoid offending other people. I am able to communicate interest in the views of others and should use this more frequently to resolve conflict.

My feelings are always restrained, and I appear solid and dependable. The degree of emotional control reduces my effectiveness in a group.

Although my humor is retained under pressure, it is used too seldom.

I do not drive others but lead them. My production would be more effective if a better framework for problem solving were developed before I dealt with details.

BILL BLACK

In trying for sound decisions, I sometimes drive too aggressively. I become impatient with the contributions of others and rely too heavily on my own preconceived opinions. This inhibits the contributions of others, which could improve the decisions. At times, particularly when I have no preconceived opinion, I become overly conservative, concerned with unimportant detail, and I delay realistic solutions and miss creative opportunities. At other times, I abdicate decisions to others to maintain good relations or reject recommendations in an agonizing inch-by-inch way. Attempts to gain support and acceptance for my decisions can lead to frustrating, overly long, post decision reappraisal.

Box 34 continued on next page

Box 34 (cont.)

I express convictions quickly and too firmly, listening to others only when I am in doubt. The inhibiting effect of this practice lasts beyond the immediate question on hand. I use unfamiliar language, verbally communicated in an overly involved way, and cut in on others while they are speaking. This, plus overbearing mannerisms, creates delay in understanding and inhibits others.

I tend to suppress conflict with win-lose responses, visible impatience, and manipulative techniques of arguing. The latter causes doubt about what I really believe and whether my real interest is in the work problem or in the pleasure of debate. At other times I appear cold and machinelike to a degree that others find unnerving. I must learn to express my feelings openly in a less inhibiting way.

My humor is a blend of cynical acid and tension-easing smoothing. My effort is high but with others it swings from inadequate followup to excessive drive. I can get more from others if I hold less of the action to myself and permit their participation rather than force it.

for a very long time. The concrete examples are what really hit home. They click. You can't dismiss them. You remember them because you experienced them. You can see the impact the action had on results and on other people. It carries real weight and has punch because it is not based on just one man's opinion. It is the accord by the other team members that gives it its wallop. When you realize that eight others are in basic agreement in describing your managerial behavior, you are really ready to listen. It's no use kidding yourself any longer."

Not all teams have difficulties as deep as these. In some cases the difficulties are even more severe. The general finding is that problem-solving teamwork in work teams rarely has achieved the quality before completion of Phase 2 which is realized upon its conclusion.

3. *Setting Standards for Excellence*

Corporate members tend to have widely varying standards of what constitutes a well done job. Some work teams evaluate

Box 35

Unobstructed Communication Is Achieved During Phase 2
Teamwork Development

Before Phase 2	Quality of Communication	After Phase 2
	Unobstructed, open, and forthright	
	Almost completely unobstructed	
	Moderately unobstructed	
	Somewhat unobstructed	
	Intermediate between unobstructed and obstructed	
	Somewhat obstructed	
	Moderately obstructed	
	Almost completely obstructed	
	Obstructed, closed, and hidden	

See Footnote, Box 32

their performance against high standards, others settle for mediocre results, and still others seem to have abandoned any real sense of pride in accomplishment. The same applies for individuals. In Teamwork Development, members measure their ways of working against standards of excellence as shown in Box 36. They answer such questions as, "Are our present standards calculated to result in excellence? Are they high, mediocre, just acceptable, or low? What evidence leads us to this conclusion? In what areas is it within the authority of this work team to set itself higher standards of achievement? What should

Box 36

Standards of Excellence Rise During Phase 2 Teamwork Development

Before Phase 2	Standards of Excellence	After Phase 2
	Sound; highest possible standards of excellence are the basis of accomplishment	▒▒▒▒
	Almost fully sound	▒
	Moderately sound	▒
▒▒▒	Somewhat more sound than unsound	
▒▒▒	Mediocre; intermediate between sound and unsound	
	Somewhat more unsound than sound	
▒	Moderately unsound	
	Almost totally unsound	
	Unsound	

See Footnote, Box 32

they be? What steps must be taken to insure we live up to the standards we set?" With relatively few exceptions, organization effectiveness is increased once work teams have expanded the scope of what they see themselves to be responsible for and have embraced standards of excellence.

4. *Establishing Objectives for Team and Individual Achievements*

Phase 2 is designed to insure that what should happen does happen. This is accomplished through setting work-team and individual objectives for change, as shown in Boxes 37 and 38.

Box 37

Work Teams Identify Improvement Possibilities During Phase 2

It had become increasingly clear that we were becoming over-staffed. In addition, from just below the top level on down there was not an effective distribution and utilization of the people that we did have. Therefore, the problem as we saw it was that the staff (these included the clerical, typing, accounting, and other people) were not organized and functioning as effectively as they might, nor in the proper numbers. We tackled this problem first and outlined the steps that needed to be taken in order to design the most effective utilization of the staff personnel. For example, there were considerations of whether each department should have a full complement of staff people supporting them or whether in some way there might be a kind of stenographic and clerical pool which could be utilized in certain areas. The strategy outlined, therefore, was to develop a study team headed by a man from the Industrial Engineering Department, one of his technical people, one person from Personnel, and someone from the General Administration area. This group would do a complete study of how personnel are currently being used. Personnel would then be matched against the job and functional requirements. Based on this study, alternative recommendations would be made to the top team. We could then see what changes should be implemented. It was anticipated that this project should be completed and fully implemented in four months.

An anticipated result was that some jobs would become redundant. However, it was felt that lay-offs would not be necessary because of normal attrition, re-training, and reassigning people, moving them into other functions which they can perform equally as well, arranging for transfers to other departments, and possibly placing those who might want to be in similar kinds of functions in other companies.

Objective setting calls for identifying important goals and for planning specifically the steps needed to achieve them. The team defines a program for getting results. They designate responsibilities. They schedule followup. They arrange for critique.

Box 38

Personal Improvement Opportunities Are Identified During Phase 2

TOM GRAY

1. Communicate Clearly

   A. Be direct, cut the frills; give the main point as fast as possible with no extraneous material.
   B. Support communication with main facts.
   C. Do not waste time with bulky detailed support unless requested, particularly in verbal communications.

2. Organize and Plan More Thoroughly

   A. Set priorities for projects.
   B. Develop a plan of attack for major projects immediately.
   C. Disseminate plans for major projects to participating departments.
   D. Review and update projects weekly.
   E. Critique progress personally, with participants, and with the boss as necessary.

3. Express Emotions

   A. React honestly and candidly. Others will accept impatience with lack of progress on tasks.
   B. When faced with conflict, interact with others to resolve it by identifying its causes.

BILL BLACK

1. Communication

   A. In discussion, focus on solving problems rather than winning points. Use a more simple, open, direct style. Gratify your debating pleasure in non-work situations.
   B. Schedule communications as any other work item. Experiment with a twice monthly 2-hour communication meeting. With this number there will be enough meat to make it worthwhile, yet the broadcast load will not be so high as to prevent reception. Use a pre-released but unclosed agenda.
   C. Both initial communication without followup and late communication on important matters are unsatisfying to others and much less useful than they could be.

Box 38 continued on next page

Box 38 (cont.)

---

2. Decision Making
   A. Identify at the outset both who is involved and affected by a decision, and whose ultimate decision it is.
   B. Insure where feasible the presence of persons involved in it: communication to those affected by it.
   C. Get key factors, both fact and judgment, bearing on the decision.
   D. Identify whether the issue is major or minor and deal with it appropriately.
   E. When the decision is made, state it clearly whether it is acceptance or rejection of a recommendation. Avoid the inch-by-inch route. State the decision clearly, then give reasons, rather than build the decisions reason by reason.
   F. When the decision belongs to others, having expressed and discussed known factors, do not continue to communicate dissatisfaction after the decision is made. Commit to it and help make it work.

Management by objectives,[3] if introduced before critical barriers in team culture are eliminated, is at worst doomed to failure and at best headed for only a limited success and probable fadeout. Opposite effects can be expected when management by objectives is introduced as the culminating action of Teamwork Development, as shown in Box 39. Once problems of communication and ·planning have been confronted and resolved and skill in the use of critique to identify and eliminate barriers and obstacles that prevent the attainment of objectives has been developed, it becomes possible for team and individual objectives to be set with the prospect of their achievement.

Management by objectives can be achieved when goals are set against the background of a genuinely work-oriented team culture, where commitment is to action predicated upon the attainment of excellence. For example, objectives introduced into a 5,5 compromising culture where there has been no Grid Organization Development are likely to reflect *status quo* thinking and mediocre standards. Objectives set against a 9,1 author-

Box 39

Achievement Motivation Increases Through Setting Objectives During Phase 2 Teamwork Development

Before Phase 2	Teamwide Objectives for Achievement	After Phase 2
	Present	▓
	Almost totally present	
▓	Moderately present	▓
	More present than absent	
▓	Present about as often as absent	
▓	More absent than present	
	Moderately absent	
▓	Almost totally absent	
	Absent	

See Footnote, Box 32

itarian backdrop are likely to be boss-directed, edict-type re-quirements. The culture of the work team must be consciously considered for its influence on objectives set or those achieved. Management by objectives enjoys the greatest prospects for success when the foundations for it are laid in a thorough manner, as set forth in Box 40.

One manager reported, "I found the greatest benefits came from goal-setting and problem-solving sessions and the followup and results of these. Work team goal setting within the team is good, because then you're committing yourself to something that is entirely within your power to accomplish. It keeps you from saying, 'We can't do anything about that because

BOX 40

Management by Objectives Is Possible Only When the
Foundations Are Solid

- Setting Objectives Which Are Motivating
  depends on

  - Releasing Commitment
    which depends on

    - Involvement with Team Goals
      which depends on

      - Effective Participation and Synergistic Teamwork
        which depends on

        - Unobstructed Communication Achieved in
          Teamwork Development
          which depends on

          - Understanding Conflict and Learning to
            Confront and Resolve It
            which depends on

            - Grid Seminar Participation

---

they won't go along,' and in that way using others as an excuse
for not doing what you should do. We found that we had a
lack of involvement that was improved some in Phase 1, but it
was really dealt with in Phase 2."

5. *Increasing Teamwork Skills*

The effective work team is the key to individual and organization excellence. In any organization, every corporate member is a member of a work team. Few members if any are organization hermits—those to whom no one gives directions,
whose work is of no consequence to anyone else, who need
not communicate or coordinate with others. If this is individuality, it is a myth, at least in the modern corporation. People are
bosses, subordinates, and colleagues. They have close inter-
workings, goals in common, and individual goals. They share

Box 41

Teamwork Skills Increase During Phase 2 Teamwork Development

Before Phase 2	Teamwork	After Phase 2
	Successful	
	Almost fully successful	
	Moderately successful	
	A little more successful than unsuccessful	
	Neither successful nor unsuccessful	
	A little more unsuccessful than successful	
	Quite unsuccessful	
	Almost completely unsuccessful	
	Unsuccessful	

See Footnote, Box 32

the need for coordination and cooperation just as each shoulders solo responsibility and effort. A work team reflects the extent to which organization members are interdependent. Box 41 shows improvement in teamwork skills resulting from Phase 2. The application of what is learned in Grid Seminars makes possible the integrated use of these skills in the performance of the work team.

The fact that people are interdependent does not necessarily mean that they are physically together. It does not mean groups or committees but means that each person is effectively contributing that aspect of the total for which he is uniquely re-

sponsible. It means that all who embrace common objectives
mesh efforts in such a way as to achieve the synergism that
sound interdependence can contribute. The football team is
the best analogy available with which to compare a corporate
team. The quarterback can move through the line if the guard
has done his job. The possibility of the guard's doing his job is
increased when he and the tackle know how to move together.
Also in parallel with the corporate team, a football team has a
common objective of winning. When this objective is deeply
embraced and when skills of teamwork have been honed to
a razor sharp edge, the extra effort which means victory can
be aroused. Individual effort under team objectives represents
a true integration of the individual into the team, whether football or corporate. In a corporation which has genuinely learned
the meaning of teamwork, the use of the word *group* or *com-
mitt*ee instead of *team* would be as incongruous as a reference
to a "football committee" or "football group" on the gridiron.

Developing team skills is one of the important Phase 2 objectives. Teamwork skills are used effectively when members of
a team have acquired several kinds of competence. They have
learned to make sound use of time. They can identify and grasp
the full dimensions of problems that need solution. They know
how to go about formulating alternative possibilities that
merit examination before a conclusion is reached. The pros and
cons of each alternative are weighed. This is possible because
members have learned that candid communication to resolve
conflict in opposing points of view is a sound basis for achieving understanding and agreement. They are prepared to implement solutions to their problems and critique the soundness of
these solutions in the light of operational facts. Under these
conditions, teamwork is likely to achieve peak effectiveness.

Learning these kinds of skills of effective teamwork in the
primary work team is a first step. Teamwork skills are equally
important in another kind of situation. This is when several persons, whose primary memberships are in different teams or
organization divisions, are drawn together by their concern for
the solution of a common problem, the scope of which over-
rides their independent responsibilities. The kind of problem
solving that takes place when temporary clusters form and
operate because persons want to solve the problem rather than

Box 42

Use of Critique to Solve Problems Increases in Phase 2
Teamwork Development

Before Phase 2	Use of Critique	After Phase 2
	Effective; team action as well as operational results critiqued as the basis of learning	▓
	Almost totally effective	▓
	Moderately effective	▓
	Somewhat effective (more effective than ineffective)	
▓	Intermediate between effective and ineffective	
▓	Somewhat ineffective (more ineffective than effective)	
	Moderately ineffective	
▓	Almost totally ineffective	
▓	Ineffective; critique not used by our team, either to improve team action or operational results	

See Footnote, Box 32

because they are instructed to do so is a hallmark of effective organization teamwork.

6. *Using Critique for Learning*

A valid critique of both past and present performance is probably the most direct way to *learn* how to make future performance more effective. Fullest learning from experience comes about when critique methods of learning have become a way of organization life. Critique also makes possible the spotting of problems as they emerge. A Phase 2 objective is to apply

critique to team performance, not only to improve the team but
also to learn the use of critique for on-the-job application in
solving operational problems. One of the largest shifts in effective teamwork, as shown in Box 42, is from relatively ineffective use of critique before Teamwork Development to much
more effective use of it afterward. This conclusion about the
heightened awareness and increased use of critique as a result
of Grid Organization Development is perhaps the most widely
reported single impact point resulting from the Phase 2 activities.

TEAMWORK DEVELOPMENT IS PLANNED APPLICATION

This description of Phase 2 provides a basis for pursuing
several questions. Why is it necessary that Teamwork Development occur after a Grid Seminar? Is it true that people do not
apply in an informal, natural way what they have learned?
Why has it been found necessary that followup steps be planned
and programmed?

Insuring That Fadeout Does Not Occur

Work team culture is pervasive. Its action and impact are
often so deep yet so silent that those who are a part of the culture do not seem to be able to change it except through a deliberately planned, programmed approach. Students, whether in
an academic or corporate setting, find little difficulty in learning facts that are interesting and personally significant. Yet
they find great difficulty in acting upon those facts, particularly
when it requires significant changes for them. Without the programmatic followup of behavior learning, this kind of personal
application is unlikely to just happen, as if by magic. It can
and does occur, however, when the strategy of development
insures that learning will be implemented with replacement of
unsound practices by sound ones.

When corporate members complete an educational experience, such as a Grid Seminar, their expectations for their own
personal performance as well as for organization excellence are
almost always uniformly high. They feel encouraged and opti-
mistic that good things can happen. Resistance to change is low

or absent. A man tries to apply his learning when he returns to work. When he meets the difficulties embedded in the corporate culture, his constructive expectations are violated. He then begins to wonder, "What's the use?" And the next step is to feel, "It won't work. To heck with it! I hope the company won't bother me with any more of this. Just leave me alone and I'll do my best." Resistance to trying to change increases.

Without Phases 2 through 6 as organized followup activities, the situation is much like that shown graphically in Box 43 when resistance increases (fadeout) if expectations for improvement are not met. The trends shown are confirmed by many reports of individual reactions at varying intervals after completion of an educational experience.

Reactions of Corporate Members to Teamwork Development

When the entire Phase 2 cycle has been completed, often a striking difference appears between participants' reactions to it and their reactions to the Grid Seminar. Understanding this can aid in providing a sense of what Teamwork Development contributes beyond the contribution of Grid Seminar attendance. A typical reaction to a Grid Seminar is one of enthusiasm, personal reward from new learning, and anticipation of working more effectively. The common reaction to Phase 2 is deeper personal gratification. It is a far more sober reaction than the usual reaction to a Grid Seminar because there is more penetrating understanding of the real problems that confront the individual. The difference is that the learning in a Grid Seminar takes place in a relatively neutral situation. A person measures himself against theoretical possibilities. He can experiment and convince himself, but he is not faced with operational realities. By contrast, in Phase 2 the situation is anything but neutral as a person has a stake in the outcome. Using theory, each person is studying himself as he has been operating in his work situation. The others, aiding him in understanding himself more objectively, are talking with him and giving him information that is based on their extended and indepth evaluation of his job performance. Beyond the serious-mindedness of individual application, it is not uncommon for work teams to discover that there are many deep seated problems that must be solved if

BOX 43

Fadeout from Learning Occurs When Expectations for
Increasing Organization Effectiveness Are Not Met

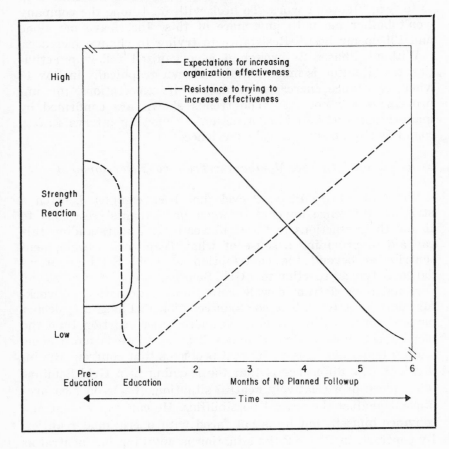

they are to gain more fully the real contribution to organization effectiveness that sound teamwork can provide.

SUMMARY

An analogy can be used to emphasize the implications of this phase for achieving and maintaining corporate excellence.

Every company must take steps to insure that physical equipment operates with maximum effectiveness. Vast amounts of time and money are spent on market development, on research and development, and on machinery and plant maintenance. A $50,000 machine with a ten-year life typically receives more attention than a $50,000-a-year man receives over the same ten years, even though his cost to the organization is ten times that of the machine and his potential contribution may be one hundred times as great.

In Phase 2, work is stopped long enough to study the effectiveness with which it is being accomplished. Each team member is aided in inventorying his work-related behavior by identifying those parts of his performance which are functioning well and those needing improvement. The team enables each man to see his own performance with the objectivity that only candor among colleagues who themselves are committed to corporate excellence makes possible. During discussions of work team culture and later in the setting of objectives for change, any cultural practices which have come to be taken for granted in the operation of the team are reexamined, renovated, removed, or replaced, or retained if sound. Because Phase 2 brings people face to face with genuine problems and in a way that means that these problems must be resolved, it is serious business. But it is rewarding because mature people seem to have unbounded energy that they are prepared to commit to dealing with serious problems.

REFERENCES

1. Patterns of corporate culture tend to stabilize rapidly. Two to three years after its formation, the culture of a company may be as firm and resistant to change as are cultures of companies after 30 years or more. The assumption that the younger a company, the less deeply entrenched its culture is unjustified. Every company has a culture and the effectiveness with which the culture is being managed is not necessarily related to company age.

2. The phrase *work team* applies to any unit that has objectives to accomplish. In this book, the *top team* is a work team just as are men who are directly engaged in physical output.

3. Odiorne, G. S. *Management by Objectives.* New York: Pitman Publishing Corporation, 1965.

6

THE QUEST FOR CANDOR

Three episodes from different Teamwork Development situations are presented in this chapter. Each highlights a different activity within the total sequence. The first shows the price paid by a top man in lack of openness and candor among others because of his tight control and suppression of conflict. The second shows how a top team, with each member operating out of his own department, had produced a cancelling out effect rather than exploiting the opportunities to achieve synergistic results. The third demonstrates how a decade of drifting had devastated the capacity of a large plant to exercise initiative with the result that many problems had become deep seated and chronic. These types of issues are generally typical of the kind that appear when organization teams confront the question of their effectiveness in the objective way depicted. Perhaps only the third could be regarded as exceptional.

I. Breaking the Sound Barrier

The team is a top team of a large, fully owned American subsidiary located in one of the developing countries within the European economic community. The company is fully integrated, having its own manufacturing, marketing, distribution, and research facilities. The top team has a high degree of autonomy in managing the affairs of its business.

The company was committed to everyone's having the experience and learning of Phase 1. Top team members had

120

Box 44

Organization Development Events Preceding Top Team Phase 2

—Seeding of six managers in public Grid Seminars

—Organization Development Coordinator attended Organization Development Seminar; another line manager attended Instructor Development Seminar

—Pilot incompany seminar conducted six months after first seeding

—Decision made for total managerial organization to participate in Phase 1 incompany Grid Seminars—180 managers attended

—Based partly on reactions to Phase 1, decision made by top team to experiment with Phase 2

---

doubts, however, about what could be gained from the Teamwork Development of Phase 2. With strong reservations among some, they had agreed with the top man to experiment with it. Box 44 summarizes the major steps taken before the top team began its own Teamwork Development.

First Line of Attack

After a rocky start, team members began to warm up to the task of reaching agreement on what a sound team culture would be. Because of previous discussions among themselves, there was a fairly high uniformity of agreement that 9,9 team action represents the soundest model for operating. They also had agreed that if for some reason this were not achievable, their second choice would be to take a strong hard line before accepting softer positions detrimental to the company.

By the time top team members began discussing their actual operation, they were deeply involved. Examples of problems in running the business came to the surface as they deliberated various aspects of their operations through examination, discussion, and agreement on how to assess themselves against the team culture instrument. What later proved to be the opening wedge to bringing about a change of attitudes was the sales manager's example of a failure to communicate and include others in decision making. The top man was involved in the example. The sales manager concluded candidly, "By your changing the decision after talking with advertising and marketing, but then not coming back to me—honestly, I was mad as hell, because I didn't know it had changed and had to get it from a third party."

At that point the top man lashed out sharply, "That's not a good example—that's not what happened at all. I checked with you before you left and told you what we were planning to do before I met with the marketing and advertising people. If you didn't agree, you should have said something then. Your own people knew. Why didn't they tell you?"

"That's not what happened," snapped the sales manager. "My own people *didn't* know. I only learned of it accidentally. You told me before I left that you were ready to go with things the way they were. You made that change after the advertising people came to you because they were unhappy with what we finally decided to do."

"That decision is final. I don't want to have to discuss it any more. You and your people are always whining and complaining whenever you don't go along with the decision that has been made. Otherwise, you're perfectly happy."

Retreat

During the short but sharp exchange, a deadly quiet had settled over the group. A few exchanged glances. Several absorbed themselves in their books. Finally the personnel manager cleared his throat. "Let's move on to the next issue." The discussion was flat and lifeless. The signal was given that the top man did not want them to be candid, particularly if it involved him. They plodded through the remainder of the work of this activity without much spirit.

The review of team culture ended with a critique of the quality of their work. They judged it fair but seemed unsatisfied with the results. Several reasons for why they felt that they had not done a good job were mentioned, but most were mechanical. No one brought up the fact that the atmosphere of candor had evaporated from the discussions or why.

As they turned to considering moving forward into the assessment of how they saw each other operating, the real concerns and reservations began to emerge. Only six of the ten were willing to move on. Even they had reservations. The others saw no value in moving forward and felt they should either spend the rest of the time on other things or pack up and go home. Many reasons were thrown out as to why the step would be of little value, but they were so obscure and guarded that the team was unable to define the problem and reach a decision among themselves.

They finally reached an impasse and were unable to decide what to do. Four held out to use the rest of the time differently or break off the meeting. The financial officer said, "One of the reasons for this activity is to enable design of followup teamwork suited specifically for our purposes. The program was designed for just any company. Who is to say that it is what is needed here? If we stay at all, I recommend that we spend the remainder of our time designing a program that will fit us and that we feel would be of value. I can't see that we'll get anything from following this kind of program." He received support from several others.

A sharp challenge was made to this last statement by another team member. "Isn't that running away from our real problem? The difficulty that we are having is not with the strategy of Teamwork Development. Being unable to be candid, we are unable to use the instruments. The problem that we must learn to solve is to be candid."

Finally the boss took over. "I don't know how we're going to break out of the log jam. I've heard enough comments about problems of discussing personal action with the boss present, so maybe one way of getting started is for me to leave. Someone had suggested earlier that you go ahead without me, but I agree with Jack that I probably know all of you better than anyone else and have more dealings with you. Therefore, you would lose whatever comments and observations I could make. Besides, I wouldn't get the benefit of your comments about me. So why don't I just leave and let you thrash it out. Let me say right now I have no feelings one way or the other. This is an experiment and I don't want anyone feeling that it will be held

against him. Whatever you decide to do is fine with me and
we won't look back on that decision. Just call me back when
you've finally decided."

Reconnaissance

After he left the room, the market research manager spoke
up. "Look, let's quit tripping the light fantastic and say what
we mean. Except for three of you, and you know who I mean,
no one was really being candid."

"Of course we weren't" the manufacturing manager said.
"Look what happened to Bob when he tried to give that ex-
ample. He got his head guillotined and handed back to him.
I'm not sticking my head on that chopping block."

"Who is *he* kidding?" asked another manager. "He came
up here with a clear goal in mind to help us go through all of
these steps. Why do you think he is pushing us on a schedule
that he has set? He wants to insure when we leave here that
we've completed everything we set out to do."

"Just tell me what we could get out of this," said another,
"except maybe cause each other more harm and even hurt our
careers. Sure, he said the purpose was to see what we could
gain in being more effective. But he's only human! He's sure
to hear some things he didn't know and hold them against us.
They're bound to influence his thinking later on."

One of the managers who wanted to move forward had a
suggestion. "You're just looking at the negative side and maybe
imagining a lot of things. Why don't you look at the positive
side. There's a lot we can learn and gain from direct discussion,
not only in our relationship with him but also in the way we're
working together. We've never tried it before. I think we ought
to give it a try."

Another supported him. "If we can't do this job openly, then
I don't see how we can solve any of our problems or even move
away from a lot of the politicking that goes on."

The discussion was animated. Everyone was participating.
"What are we going to do? It's clear he doesn't want us to be
honest, particularly if we are talking about him. That's typical
of the way he chops us up back on the job. Let's not kid ourselves," another manager said.

"I think we ought to go ahead," said another. "At least we should discuss one or two of us and if the same thing happens— if we don't feel it's worthwhile—we can still quit and do something else or go home. But now that we're up here and have gone this far, I think we ought to at least try it."

"If I thought he would be more receptive," said a dissenter, "I wouldn't mind going ahead. I'd be willing under two conditions: 1) if he would quit pushing us on his private tight time schedule so that we could really do a good job, and 2) if we decide it's not worthwhile, then we stop wherever we are and talk about how we could do something else. I am convinced that there is a lot of value to be gained and would like to do the same kind of thing with my subordinates."

"I would have this proviso. Before we get started, we decide just what things we are going to talk about and what things we aren't. We need to establish ground rules so that someone doesn't talk about things that are irrelevant or inappropriate or better done in a one-to-one situation with the person concerned."

"I would go along with you except we come right back to the main problem—he just isn't willing to listen and will cut us off when something comes up that ought to be said but he doesn't want to hear."

The discussion continued for nearly two hours, as members talked back and forth about getting into personal assessment. Each time the discussion would come back to the boss's closing his ears to what he did not want to hear; to cutting people off sharply and sometimes using ridicule so that they had no zest for pursuing the matter. This issue was particularly important to solve because when critical work issues were involved, good ideas were cut down in the same way.

Second Maneuver

Toward the end of the discussion, the Grid Organization Development specialist working with the group said, "What would be the pros and cons of telling him directly when he comes back that you want to move forward but only under the conditions that he listens to what's being said and that you reserve the right to challenge him whenever he moves in and tries to cut someone off. If you're not candid with him, how do you expect him to act any differently?"

"Maybe we ought to level with him first," someone suggested.

"I don't think we could," the sales manager answered. "You know from Phase 1 that it takes a while to get moving and to develop some candor, and I don't think we would be candid with him if he were first. And so we wouldn't gain anything and he wouldn't either."

"Why don't we just tell him point-blank what our provisions are for moving forward and then discuss him when we feel like we have developed a good degree of candor. But we may not know how he really feels until we've seen how he reacts to our assessment of him."

The Grid Organization Development specialist had a suggestion. "Why not begin with one of you who you agree is neither the easiest nor the hardest to do or someone you feel is a little more thick-skinned than others. Then do the boss second or third so that you do not have a continuing concern about him, thus relieving any dampening effect on your discussions."

"What if he wants to go first?" someone asked.

The sales manager had an answer. "Then I think we ought to put among our provisos that we want him to be one of the early ones but don't feel he should be first and give our reasons. I suggest that we call him in and tell him without hedging that we want to try the activity with a few of us, including him as one of the early ones. We feel if he behaves as he did in earlier discussions—cutting people off—it would not be worthwhile to go on. We should also say that we want to be thorough, and so he should not push us under his private time schedule. This kind of thing is too important to rush through."

Several were far from convinced but agreed to the plan. The boss was invited back. They reviewed the discussion and conditions under which they felt they could continue.

"I think you came to a good conclusion," he said. "I was hoping you would want to go ahead, but I didn't want to impose it. As far as calling me down, if you feel that I am being unjust and not listening, I've always wanted you to do this. But usually people back down and I assume that they don't have enough conviction to feel that they are right. Therefore, I see no reason for changing my mind once it's made up."

Box 45
Attitudes of Top Team Members About Candor

Reservations and Doubts	Beliefs and Convictions
What rights do subordinates have in criticizing the boss?	A subordinate has the obligation to assist the boss in being more effective.
People should not criticize others, especially in front of the boss.	If criticism is based on fact and not prejudice, it should be constructive, not destructive.
The boss may learn something he did not know about a subordinate and hold it against him.	There is an even chance that unknown strengths of subordinates will be revealed.
Candor could harm a person's career; people might be too candid and do more harm than good.	Honorable honesty which results in a person's striving for improvement will enhance his career.
Candor is only possible in one-to-one situations.	This is a contradiction of terms. Candor is only candor when it can be exposed to the light of day.
We are not a team; therefore, we cannot judge how each person is operating.	If we are not a team, we had better find out why and take appropriate corrective steps.
A person won't accept what he hears because they are only impressions, not facts.	One of the ground rules should be talking from fact and identifying impressions when they are only that.
We can work on problems and goals without doing personal assessment.	If we don't identify the communication barriers created by personal behavior, we probably will not get down to the real work problems.

Before beginning, the top team members spent some time talking about how they would work and reviewing some of their attitudes about candor which could affect the quality of the discussion. Attitudes held by one or more persons are summarized in Box 45.

The Point of Breakthrough

The sales manager was first. The team surprised themselves by getting into the activity more easily than they had imagined. When they finished their description of him, they looked back and were pleased with the results. Yet they agreed that the quality could have been higher and they could have given him greater insight if they had been even more candid.

As they reviewed their discussion, the personnel manager suggested, "Let's do one more, namely myself, and then discuss the boss. If we're talking about being candid, I for one know that I've been holding back some, and I probably will continue to until I know where he stands."

His suggestion was followed and they completed their review of the personnel man. There was some improvement in discussion, they felt, but it still was not as candid as it could be to be fully effective. At that point the boss said, "Well, there's no need putting it off any longer. Whether you do a good job or not, it's time for me to get in the saddle." The team took a deep, collective breath before describing to the boss how they saw him in action.

They began cautiously. The third comment began, "I have noted down some things since we got here which I think need to be said." With that the speaker went into a detailed description of how the top man vacillated from one approach to another, on occasion forcing his will with an iron fist, leaving little or no room for challenge or questioning. At other times he seemed to manipulate people and not make a decision, saying it was up to them and letting them guess his convictions, thus creating friction among managers and a feeling that they were being "used."

With that the group seemed to loosen up. Others endorsed what the third man had said and were able to cite many examples. These were talked through, with the men giving their

feelings and reactions to them in a thorough way. They had
now reached a high level of candor. From time to time the boss
would ask for examples, not in his typical challenging or ridi-
culing way, but in a way that indicated an interest in understanding better some of the reactions and feelings under discussion. They spent nearly three hours discussing how he
operated and some of the problems he created for them. The
boss reacted in such a way that obviously communicated to them
that they could be more open. Upon completion of this discussion, the atmosphere had clearly changed. They began to move
forward with a much greater sense of involvement.

Victory

The final test of the extent to which they could openly discuss
their problems was in the description of the actions of the
research and development manager, who seemed to be at the
heart of many of the problems of coordination between departments. They knew this would be difficult and that he represented
the last hurdle for their achieving candor. They laid it on the
line. They neither minced words nor held back their feelings.
He was told how he appeared to want to extend his lines of
authority more and more into other areas but closely guarded
and rejected anything that even implied that others might be
making suggestions about the work of his department. Schedules and plans were delayed until the last minute because he
did not exert the effort other departments did to meet tight
time schedules. His unrealistic and idealistic standards and
thinking along textbook lines prevented them from making
sound business decisions. They showed that he and his department demonstrated little concern for profit as long as professional standards were met, standards that were not appropriate
or were too costly for the payoff that could be realized. He
was told many other things and in a forthright manner. He
obviously found great difficulty in absorbing the impact of what
he had been told. It was also clear that inconsistencies had been
revealed in what he believed he had been doing and what
others had said they had seen. It would be some time before
he worked through in his thinking all of these inconsistencies.

He admitted that he could see many problems that had arisen through his own doing.

His reaction was, "I've heard a lot of things that could create problems with you. I have them all listed. Some I don't understand yet. I'm not sure that I agree with them, but one thing is clear. Many of the issues you have mentioned need much more discussion and better understanding on my part. Many of the points have dollar signs on them and if they can be resolved, expense reduction and profit improvement are surely to be expected as results. Therefore, I would like to be able to get together with some of you individually to pursue more deeply some of the things that have been said and to discuss the problems you see in my department as a result of the way I have been operating. This could be the most beneficial thing that has ever happened to me."

The crisis had been reached and passed. Without saying so, team members knew that if they could be candid with this person, they could be candid with everyone. They knew they could discuss openly interdepartmental problems which they had previously denied and said did not exist. They were through the crisis. They had the confidence that they could do the job that needed to be done.

From then on, tension was absent from the atmosphere. Individual behavior and problems were discussed freely, directly, simply. Problems which had not been openly or fully explored during the examination of their culture were approached in a way that could lead to real resolution. Before leaving, they made plans for continuing with the activities as soon as possible. Individually they were also formulating plans for beginning Phase 2 Teamwork Development with their own teams.

II. DIVIDED WE FALL

"We may be called the 'top team,' " the plant manager said, "but I am not so sure we are a team. I know each of you is working hard at your own job, but efforts just haven't been adding up as they should. We here at the plant have only been contributing increases in costs to the corporate picture."

This is the way the plant manager opened his Phase 2 Teamwork Development. This plant is one manufacturing unit reporting to a vice president of manufacturing. It has three production departments. Their managers, together with the industrial engineer, the administrative manager, and the industrial relations manager, make up the top team of the plant.

The Influence of Headquarters

This fact of high cost with hard effort was known equally well by other team members.

"We know how to get those boxes out of the back door in a streamlined way," one manager said, "but if I were on a profit center basis and didn't have to depend upon requirements and services from outside, there are a lot of things I guarantee you I would change. We get results and that's primarily what we're concerned with around here." Another department manager supported him, "But we sure don't worry about how we get them either from the standpoint of costs or demands that we pressure people with."

"We know what side our bread is buttered on," another department manager said. "Our performance is judged at headquarters by whether we meet production objectives. We wouldn't be human if we worried about anything else."

The industrial engineer said the same in another way. "It's no different in my situation. I have performance standards and ways of doing things and processes and procedures and new methods to sell to you people which are developed in the headquarters engineering division. That's why I'm here; I'm expected to be the link for the industrial engineering division to see that sound operating procedures are developed, established, and used within the various production units. Now I can't force them on you, but my responsibility is to make them available to you."

A Group Is Not a Team

At the beginning of Phase 2, this particular group saw no compelling purpose for meeting. The prevailing attitude among members was, "You run your shop and I'll run mine." One department manager summarized the situation by saying, "We run a 5,5 organization in a 9,1 way." Overall they were implementing many routinized operational practices with minimum involvement in thinking through how best to accomplish plant objectives.

In terms of mechanics of running the operations, it should have been a well functioning system. Production costs were set for each particular segment of the organization. Up and down the line each person, including top team members, had a job description which clearly outlined his responsibilities within his span of authority. On paper there were no gray areas. Because of this rigidity, departmental objectives seemed to be at variance at times. As a result, employees felt stresses and strains that caused them to drift ever further apart. Characteristics of the corporate culture that reinforced the stresses and splits are described in Box 46.

From a mechanical, manning, and equipment point of view, the organization was well designed, but the designing was done without thought for strategies relative to the human organization that could make the design work. The top team members viewed their purposes differently, even those related to running their separate departments and units. Some, for example, believed they had only production responsibilities. Others thought they had responsibilities not only for production but also for safe conditions, job security, and adequate benefits to subordinates. The plant manager felt his obligation was to the plant organization and also to corporate profit goals. Whatever the definition of purpose, the result was that various persons were looking at different things and placing weight on different elements with respect to objectives to be achieved and problems to be solved.

This loosely knit group was held together by a tight grip on the reins of the top man. An engineer by training and profession, he is recognized as knowing the business from the ground up. The Grid Organization Development specialist who observed these sessions recognized that the plant manager reached his decisions quickly. Once his convictions were formed, they seemed almost unshakable. His pace and energy belied his sixty years. He was a large powerfully built man with a booming voice. His face looked like it had been chiseled out of rock. When he became angered, his reaction was like a thunderclap. He relied only on himself and dealt with subordinates strictly on a

Box 46

Characteristics of Corporate Culture Affecting
Management Behavior and Performance of the Top Team

Rigid, "tried and true" traditions and practices imposed on plant by headquarters

Fixed, functional lines that create split loyalties, interpersonal frictions, and intergroup splits within plant

Planning, policy formulation, process and product development, and financial control highly centralized in headquarters with minimum regard or involvement of plant management

Lack of open, candid communication between headquarters and the plant

---

one-to-one basis. He disliked conflict with others or between them and cut it off sharply.

Only in alliance against "common enemies" did this top group react with any degree of cohesion. At times headquarters demands brought it together for mutual support. Marketing criticisms of poor production occasionally spurred a united reaction. These actions represent only momentary joining of forces. Most of the time, top team members found little reason to bind themselves together in a concerted way.

Mutual Protection Society

Because of the "you run your shop, and I'll run mine" attitude and the 9,1 leadership of the top man, there seemed to be an implicit understanding that no one would talk about the way things were being done in another department. Everyone was sensitive about not stepping on others' toes. No matter how bad the situation, criticism was usually held in. The situation was tolerated. If a condition in one department affected another, the affected department manager would go to the boss. This resulted in the top man's spending an inordinate amount of time serving as an arbitrator when differences arose between departments.

His action as arbitrator widened the cleavages between departments, intensified win-lose attitudes, and created ill will and animosity.

Clarifying the Work Culture

Because of the problems with its culture, this team spent over two full days analyzing it. The result was a clear focusing and crystallizing of traditions, norms, past practices, values, and attitudes that had helped shape the team's thinking and behavior.

Box 47 summarizes the analysis of the work culture. The 9,1 management by the boss and the extreme isolation of work team members together with a larger cultural background of "engineered mechanisms" and sharp functional lines had resulted in mutual suspicion and distrust among colleagues. In the past there had been wholesale "politicking" by cliques and temporary alliances governed by the particular gains derived or the frustrations of the moment. Departmental membranes were no longer permeable but had become blocked. Horizontal communications were non-existent. Top team members wore a mask of bland tolerance while suppressing feelings of resentment and distrust. Superficial discussions of trivial matters took place between departments, but critical issues that required cooperation between top team members were avoided.

Studying Personal Behavior and Performance

After the team's culture had been examined, the team moved on to an examination of each member's managerial behavior and performance. The plant manager set the pace by asking that his managerial actions be studied first. He was determined to use the session in the most constructive manner. He said, "This task gives us the opportunity to sweep away the complacency we have in ourselves which clouds our thinking. As we have worked together, we have become too accustomed to each other. We have settled for being predictable at the expense of outstanding performance. I'm sure that many of my own ways of managing are ones that I've persisted in, not because I necessarily believe that they are the best ways to get results, but because I've

Box 47

Description of the Work Team Culture

Traditional ways of doing things are rarely questioned; they represent the tried and true operating standards.

Plans come down from the boss without opportunity to review, evaluate, or recommend changes by those who implement them.

Persons only do what is expected of them. Each man runs his own shop. The boss calls the shots.

Results are what count no matter how achieved.

Followup is by the boss on a one-by-one basis but discussion on a surface level.

Persons exercise initiative only when policies and guide lines are clear; otherwise problems are passed to the boss for decision.

When problems arise between departments, people are careful to maintain neutrality, settling for halfway solutions.

---

become set in my ways. The benefit I see in your writing a good, accurate description of my managerial behavior and performance is in being able to dig beneath the surface of superficial politeness. If we can get this kind of objectivity into the descriptions of each of us then we're in a strong position to do improvement planning, and that's where the payout is."

The discussion began with a description of his strengths as a manager. There was clear acceptance that he probably knew the business and its many parts better than anyone else. He could penetrate a problem in an incisive, direct way. Although his ability was recognized, the way in which decisions were reached and implemented came under analysis. "You don't communicate your decisions to us," said the first department manager. "No one is quarreling with your right to make the decision, but sometimes you've reached it before we even know what's happened, and then you just say, 'This is it' without a word of explanation or reason or anything else."

"That's right," agreed another. "Sometimes, when I talk with you about a problem, the discussion is over before I even think it is begun. Sure, I find out later or become convinced later that it was the right decision, but the result can be foot dragging and, I don't mind admitting it, low commitment where I'm involved."

"I agree," said a third. "If you wouldn't just announce a decision but tell us why you came to that decision and the facts behind it, and furthermore what the alternatives were and why they didn't stand the test of analysis, I'm sure we'd have a better basis for supporting it. But the way it is done now, people just say 'what the hell'—a guy just naturally isn't going to run out of here and knock himself out to get results."

"This kind of unilateral decision making without discussion also happens in our meetings," said the industrial relations manager. "We sit in here and say little or nothing. You draw your conclusions and don't even ask our reactions. And I know all the rest of us, because I have too, will leave when a decision has been made that we do not agree with and then raise all kinds of holy hell and objections in the hall."

The industrial engineering manager described another aspect of the problem. "Let's face it. We all have been guilty of the same thing. We line up our allies and then we bring our recommendations to the boss for decisions. We present the data that will bolster our position and disregard or hold back other points that may be important. Backed up with a long laundry list of facts, we try to maneuver him to make a decision in our favor. But all of this we do behind our closed doors."

As team members began to open up with the boss, he gave evidence of listening for recurring themes. He made a genuine effort to avoid being defensive and to refrain from denying what was being said to him. Because of the tone set, team members were encouraged to go forward and review the managerial behavior of each man in turn.

The descriptions below of other members of the team are not the actual paragraph descriptions written by team members. Rather, each represents background information for the improvement objectives selected by each manager.

First Production Department Manager. On the surface he appears to be a rather mild person. He has rigid and deep-seated private values. The chief among these is the belief that "civilized people do not criticize one another or talk to another person about personal aspects of his behavior." He also believes that a manager is paid to think and act independently in his job. If he can't do the job, he should be replaced, but as long as he is in the job, he should be allowed by his boss or colleagues to run it in the manner he sees fit. He sees no value in involving subordinates in problems. He sees them as out to get by with as little as possible. In summary, he privately holds strong 9,1 attitudes and assumptions about other persons and about his role as a manager. He is a loner.

Second Production Department Manager. Although not slow to develop convictions, he is deliberate about taking a stand and is almost exclusively influenced by facts—things that he can see, touch, or smell. Once he has taken a stand on what he feels to be a completely factual basis, it becomes almost impossible to shift his thinking. He is difficult to move even though he is presented with added facts or contrary facts. Although he is serious-minded he is open and spontaneous in expressing his thoughts, reservations, and feelings.

Third Production Department Manager. The only person in the top team who has spent much of his working life with the parent company, he knows the corporate culture inside and out. He has a strong air of pessimism. His initial reaction to a situation is, "It can't be done." He will push a point of view in a rather outspoken way for a sustained period of time but will almost unnoticeably withdraw when he sees he is not achieving anything. The result is that when others feel he is finally convinced, he seems suddenly to return to his original position and is just as unconvinced as when he started.

Industrial Relations Manager. A sincere and intense man, he sometimes is seen as idealistic in his thinking. He is highly motivated and exerts himself when personally involved, but if an organization issue does not capture his fancy, he tends to go along too quickly and seems to feel little hesitation in compromising his thinking.

Industrial Engineer. A soft spoken man, he is a person who can be in a group and go unnoticed. Quietly and unobtrusively he places an idea on the table with little or no comment or fanfare. If the thought is unheard, disregarded, or brushed aside, he will merely pick it up again and try once more. His approach to influencing others is like water dripping on a rock.

Business Services Manager. With his high technical skills and competence in accounting, computer, and other business sciences, he concerns himself only with these areas and seldom gets involved in issues outside his field. He tries to use persuasion in getting procedures and practices adopted within the various departments. If this cannot be done, he goes to headquarters to exert pressure from the top business services officer of the company. He acts as if he were on detached service to the plant rather than being a part of the team.

Following agreement on how they saw the person operating, the team identified three or more improvement areas for each. These served as a basis for each manager to develop a plan for changing his style. Box 48 summarizes one improvement objective selected by each person.

At the end they agreed that this kind of review and examination should be made a part of their regular work activities. A specific date was set about two months later for a critique of progress using the written documents produced here. The aim was to review with each person the character of his contribution in order to identify where needed changes were being made and where recommended changes had not resulted in progress.

Team Objectives

Up to this point team members had examined their ways of operating and both the team and individual barriers to effective

Box 48
Improvement Objectives for Team Members

Person	Improvement Area	Plan of Action	Probable Barriers to Achievement
Plant Manager	Give background thinking to decisions reached—involve department managers more in thinking through and testing implications before decisions are finalized	When necessary to announce decision, follow up with written memos detailing rationale and background Encourage questions in sessions Seek out disagreements or reservations Identify problems of others in implementing decisions and give active support	Strong feeling that subordinates should be committed to action without having to know reasons why Impatience to move to other things
Department Manager 1	Delegate more and involve subordinates more	Give more routine and detail work to subordinates Insure subordinates know what, how, when, and where of assignments so more confidence in results can be extended Involve others in critical as well as minor issues	Deep convictions he should "go it alone" Lack of confidence in abilities or intentions of others
Department Manager 2	When wrong, shift thinking more quickly—less win-lose position taking	Take less of a department view Probe for the possibility that others have opinions and facts to contribute Don't take differences personally or as rejection of self Give others more benefit of own thinking and facts, not just conclusions Be less defensive and aggressive to others personally Curb "sharp tongue" that solves nothing	Defensiveness Strong identification with own viewpoints rather than with problem Overpowers others as a weapon; cuts off facts

Box 48 continued on next page

Box 48 (cont.)

Person	Improvement Area	Plan of Action	Probable Barriers to Achievement
Department Manager 3	Whenever you feel, "It can't be done," remind yourself we see this as pessimism and force yourself to think of alternative possibilities	Think through problem fully and clearly Organize thoughts and present in logical manner Be more straightforward. Don't hedge on touchy issues or possible areas of contention	"Can't do" attitude Quick acceptance of things as they are Readiness to go out on a limb—away from "middle"
Industrial Relations Manager	Make fuller contribution—resources and time not fully used	Identify areas (however uninteresting) that need development Increase knowledge in labor relations field Contribute more in areas outside personnel Work closer with Department Managers to see where greater support can be given Initiate needed new training programs Set department objectives with subordinates	Sees some aspects of work as unchallenging or uninteresting
Industrial Engineer	Formulate reports, plans, schemes, processes, etc. in less technical language so others can understand	Put self in other's shoes—make recommendations in terms meaningful to them Don't hide behind expertise Don't "snow" with technical terms Be more explanatory and firmer in convictions Face possibility of rejection of ideas	Distaste of conflict Narrow interests Strong loyalty to headquarters engineering

Box 48 continued on next page

Box 48 (cont.)

Person	Improvement Area	Plan of Action	Probable Barriers to Achievement
Business Services Manager	Make fuller contribution of management science skills	Work with the other departments to solve production and other problems they have Investigate own staff procedures to see if they can be changed to be of greater value to other departments Be less defensive of own staff's work Involve self more in overall plant problems Use headquarters less as a pressure device to get ideas or system bought at plant Involve line and other managers in developing procedures and systems	Functional loyalty Visible impatience with those who are not "experts" in area Failure to see how to contribute to overall plant objectives

problem solving that needed to be removed. Their next step was to specify objectives. They were concerned with (1) developing objectives that would aid them to improve their effectiveness as a problem-solving team no matter what the problem, and (2) developing operational objectives to be achieved if they were to reverse rising costs.

"We need to do much more joint planning than we've done in the past," the industrial relations manager said, then directed his remarks to the plant manager. "We think you can do better planning and come up with stronger objectives if we do this as a team rather than your just piecing together the separate thinking by each of us. We've all gone our separate ways instead of taking united action on anything. This can only lead us downward. If we keep on being divided like this, we'll all fall down. We've always let each production department worry about its safety program, training, and cost reduction. I bet if we examine these across departments, we could get stronger commitment to changes and improvements in increasing production efficiency and decreasing costs and wastes than we have in the past when each of us has been left to work this out for himself. Just to give you one example, each of our departments has its own laboratory section and technicians, but they're all doing the same kinds of jobs. We probably have 30 to 40 percent more technicians than we need. Some of our raw materials shipments get tested in each department on every shipment so that we've tripled the man hours on that one testing step. We could name a hundred similar situations like that if we wanted to."

Over a dozen team effectiveness improvement areas were identified and more than twenty operational objectives and problems pinpointed. Included among the team effectiveness objectives were the development of clear guide lines by this team and subordinate teams for the use of team action for areas where there should be common objectives. Specifically, these included more effective use of critique, better use of time, facing up to conflict rather than turning aside or discussing differences behind one another's back, and stronger and more effective use of meetings. Box 49 summarizes the plan of action for achieving three of these objectives. Also shown are some of the probable barriers that would prevent real success from being achieved.

They discussed two operational objectives, set target dates for these, made specific plans for others, and identified problems for work in the future. These included increasing and improving customer service, achieving better safety practices within the various production divisions, establishing overall plant cost objectives, improving communication throughout the organization, and upgrading technical and other training programs.

The team adopted a new way of planning. In the past, overall objectives had been defined by the plant manager. He would split up the problem and give each department that part it could best handle. Recommendations were passed back to the top man who would then sift through them and announce the final plan of action. The approach during Phase 2 was for the team members first to agree that the objective to be achieved was realistic and necessary. Second, they defined what knowledge, skills, information, and other resources would be needed for them to do the best possible job of examining approaches.

Box 49

Team Objectives and Action Plans Set During Phase 2

Objectives	Plan of Action	Probable Barriers to Success
Operational: Improve efficiency of laboratory services	1) Create task force to establish what functions best handled centrally by labs; what functions best handled by direct operator 2) Determine minimum essential staffing 3) Have plan for relocation 4) Review alternatives and recommendations with top team 5) Make decision and communicate with background reasons 6) Insure sound transition 7) Complete within two months and critique	
Improve effectiveness of staff and clerical functions	1) Use team action task force to develop information on job requirements, current job descriptions, etc. 2) Determine if more or less skills are needed for each job and where demanning is possible 3) Secure policy position from headquarters if needed 4) Establish time schedule for above 5) Communicate statement of intent to plant. If needed, have developed plans for demanning, transfers, aiding employees secure new jobs, etc. 6) Complete above in four months and critique	1) Possible pressure from union 2) Lack of support from headquarters 3) Protectiveness of own departments
Team Effectiveness: Make better use of team action to increase effectiveness of top team planning and reduce crises	1) Identify major decision areas 2) Analyze overriding responsibilities of department heads 3) Determine what types of issues are best resolved at department head level, which need interdepartmental planning by top team before programs are initiated	1) Press of day-to-day problems 2) "Firefighting" reflex 3) Top man's failure to initiate and set example
Make better use of critique	1) Build into work and meeting schedule specific plans for critique 2) In two months, evaluate effectiveness of critiques and make necessary adjustments	1) Work pressures and lack of full commitment

Box 49 continued on next page

Box 49 (cont.)

Team Effectiveness: Make better use of resources and time	1) Preparation by individuals before beginning work on problems 2) Develop agenda of when meetings are to be held 3) Establish priorities 4) Establish and live up to time commitments 5) Use critique	1) Insufficient time devoted to clarifying objectives or problems and bringing up issues on too short notice

They then set up a task force. It included personnel from this team as well as from lower levels of the organization. Another difference in their approach was that they were not content with expressing the objectives to be achieved in general terms but rather developed a clear definitive statement of the problem and the final product.

Headquarters Reappraised

By the time team objectives had been set, this team was no longer divided. It was united by its knowledge that better results could be achieved through concerted action than had been accomplished in the past. Their changed attitudes were reflected in the plant manager's conclusions about headquarters.

"I think we can now see that we have a lot of latitude in how we want to do things and how we want to run this plant. If we'll just admit it, we've taken the easy way out by saying . . . 'that's the way *they* want it and that's the way it's always been,' and let it go at that.

"There are two things, at least, that we can do that we haven't done in the past: one is to get off our backs and make those changes where we know we have the obligation to do so. Second, and I think this would be expected by headquarters, we should look for procedures or policies or standard operating practices that aren't sound or need to be changed to make it possible for us to be more effective. Once we find them, I think, we have the responsibility to determine what changes need to be made and to take them upstairs and get them approved. We've done this before, but only when we were driven to the wall or really felt hot about something. When we have our facts lined up, we can expect that headquarters will be eager to give us the green light."

III. A DECADE OF DETERIORATION

"Whose responsibility is it?" the plant manager asked.

"Purchasing's, I guess. Who else?"

"I don't think we can hold Tom (the purchasing agent) at fault. He's not really a store manager. That's not his job and he's not trained for it."

"I buy what's on the books," said the purchasing agent. "If something's not being used anymore, I don't know it unless the department using it tells me."

"That sounds 1,1 to me," said the production manager (John).

"But, four years—automatically buying the same obsolete stuff?" interrupted the plant manager. "You knew it, John. Why didn't you say something to Tom?"

"I figured he knew from his books. He could tell from requisitions we hadn't picked up one of those parts in nearly two years."

"It's nobody's fault," smoothed the industrial engineer. "We need an inventory system. We're still operating the way we were ten years ago. It's too much for one person now. We need a modern inventory control system. Tom isn't a store manager. We need to get one."

"That's a lot of baloney," the plant manager cracked. "That's not the problem. The problem is no initiative. Nobody takes responsibility. Everyone says, 'Let George do it.' We were kidding ourselves yesterday when we said we're facing up to our problems now. It's business as usual. What is our inventory variance?"

"You all have a copy of the book," said the purchasing agent nervously. "I'm not authorized to make changes in it. I only buy according to what's authorized."

"What's the variance?" the plant manager said impatiently.

"All right, let me just give you the facts," the purchasing agent said. "The book inventory is authorized at one million dollars. As of the first, we had 1.8 million dollars in stock. The variance is eight hundred thousand, but that will go down when we complete installation on the new production line."

"Let's get all the facts on the table," said the production manager. "Nearly everything has been drawn out of the stock for the new line. You correct me if I'm wrong, but your assistant told me the other day that we had nearly 4,000 store items that have practically zero turnover."

"Well, we need some of those parts because they don't make them anymore. If one broke we'd be in a spot," the purchasing agent explained.

"We could have greater interchangeability if we wanted," the production manager said. "We never have tried to standardize. We buy whatever the salesmen put in front of us."

"Production draws up the 'specs' and we buy from that. I can't change anything in the books till somebody tells me to."

"I don't want to change the subject," said the manager of engineering, "but this is the same thing as the foreman problem. We've sat back and moaned about the lack of commitment of first level supervisors and not really asked why. We said yesterday we're better informed since going through Phase 1 of the Grid, and all we have to do is get the rest of the company going. But we're just not taking responsibility for our role in the situation. It's easy to blame past leadership and say, now we have a new boss and everything is dandy, but if we ourselves are not the past leadership, who is? There's lots we could have done in the past but we blame the old boss and go on griping. We'd better take a closer look at ourselves because nobody is going to do it for us. It sounded more like complaining than commitment."

No one except the plant manager seemed to want to say more or face up to the facts. Finally he spoke. "At lunch yesterday Harry (the Organization Development specialist) suggested we take another day and see if we can't get a real start on plans to solve some of our critical problems. I suggest we do it."

This was the way Phase 2 was proceeding in the top team of a manufacturing plant. Progress in digging into the roots of the old team culture was being made. What lay behind this apathetic, deeply gloomy culture of a pessimistic group that should have been a leadership team? Why had they resigned themselves to failure as a fact of life and learned to take organizational setbacks in stride and without question? Why the lack of candor or past absence of signs of vitality?

A Period of Pussyfooting

Under a series of plant managers, each of whom had remained in his position for only a year or so before being replaced, control and authority had become more centralized in the plant manager's office and middle management's strength had deteriorated. It had been a vicious circle. As pressures had increased, the management team had grown weaker until it yielded to the pressures more easily and quickly. The union-management situation was a good example.

If the plant's continuous production lines were to go unattended for three shifts, the entire process would have to be shut down. Not only tremendous damage to the product and the production equipment but high costs in hours of labor to get back into production would result. Within the last year, there had been a union walkout over the question of early wash up time. Since management had traditionally yielded quickly to union pressures to assure uninterrupted production, the workers knew their demands would be met immediately. This is precisely what took place. Soon after, they had walked out again. During this walkout, the company was adding a new production line but top management at headquarters had decided to call the union's bluff and shut down the operations at a cost of over 10 million dollars. Management backed down again and operations were resumed in a few days but after the 10-million-dollar loss had been incurred. A short time later, the plant manager was replaced, the usual headquarters reaction to the recurring union-management crisis.

When the new plant manager arrived, the plant's operating budget was five million dollars in the red with this unfavorable variance on the increase. This generated on him a pressure that each of his predecessors had experienced. He also clearly saw that it was his responsibility to prevent another union crisis. He had tried to avoid the mistake of others before him—taking over with an iron fist, dictating and trying to control the thinking of the department heads. When he sat back and waited for them to take the initiative, department heads were unsure of where he stood and had become even more cautious and guarded than they had been before, exerting less and less initiative and paying little attention to the problems of supervisors at lower levels. No one would make a move without a signal from the top. Union grievances were invariably decided in the union's favor. First level supervisors saw a need for greater control over the wage earners but did not expect support from above. They too had thrown up their hands in despair. The lethargy had worked its way down to the bottom and back up again.

Management had rationalized themselves into a tolerant attitude. "It's the nature of the business we are in. Our hands are tied." They found fault with and blamed their troubles on past managers, lower level supervisors, and the union. They had given up on improving the situation.

With the union it had become a deadly serious game that had a little of the risk of Russian roulette. "We got rid of the last plant manager in eighteen months. Let's see if we can't get rid of this one in twelve." The union irritation was one of many inherited by the new plant manager. The fundamental problem, however, was the lethargy of the supervisory group and the fact that they had abdicated responsibility for the effective operation of the plant.

Phase 2 Activities

By the time the team discussion of the purchasing and inventory problem took place, several Phase 2 activities had been completed. At the beginning, team discussion centered upon the subject of how members saw the new plant manager operating, based on his first six months at the plant. The plant manager had confided in them that one of his first goals had been to build up their confidence as managers and decision makers, but he had resolved not to make their decisions for them or to tell them what needed to be done to correct problems within their departments. "I was absolutely determined," he admitted, "that if it became necessary I would force you people into making decisions and if I decided you were procrastinating or leaning on me too heavily, I was going to see to it that you took more decisive action."

"Sure," said the industrial relations manager, "we know you want us to make our own decisions, but look how it ends up when we reach a real impasse. Rather than sitting down with the three of us to thrash it out, what you usually do is say, 'Look, I can make the decision. One of you probably won't like it and maybe both of you won't, but I'll do it if that's what you want. However, I would think that you two are intelligent enough and grown up enough to resolve your own problems.' So what happens in the end? You get a 5,5 decision. We would rather find a compromise when you say that than come back to you and admit that we wanted you to make the decision for us. That would mean we weren't intelligent enough or grown up enough to do it ourselves."

"I am beginning to realize, as I listen to you discuss this, that though my intentions were good, I swung the pendulum too far from the way things had been done in the past. It was my determination to have us, as a team, stand on our own two feet," said the plant manager. "I am also eager," he continued, "for us to set specific objectives and work together toward achieving them. All of you have some ground rules and goals you have been given to manage by. But you are all going your own separate ways."

This had become clear to all the top team members during the Phase 2 sessions. They had seldom before discussed or openly faced why they had not been meeting their cost goals or other goals. One after another they had explained how other departments' actions had prevented them from getting results. They had also referred to times when conditions had become so difficult that there had been a flare up of tempers and then they had quickly drawn back to prevent future explosions. As they described each others' personal behavior, it became evident they had all been guilty of withdrawing from conflict to prevent annoying others. They had depended upon the exchange of pleasantries to help them avoid discussing real issues.

During personal feedback, they rationalized away the ineffective behavior, they made excuses for one another and gave each other the benefit of the doubt until finally the industrial relations manager said, "You know, I have been sitting here listening to all of this for the past two hours and I have come to the conclusion that we were just kidding ourselves when we said we typically operate in a 5,5 way. All I have heard here is a bunch of 1,9 back slapping. I think there is a hell of a lot of 1,9 in every one of us, or else we would really tell each other what we think instead of handing out bouquets the way we have been doing."

It was here that the discussions took a turn toward becoming more objective and open. The issue of being candid and critical of one another at first had not been seen as a problem. As the personal feedback began, one manager had said, "It won't do any good. All you do is create a more uncomfortable situation for yourselves by criticizing others for what they are doing. This is nothing more than griping and we have enough of that as it is." Another had echoed, "If you can't say something nice, don't say anything at all." Reluctance to be forthright had been a formidable barrier throughout the Phase 2 discussions. This barrier had begun to break down after they debated the possibility that the industrial relations manager's comment on their 1,9 back slapping had real merit. They tried to recall anything that had represented a kind of critique of individual or team operations. They agreed that it had been a way of life to deal with problems according to a fire-fighting approach and that critique had been non-existent. This was the second high point in the behavior change of the top team of this plant.

Looking Ahead—Planning for Improvement

After five days of intensive teamwork and diagnosis, the team had emerged from its cocoon. It had developed a more realistic and objective picture of itself. There was greater readiness to change conditions which they were no longer able or willing to rationalize away. Dimensions of their problems were clearer and a significant shift in their thinking had occurred. No longer were all of their problems placed on the shoulders of past plant managers. They recognized that the apathy and lack of skill at lower levels of supervision was not inherent in that group but a direct result of their own lack of leadership and support. They saw how they had dodged their trouble by comfortably blaming the technological complexities of their business for many of their problems with the wage and hourly employees. They saw how their concern for maintaining pleasant relationships had caused them to set production standards which neither demanded much effort nor caused embarrassment if not achieved. Box 50 lists the significant Phase 2 shifts in attitudes.

A Herculean task lay ahead of the team once the step of squarely accepting the responsibility for their problems was be-

Box 50

Emergence of the Top Team from its Cocoon

From	To
Past leadership is to blame.	We have been instrumental in creating current conditions.
Lower level supervisors are disinterested and untrained.	We have not provided the leadership that would strengthen lower level supervisors.
The nature of our business creates too many uncontrollable factors.	We have hidden behind this aura of mystique about the business.
The union has us over a barrel because we cannot operate without their skilled workers.	We have a serious problem with the union because we have let a serious problem arise. If we manage with responsibility we can create a condition where the union will react in a responsible manner.
It is not proper to criticize how other departments are run—"live and let live."	Each department manager has a responsibility to challenge ineffective action in another department which affects interdepartmental effectiveness or plant performance.
Industry norms are the best guides to how we are performing.	Standards of excellence we develop should be the guide to "how good is excellent."

Box 51

Improvement Opportunities Identified

—Planning—lack of clear, explicit company-wide goals
—Lack of inventory control system and cost control
—Need to face up and deal with incompetent managers
—Poor managerial skills and commitment of first-level supervisors
—Lack of understanding of technical aspects of production
—Control of equipment, property damage, and loss
—Poor quality standards
—Poor housekeeping, maintenance planning and scheduling
—Lack of coordination between Production and Engineering and Industrial Relations on job content
—Lack of system for assessing supervisory talent
—Insufficient use of modern business techniques
—Poor technical skills of craftsmen
—Lack of technical development of equipment and processes
—Poor contract with union

hind them. For the first time they found the impetus to overcome past inertia. Unhappiness and a sense of urgency had replaced the feelings of resignation and tolerance which had characterized the team members earlier.

Having placed their past operations as a team without teamness into perspective, members concentrated on identifying improvement opportunities that called for their thinking, planning, and initiation of new effective action. Major areas for improvement are listed in Box 51. In designing a demonstration project to test how to resolve these problems, the team agreed to select as tangible and measurable a project as they could think of, and one which could make a significant contribution to the profitability of the organization. They decided to tackle the inventory problem.

Box 52 shows the summary of the team's analysis of the inventory problem, objectives to be achieved, and the plan of accomplishment.

Achieving a readiness to face up to critical situations, although essential, provides no guarantee that the problems will be solved. The team was hampered by its members' lack of skill in pooling and organizing their thoughts in the form of objectives, their lack of experience in working other than individually, and their tendency to react quickly to surface appearances. It took them almost an hour to define the inventory problem. The plant manager saw the surplus materials in the inventory or the lack of a cost control system as symptoms.

"Our varianace," he pointed out, "is not the problem either. It's really just a measure of the extent of the problem. I think the problem is that Tom, who is most directly responsible, and John and his people in production, and the rest of you have not taken the initiative and responsibility to correct the situation which has obviously been with us for a long time. This same thing can probably be said in many of these other improvement areas that we have identified. With respect to inventory, for example, we could have Tom look for a new system, set it up and assume everything would then straighten itself out. I don't think that would solve the problem. We need to define the problem in such a way that makes us approach it so that responsibility is clear, so that those who should be involved are, and so that we can take steps to insure real operational understanding and commitment by everyone affected. If we approach the problem from that angle, I think we will be less likely to correct only a piece of it or deal with only one part."

"If we only think of reducing inventory or getting a new system," agreed the industrial relations manager, "we won't get at these more basic causes."

When they had agreed on the definition of the problem as one of initiative, they had created the essential condition for action. They tested their plan with questions such as, "Have we assigned responsibilities to the right men? Have we involved those who should be involved? Have we planned for coordination and insuring understanding by those who must implement the plan and the system? Do we have a means for measuring results?"

An important aspect of the completed plan was that they did not leave the question of operational understanding to those at lower levels of the organization who would be affected and would have to implement it. Instead they designed a team action strategy to insure the active involvement of others in learn-

Box 52

A Model Plan for Accomplishing a Team Objective

Project—Inventory Control

To replace an ineffective inventory system coupled with a lack of management initiative and responsibility with a modern inventory system fully supported by management.

Nature of Problem: Present system is outdated and costly. There are over 4,000 stock items which have practically no use. People in the store rooms and other departments are maintaining an archaic system by the book.

Extent: Problem extends throughout store rooms and inventory control, production engineering, and maintenance departments from top management down through the wage ranks.

Impact: $800,000 variance from standard. Misunderstandings across departments that result in friction. Costly production and maintenance procedures.

Causes: Lack of top team leadership. Lack of commitment and feeling of responsibility at lower levels. Outmoded system. Poor coordination.

Objective

Reduce inventory by $800,000 by end of fiscal year. Fully effective inventory and control system to be completed within four months.

Action Step	Responsibility	Jointly or Coordinated with	Product(s)	Comments	Completion Date
Fact finding and data collection	Department Head—Stores and Inventory	Production, Engineering, Maintenance and Accounting	Detailed cost analysis	Report distributed to top team	July 3
Establish task force to design new inventory control system	General Manager	Department Head—Stores	Memo to those assigned. (cc: top team)		July 7

Box 52 (cont.)

Action Step	Responsibility	Jointly or Coordinated with	Product(s)	Comments	Completion Date
Orient task force; task instructions	Department Head—Stores		Agenda fact-finding report, task paragraph	Review with top team July 11	July 12
Design model recommendation for inventory control system	Task Force Leader	Department Head—Stores	Inventory control systems, manual	Review progress with top team August 18	Sept. 1
Approve final system—establish measurement criteria	General Manager	Department Heads	Approved, revised manual with established measurement criteria.	To be sent for pre-study to top team prior to September 6	Sept. 8
Design team action plan to distribute to department managers and supervisors involved	OD Coordinator	Task Force Leader	Four-hour team action design with materials (prework, etc.)	Test with sample group prior to September 22	Sept. 22
Conduct inventory Team Action Seminars in appropriate departments	OD Coordinator	Department Heads	Report on potential problem areas identified in seminars	Submit summary of report to top team	Oct. 1
Convert to new inventory control system	Department Head—Stores	Department Heads	Transition plan	Monitor transition	Oct. 16
Review and critique system—measure results	Department Head—Stores	OD Coordinator, Department Heads	Critique report	Distribute to all managers and supervisors	Dec. 15

ing the new system, identifying problems and obstacles that might be encountered, either in implementing it or during the period of transition. Steps were taken to insure that progress would be measured quantitatively.

The demonstration project was completed. It was apparent to all that progress had been made. It was equally evident that making up for a decade of managerial deterioration would not be easy or be accomplished overnight. The magnitude of the task can be seen from the range of problems identified of which the inventory situation is but one.

SUMMARY

These Phase 2 episodes show some of the problems facing key members of managements in different organizations. Different problems confront different teams. These examples are of the kinds of situations dealt with in Teamwork Development.

Communication is a major problem. The solution to it is a solution that involves invoking different theories of managerial behavior than those which managers have unwittingly applied in the past. Use of 9,9 theory increases the prospect that mutual understanding will be achieved. With mutual understanding, the likelihood is increased that unobstructed communication can take place and stronger and more worthy objectives can be set. With shared commitment to attaining these objectives, there is a realistic prospect that improved results should be forthcoming.

Difficulties of planning are also reflected in each of the three episodes. But the solution to planning as a difficulty depends on solving the communication problem. With the communication problem effectively eliminated, a foundation of interaction has been laid for sound planning and for achieving commitment to the execution of plans which can have operational consequences.

Without planned, deliberate, organized followup, the insights into managerial behavior acquired from a Grid Seminar are unlikely to find their way into operational action. With Teamwork Development the likelihood that behavior theories will work their way into daily use is strengthened by contributing to the removal of operational barriers to the attainment of excellence.

From these three episodes, it may be evident why the reaction to Teamwork Development tends to be serious. When organization members come face-to-face with solving problems that limit effectiveness, they often find that the demands upon them for the initiative, energy, and genuine commitment to organization objectives are substantial.

7

RESOLVING CLEAVAGES
THAT PREVENT
INTERGROUP COOPERATION

Corporations are organized into groups, divisions, departments, sections, or units. One segment has responsibility for marketing and sales and can concentrate its energy into that area. Another deals with manufacturing and can mobilize its resources toward achieving production objectives. Throughout the entire organization there is compartmentalization of responsibility, with a research and development department for inventing and designing new products and processes; a personnel department for wage and salary administration, employment, labor relations, benefits, and so on; and other segments organized similarly to carry out specific functions of the enterprise. This dividing of the corporation into compartments to separate functions is so widely accepted that little thought is given to its implications. But the corporation is still a whole—a unity. No department is in business for itself. All must eventually mesh with the others with whom effort is correlated if each is to fulfill its part of the total responsibility. The resulting flexibility provides the sound basis for unobstructed communication and valid planning that is present in an excellent corporation and can be seen when there is a fluidity through man-to-man exchange and functional problem solving across intergroup lines. Corporate synergism is achieved when a "within-department" concentration of effort is reinforced by a "between-department" coordination of effort. The total capacity of the corporation to achieve is then more than the sum of efforts of each department considered singly.

Because each has a singular responsibility, corporate members of departments or divisions tend to think more about their individual components and less about the whole. They may act and react more in the interests of their departmentalized units than in the interests of the entire company. People can see most clearly those interests which they feel most immediate. From inside the department, this is viewed as selflessly serving the corporation. Such preoccupation of men with their own departments may mean less of their attention is paid to other departments. Then when one department must cooperate with another, people in the second tend to see those in the first as motivated by selfish considerations, particularly when needed cooperation does not seem to be forthcoming. The second department may ask, "Why are they dragging their feet? Why are they unable to provide the service we need, which is the reason for their existence in the first place? Are they slighting us or are they deliberately disregarding our requirements?" These kinds of attitudes are born of frustration and can quickly promote negative criticism. A man in the second department may pick up his phone in irritation, "What's the matter with you birds? Why can't you meet your deadlines? Don't you know how to manage?"

The answer comes back, "Who do you think you are? Can't you remember last week? One of your saints miscalculated on a job that forced us into needless overtime and screwed up our schedules, but good!"

Such intergroup attitudes are easily provoked and, once formed, easily inflamed into win-lose power struggles. When this happens, needed cooperation is sacrificed, information is withheld, requests are received as unreasonable demands. When corporate members are asked what their problems are, they tend to answer, "Poor communication between departments." However, the underlying problem of relationships must be dealt with before any fundamental change in effectiveness of communication is achieved.

Box 53

Typical Attitudes Between Company Units That Reveal Intergroup Cleavages and Conflict

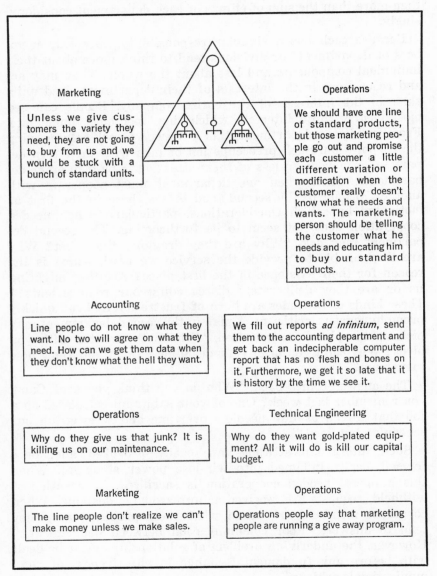

Marketing

Unless we give customers the variety they need, they are not going to buy from us and we would be stuck with a bunch of standard units.

Operations

We should have one line of standard products, but those marketing people go out and promise each customer a little different variation or modification when the customer really doesn't know what he needs and wants. The marketing person should be telling the customer what he needs and educating him to buy our standard products.

Accounting

Line people do not know what they want. No two will agree on what they need. How can we get them data when they don't know what the hell they want.

Operations

We fill out reports *ad infinitum*, send them to the accounting department and get back an indecipherable computer report that has no flesh and bones on it. Furthermore, we get it so late that it is history by the time we see it.

Operations

Why do they give us that junk? It is killing us on our maintenance.

Technical Engineering

Why do they want gold-plated equipment? All it will do is kill our capital budget.

Marketing

The line people don't realize we can't make money unless we make sales.

Operations

Operations people say that marketing people are running a give away program.

Box 53 continued on next page

Box 53 (cont.)

Operations

> What do those R&D long-hairs do with themselves all day long?

R&D

> These guys want instant miracles.

Operations

> That bunch in their ivory tower don't know what's going on here. If we did what they say to do, we'd ruin the company.

Headquarters

> That bunch out in the plant are running their own show.

Personnel

> The line doesn't realize we have all this information on what the going rates are in the community.

Operations

> We can't get the kinds of people we need because of the salary levels that are set.

Operations

> That case-study stuff they give us just isn't practical. They ought to know what it's really like when a job has to get done—Give us economic justification. If you can't measure it, we don't want it.

Training

> Line people don't understand what we can do for them. How can we help them if they don't tell us what they need? It is unrealistic to measure the impact of this sort of thing. Why do they pick on us? They don't try to measure other things around here.

Headquarters

> The field doesn't try to face up to its responsibilities.

Operations

> Headquarters tries to judge all plants together and we shouldn't be judged in this way because we are different. There isn't a basis for comparison between us. Overall we are doing a good job; they are taking the things we are good at and ramming them down the throats of other plants. They are playing us against each other.

Box 53 continued on next page

Box 53 (cont.)

Union	Operations
We need to be realistic. The line doesn't know the whole story. We have to compromise at times to move ahead.	Why should we support and develop convictions over certain issues because when it gets in the bargaining committee they are going to cut the rug out from under us.

INTERGROUP CLEAVAGES IN INDUSTRY TODAY

All too often situations such as these corrode communications and coordination linkages between the departments of an entire corporation. Box 53 shows some common intergroup cleavages in industry today. These are evident not only in the United States but also in Great Britain and Japan, and other countries. Such "we-they" attitudes, coupled with inability to understand their causes, have been the reason for antipathy, antagonisms, and even open warfare in all areas of life. In corporate life, such splits may not be reported in newspapers, but they are no less real. Once attitudes of criticism, recrimination, attack, and counterattack have become common, the pursuit of solutions that would serve the interests of the corporation as a whole tend to be sacrificed under the justification of moral indignation for mistreatment. Sometimes conflict is relieved because departments draw apart and cease to fight. Surface harmony prevails as each keeps its distance from the other, doing the minimum necessary. This insulation is as unhealthy as the situation in which negative feelings are open and obvious.

These are the kinds of intergroup cleavages that take place between divisions within a company. Similar ones prevail in other areas of corporate life, such as between a union and management, headquarters and plant, line and staff. The union-management attitudes depicted in Box 54 are not unusual in many corporations today.[1]

Box 54

Images Developed by Management and a Union
During Phase 3 of Grid Organization Development

Management's Image	
Of Itself	By the Union
1. Concerned with running the business effectively	1. .... (an issue not considered)
2. We show equal concern for production and people	2. Management is concerned only with production
3. Autonomous decentralized decision-making body	3. They follow all of headquarters' policies and dictates
4. Want to learn to work better with international	4. Opposed to all organized labor
5. Prefer to deal with independent unions	5. Prefer to deal with independent unions
6. Strive continually to upgrade supervision	6. ....
7. Goal is to establish problem-solving relationship with the international	7. Their goal is to drive us out of the plant
8. Maintain flexibility in areas concerning our "rights to manage"	8. Management wants power and control over every aspect of a worker's life—they are fatherly dictators
9. We are inconsistent in how we treat independents and the international	9. They treat the independents one way and us another
10. Honest and aboveboard in our dealings	10. They are underhanded and they lie.

Box 54 continued on next page

Box 54 (cont.)

Union's Image	
By Management	**Of Itself**
1. Little concern shown for the profit picture of the company	1. Concerned primarily with *people*
2. They are skillful and have intense pride	2. Proud of our craft and skills
3. Controlled by a scheming professional leader and a minority clique	3. Governed by the will of the total membership
4. Legalistic and rigid in interpreting contract	4. Approach problems and contract with open mind
5. The union pushes every grievance to the point of arbitration. When they want to establish a precedent, they want to arbitrate	5. Do not want to have to arbitrate every grievance. We want to work them out with management
6. They want to prove they can "win"—they don't care what, just so it is something	6. We want good relations and to solve our problems with management
7. They want to co-manage. They want a say in every decision we make	7. We want a voice in those areas that directly concern us
8. The union wants the training of their people back under their control	8. We want joint control of the training and apprenticeship program
9. The union does not communicate internally. Their people don't know what is going on	9. Our people always know what is going on and what important union business is coming up

Box 54 continued on next page

Box 54 (cont.)

10. Union is concerned only with seniority and job security. They are not concerned with our problems

10. We want greater consideration for our skills and what we can contribute to the plant

The two views of the *actual situation* are radically different. The extent of difference demonstrates inherent sources of difficulties between this union and the management, as their representatives tried to reach agreement on a contract with these kinds of culturally-rooted antagonisms embedded in each word spoken. Only *after* these attitudes were exchanged and worked through in a genuine effort to develop understanding was it possible for these particular groups to develop a problem-solving relationship.

Intergroup problems are becoming ever more conspicuous between a parent company's headquarters in one country and a subsidiary in another, as illustrated in Box 55. This is taking place particularly as American industry grows more aggressive in pursuing business in other countries. Similar cleavages exist in developing countries between foreign-owned industry and the government of the host country. Grid Organization Development has been found useful in bridging the cleavage between Americans who are serving as resident managers in a host country and the nationals residing in that country as shown in Box 56.[2]

The effectiveness lost when human energies are diverted into maintaining and extending these intergroup disputes defies measurement and management. Such disputes severely narrow and restrict the number, quality, and creativity of solutions needed for the resolution of problems if a company is to achieve corporate excellence.

BOX 55

*How the Relationships Between a New York Headquarters
and a South American Subsidiary Shifted from
Mutual Disrespect to Confidence*

Subsidiary Image of Headquarters

New York's attitudes are naive and uninformed. Headquarters personnel rarely visit. Their pressures for increased return on investment are unreasonable, unfair, unrealistic. Their attitudes are arbitrary or demanding. They don't really understand the political climate of business decisions made in this country.

They are unable fully to appreciate or understand our problems from our point of view.

We have ceased to expect recognition of accomplishment. We expect our situation to be viewed unsympathetically and often criticized in a manner that provokes our hostility rather than cooperation.

Headquarters Image of Subsidiary

It is a company which has done an outstanding job in the past, but it is now falling behind.

The management is overpaid, underworked, living a soft, easygoing life, with lax and loose practices. They have self-satisfied, smug attitudes, with little desire for improvement. They take security from progress made in the past. The top leadership is indecisive. It is being confronted with problems it had not sufficiently anticipated and has no plans for their solution. The organization is overmanned, not firm enough in dealing with the union, and takes a least-resistance path in dealing with personnel matters. Unless they can reverse their situation, we shall be forced to pull out our investment in two years.

Box 55 continued on next page

Box 55 (cont.)

Four Years Later
Headquarters Description of Subsidiary

Their operation is one of our fastest improving operations anywhere in the world. They have become lean and keen and have expanded their product lines. They have advanced resident nationals to responsible positions of management. Their decisions show statesmanlike concern for issues of government, but there is no kow-towing to avoid causing a ripple. As can be seen from our last budget, we plan to increase our investment as this operation is now a sound business proposition.

THE PURPOSE OF INTERGROUP DEVELOPMENT AS PHASE 3

Grid Organization Development provides a basis for repairing intergroup cleavages. The objective of Intergroup Development, Phase 3, is to bring intergroup problems into focus and confront the conflict contained in them so that their causes are identified, their consequences assessed, and their cures designed and implemented.[3] The Grid provides an intellectual framework for analyzing relationships between segments of a company and evaluating alternatives for changing ineffective intergroup relationships into sound problem-solving ones. These are shown in Box 57.

Intergroup conflict of the 9,1 kind is the most obvious. Relationships stabilized under a 1,9 circumstance of peaceful coexistence or a 1,1 attitude of mutual withdrawal and isolation are not so easy to identify but no less in need of correction. They are more difficult to recognize because the heat has died down, but they are equally important because the loss in operational effectiveness may be great. Relationships of a 5,5 bargaining and compromise character also are hard to dig into be-

Box 56

Grid Organization Development Contributes to Improved Intercultural Understanding as Shown by Change in Understanding of Each Other by Resident Nationals and American Citizens Employed in Two Foreign Subsidiaries of a Large American Corporation

Percent Reporting	Decreased Understanding		No Difference in Understanding		Increased Understanding	
	Indonesia	West Indies	Indonesia	West Indies	Indonesia	West Indies
Resident nationals	3	0	10	25	87	75
American citizens	0	5	0	0	100	95

One of the two experiments was conducted in the West Indies, where the unit employs several thousand in chemical process manufacturing. The ratio of American citizens to resident nationals to third country nationals is 2:5:1 for managers. All of the company's 400 managers were participating in Grid Organization Development. Data are from 36 managers who represent a random sample of about 10 percent. The second unit employs several thousand in similar operations in Indonesia and the ratio of Americans to resident nationals to third country nationals is 3:19:1. In this case, data were gathered from 55 members of executive and managerial levels.

cause responsible persons in the two groups usually feel that the relationship is good enough. Slow but steady sapping of organizational vitality is the result.

The behavioral logic of Intergroup Development for changing relationships of conflict, peaceful coexistence, isolation, or compromise and bargaining to conditions of problem-solving effectiveness is clear. It is that problems between groups are caused by intergroup attitudes embedded in the cultures of the groups

Box 57

A Basis for Analyzing Approaches for Resolving Intergroup Disputes Is Provided by the Grid

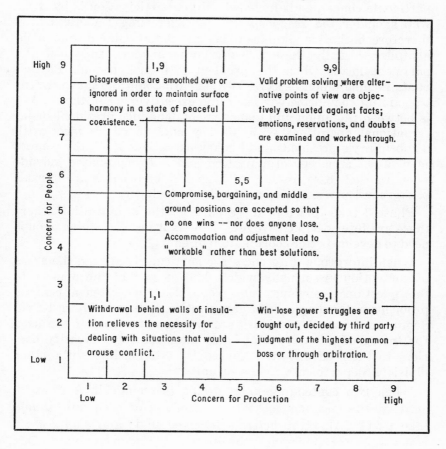

themselves. People defend their attitudes because they "make sense." Indeed, anyone within a department who sees the situation differently from the rest is subject to criticisms for acting out of selfish interests rather than departmental concern. Valid communication is sought rather than communication between groups which is distorted by intergroup loyalties and a history of misunderstanding.

How Intergroup Development Takes Place

In Phase 3, culturally rooted attitudes, thoughts, and emotions causing difficulties are investigated. Not everyone in the departments concerned is included. Direct participation is by those who shoulder the responsibility for exercising leadership and therefore authorize significant action, shape opinion, and mold attitudes. Usually these are division managers and their department heads when the problem is interdivisional. Participants include union officers, key stewards, and the management bargaining committee with key line executives when the conflict is between the union and management. The vice president of international operations with his key staff members meet with a subsidiary's president and his key executives when the conflict is between a parent organization and a foreign-based subsidiary. In each case, others with special knowledge or unusual background on a situation might also be included.

Phase 3 takes place in those parts of the organization where there are intergroup cleavages. "How is it decided which groups need to develop better coordination of effort?"

When intergroup differences are particularly strong, the areas of contention are usually widely known so that the answer to this question is obvious. Intergroup cleavages often appear as problems in the diagnosis of organization culture in Phase 1 Grid Seminars. Phase 2 provides an excellent barometer of the need for Intergroup Development when team members identify barriers to their effectiveness caused by relationships with other divisions, departments, teams, or units.

When two contending units decide to engage in a Phase 3 activity, the question is, "Which members of each unit should take part?" All those *actively* involved in it and *significantly* responsible for achieving coordination should participate. This means including corporate members from the lowest level of the organization at which decision making basic enough to resolve problems can take place. For example, if an intergroup cleavage is between two departments, the department manager and his immediate subordinates are the persons who probably should engage in Phase 3 activities. If the cleavage is particularly deep, representatives from lower levels may also take part so that the problem can be analyzed and understood in its full scope and steps of coordination planned.

Intergroup Development is not necessarily limited to two units. Sometimes the coordination problem involves a three-way interrelationship and under exceptional conditions may include even more.

The first Intergroup Development activity is best thought of as a demonstration model of how to implement Phase 3. The assistance of a Grid Organization Development specialist therefore is desirable.

The ideal point for applying the first Phase 3 is with two groups which have a 9,1 win-lose type relationship. Unsatisfactory relationships where heated conflict is apparent are usually easier to solve than others from a development point of view because the motivation to confront and resolve the tensions is greater. When all work teams in the units have successfully completed Phase 2 activities, their members are prepared to turn their attentions to unproductive relationships between themselves and other units.

At first, a period of about three to four days is needed. This is ample time for those who participate to study the historical roots and continuing causes of the problem and identify concrete steps for increasing coordination. Implementation may be achieved in a few weeks, but it is more likely to take several months. Full completion may take many months or even years, depending upon how deeply rooted are antagonisms and how much change is needed in concrete operational matters.

Steps of Intergroup Development

It might seem that by this stage in Grid Organization Development, the best way to tackle problems would be to bring together the people or groups having difficulties of coordinating effort and let them confront their cleavages directly and informally. Rather than taking this approach, however, Phase 3 uses a sequence of rather precisely planned and tightly controlled steps of contact. Attitudes are anchored in misunderstandings and misconceptions of history and group membership. To search out complexities of relationships between groups needs far deeper study than is likely to come about merely through discussion of problems as though they were in no way related to these deeper causes.

The sequence used in Phase 3 proceeds through a series of steps. First, in advance of the sessions, each person from the two (or more) groups in conflict completes his prework. This calls for a written description of the *ideal* working relationship as contrasted with the *actual* situation—between a manufacturing department and a marketing department, for example. Then the group, which includes the manager from each department and those under him who have operational responsibility for working with the other department, isolates itself from operations for two or three days. The intergroup sessions begin with an orientation to the objectives and methods. Each department *by itself* then formulates its views of the ideal and actual relationship. During this step each department works separately on its own. The next step is a joint activity. The two departments meet and compare their views of what *is* in contrast with what *should be*. Each department selects a spokesman to present its points of view. All members of both groups are present so that everyone can simultaneously gain understanding, yet personal feelings of individual members are not drawn into the situation. The purpose is to examine for validity attitudes shared by all members of each group as opposed to attitudes representing unique points of view. The reason for this controlled communication is to reduce the likelihood of defensive reactions, abrasiveness, and justifying of positions.

During these exchange sessions, interaction between two departments generally is limited to descriptions and questioning for clarification of intention. The aim is unobstructed communication leading to genuine understanding. While achieving agreement on what *should be* usually is not too difficult, gaining agreement on what *is*—what the current problems are, their causes, and so on—is far more difficult. Yet it is possible, based on confrontation techniques, to achieve examination of the relationships and the issues underlying the cleavages. With agreement on what *is* and what *should be*, the final step is to establish in concrete and operational terms the actions needed for shifting the relationship from what it *is* to what it *should be*. This phase of intergroup problem solving is not completed until both departments know clearly what action each will take to achieve a sound relationship and until followup is arranged to insure that operational consequences will result.

WHY PHASES 1 AND 2 COME BEFORE PHASE 3

A frequent question is, "Why not use the Phase 3 Intergroup Development strategy with departments in conflict even though Phases 1 and 2 have not been completed?" This can be done, but the reasons for there being serious reservations about doing so lie at the heart of Grid Organization Development. In Phase 1, organization members develop understanding of Grid theories of behavior. When they have learned the 9,9 theory and gained practice in applying it to on-the-job situations in Phase 2, they have such values as unobstructed communication and confrontation of conflict, and a deepened sense of urgency about the corporate objectives of productivity and profit. These values are vital for resolving issues of intergroup cleavage and for insuring that once solved, they will remain solved. Phase 2 precedes Phase 3 so that every team can deal with those barriers to effectiveness which it controls before it attempts to solve problems which require coordination of efforts with people outside its boundaries. If a department or division has failed to solve its team relationship problems, attempts to deal with intergroup situations are likely to cause not only greater internal difficulties but also to rupture already tenuous relationships. These ruptures are very difficult to heal.

Not all points of friction between departments require application of the formal development steps of Phase 3. For instance, many operational difficulties can be resolved easily when those aware of them take the initiative to solve them, particularly when the problems are caused by little more than failure to see or seize opportunity. Phase 3 Intergroup Development is only necessary when there is a history of poor relationships, of conflict, or of isolation and when ineffective relationships have come to be accepted as a way of life.

SUMMARY

By its very nature, organization structure sets up divisions, departments, sections, and units within a company. Doing so is calculated to concentrate energy and effort around operational and production objectives. It also creates conditions that can lead to interdepartmental rigidities and cleavages which prevent the interdepartmental coordination of effort essential to accomplishing overriding corporate purposes.

Intergroup Development as a Phase 3 activity provides a way to resolve intergroup rigidities and cleavages. Causes of conflict are confronted directly by those involved. The purpose is to change the traditions, precedents, and past practices anchored in group membership in which ineffective relationships have become embedded. This makes it possible to promote a climate of intergroup relationships which can sustain flexible man-to-man intergroup problem solving on a day-by-day basis. In this way the obvious advantage from corporate structure of concentrating energies within departments is retained and yet flexibility of interdepartmental communication and planning so necessary in achieving corporate excellence can also be preserved.

REFERENCES

1. Blake, R. R., Shepard, H. A. & Mouton, J. S. *Managing Intergroup Conflict in Industry*. Houston: Gulf, 1964, p. 173.
2. For complete study, see: Blake, R. R. & Mouton, J. S. International Managerial Grids. *Training Directors Journal*, 1965, *19*, 8-23.
3. See: Blake, Shepard & Mouton. *Op. Cit.*

8

FROM PATERNALISM
TO INDUSTRIAL
STATESMANSHIP

The following episode depicts the application of Intergroup Development. It takes place in a situation of controversy between a management and its union. A union-management example has been selected because this is such a common source of sharp cleavages in business corporations. The strategies of Intergroup Development which are revealed here are basic. They are not restricted to the union-management situation, but have utility for the resolution of intergroup cleavages of many kinds.

The stakes were high when the management of this $600 million business and its major international union confronted each other in the Phase 3 activity. The union represented 4,000 of the wage and hourly personnel. Failure to come to grips with basic problems could only mean that the already existing antagonisms would be inflamed with the repetition of a pattern of costly strikes to be anticipated. Success in solving problems that had become sources of contention could mean the beginning of a new era of industrial statesmanship. For management, there was a shrinking profit margin which would become a loss if a pending organization-wide employee walkout were to occur. For the union and its officers, long term continuity and the opportunity to represent its membership were being challenged from both within and without. Although not actively sought over the years, a situation requiring mutual cooperation faced the management and the union. It was created partly by outside factors over which neither had control. The seeds of the conflict were sown long before and had matured in the rocky soil of paternalism. Both management and the union felt that to survive they had to act. It was in this atmosphere that the Grid Intergroup Development activity was seen as an opportunity to learn to act in concert. Phase 1 had been completed and Phase 2 was well on its way down through the middle levels of management but had not yet reached the first level of supervision. A readiness to face up to issues, however disagreeable they were, was evident. Confronting squarely the growing problem with the union was one example of this readiness. How did it start?

BACKGROUND

"We knew we had a long way to go," the director of personnel recalls. "The company has a history of 'playing' with any and all 'new fads' that come along. Not all were sound, but they got the same 'fad' treatment. Everyone would get excited, say, over a new communications or human relations course. We would adopt it for our training curriculum, but before it was half finished, along would come someone with something different. Our training people bombarded line management with one program after the other. We never found out if any of the training would work. People didn't have time to try to implement the new learning because they were busy learning something else. When I took over as director I was determined we would see our next development step through to completion and that we would take enough time to implement it and measure the results.

"When we began to look seriously at the Grid, suggestions for doing 'other things' at the same time came across my desk. Many of our managers who attended early Grid Seminars were enthusiastic over the potential they saw in Grid Organization Development. They were pushing me to take short cuts to move into later application phases. But I stood firm."

Box 58

Steps That Made Intergroup Development Possible

Grid Organization Development initiated in company by management
—Top executives seeded in public Grid Seminars
—Strong Personnel Department supplied consultative support to Phase 1 and later phases
—Widespread line participation in Phase 1 Instructor Development program
—Line instruction in Phase 1
—Phase 2 initiated at key executive level and carried downward, throughout managerial and supervisory levels.

Strong desire of Personnel Relations Director to involve union in Grid Organization Development
—Union officers investigate Grid through seeding in public Grid Seminars
—Union officers recommended Grid learning for other union officers and members
—Incompany Phase 1 Grid Seminar held involving 20 union representatives, 20 managers.

Two-day labor-management conference conducted to study current labor relations issues with time devoted to theory of intergroup dynamics. Three of the twelve union officers attended.

One union officer saw potential for solving problems more effectively with management and influenced thinking of other officers.

Phase 3 proposed by management; union leadership agreed.

Preconditioning provided the foundation for later action. It was primarily through the personnel manager's efforts. "We stuck pretty close to the suggested model for testing the Grid and moving forward," he reports. The sequence of Grid Organization Development steps followed by the company is shown in Box 58.

Box 59

Attitudes, Reservations, and Doubts at the Beginning of Phase 3

Management Doubts

—A few union officers were believed to be loyal to the company but one or more were "known" to be trouble makers, ready to sell the company down the river for their own selfish gains.

—Much union officer behavior was interpreted as "politically" inspired.

—Past paternalistic thinking dominated management actions; treating union officers as equals was a new and dangerous thought; to do so would be tantamount to inviting the union to help manage the company.

—There was disagreement as to who was responsible for day-to-day relations with the union. More emphasis was being placed on first line supervisors than before with less dependence on the Personnel Relations Department. This led to uncertainty about who should do what toward altering the situation.

Union Officer Doubts

—Management's motives were suspect—little possibility for progress was seen.

—The initial attitude was, "If management wants it, watch it. If it's good for them, it can't be good for us."

—Long range or basic problem-solving implications were not apparent—Phase 3 was an opportunity to confront top management with immediate, concrete problems on which the union was getting the runaround.

—How members would judge union-officer actions was a constant worry.

A significant impact from Grid Seminar learning in this situation was a new perspective on conflict and its management. Concepts of conflict as "bad" and to be suppressed were replaced by concepts of conflict as inevitable but capable of resolution. Insights regarding the causes and negative consequences of conflict, which prevent rather than permit sound communication, provided the intellectual foundations for openly confronting it. Conflict as the seed of creative thought gained increasing value in the thinking of those who participated. Finally, the significance of conflict in organization life became more and more apparent. Its ineffective handling was ranked as a major organization problem. In spite of this, there was not a strong or unified conviction that a Phase 3 Intergroup Development activity with the union would be a sound move. Before and during the Phase 3 confrontation, both management and the union were doubtful about it. Box 59 summarizes the mixture of feelings and counteracting forces acting on management and the union at the beginning of Phase 3.

ORIENTATION

"This first general meeting will be brief," said the Grid Organization Development specialist. "The time available is very short and we want to make the most of it. That is why we are beginning tonight rather than waiting till tomorrow morning.

"There is little doubt you are all aware of chronic, immediate problems that need solving. I'm sure we could spend the next two and a half days just on these kinds of issues . . . But if experience is any guide, the chances are you would only be fire-fighting. We could try for temporary relief but it is unlikely that the underlying causes producing the immediate problems would be brought to light. The objective, therefore, is to set aside more immediate symptoms of friction and misunderstanding and examine basic issues that lie beneath them. This objective will be sought in three steps: one is to evaluate whether conditions exist or can be created that would permit management and the union to establish a sound way of working with one another. We'll begin this step tonight. Both groups will work separately to develop a description of what they believe would constitute the *soundest possible* relationship between them.

"Assuming joint agreement can be reached later regarding the behavior that would be involved in a sound relationship, the second step will be to develop a common understanding on the *actual* relationship between the two groups—that is, what has been and still is typical of management's actions and what has been and still is typical of the union's at the present time. Here we will be particularly interested in the attitudes, assumptions, and behavior you see in each other and in yourselves.

"If agreement can be reached on the character of the present relationship and the areas of misunderstanding that exist, the final step will be to explore how the relationship can be changed from what it is today to what is agreed is the best possible one."

IDENTIFYING AN IDEAL RELATIONSHIP

Each group spent nearly eight hours of independent deliberation in formulating only the bare rudiments of what would constitute a sound relationship between them. Such thinking did not come easily. Often they had to place themselves in the positions of the other side. They had never done this before. The result was two statements of how they should relate to one another. There was agreement and deep commitment on both sides. Box 60 summarizes management's formulation of a sound relationship, showing how management would operate and how the union would operate. Box 61 summarizes the union's formulation.

Although the definition of the ideal relationship by management differed from that of the union, there were no points of contradiction between them. As revealed in its description of an ideal relationship, management saw the major barrier to contract bargaining and problem solving as lack of economic understanding by the union. The implication was that if the union understood the economics of the industry and the company, it would exercise greater objectivity in defining its demands.

The union, as demonstrated by the points emphasized, believed a basic condition of a sound relationship is a management that is fully informed on the contents of the contract and prepared to implement it soundly. The differences in barriers were identified and evaluated. This led to each side's having a deeper appreciation of the views presented by the other. An expanded definition of the ideal relationship was agreed upon, one which integrated the points of view presented in each of the independent definitions.

Box 60

*What a Sound Union-Management Relationship Would Be
as Described by Management*

The Management Would:

Maintain open communications with the union in the following areas:

Economics of industry and company
Goals and objectives of company
Long range company plans
How company profits handled and distributed
Problems facing company
Growth opportunities—company and individual
Security and development of employees
Employee induction and orientation—where person fits in total scheme of things

Participate in prebargaining discussions to:

Identify and clarify current economic climate
Identify and understand company's competitive position
Assess and evaluate indexes for productivity
Identify and agree upon appropriate and objective cost of living standards
Identify and understand employee attitudes and concerns
Assess strengths and weaknesses of present contract
Identify possible obstacles and barriers that could arise during negotiations

Adopt bargaining strategy to:

Develop frame of reference for agenda
Explore problem areas jointly
Explore opportunity areas

Have more *joint* problem solving—e.g., on:

Evaluating impact on employees from operational changes
Work simplification
Benefits and pension programs
Techniques of training
Job safety

Handle complaints and grievances as follows:

First line supervisors would discharge responsibility for resolving complaints and grievances and act with dispatch

Box 60 continued on next page

Box 60 (cont.)

Participate in continuing joint efforts leading to clear interpretation and uniform application of contract clauses at working level

Maintain open door policy—union executives have free access to management executives and vice versa

Establish and maintain open, upper level labor-management dialogue—ongoing critique

Endeavor to understand problem confronting union officers within their frame of reference in their relationship with membership.

The Union Would:

Develop comprehensive understanding of specific nature of the business and concern for it

Understand and consider nature of competition as it relates to company performance and needs for change

Develop understanding of relationships of productivity to wages and benefits

Because of peculiar nature of industry, understand long range impact on both company and employees from work stoppages

Recognize implications of taking fixed positions in approaching problems—win-lose trap

Recognize harm in intragroup (within union) conflict resulting in company and employee backlash

Subdue personal interests in favor of overall company and union objectives

Accept responsibility to communicate facts to employees without prejudice.

IDENTIFYING THE ACTUAL RELATIONSHIP

Examining the *actual* relationship as a step toward making *ideal* concepts operational was the next task. Working sepa-

Box 61

*What a Sound Union-Management Relationship Would Be
as Described by the Union*

The Management Would:

Exercise authority on complaints, grievances, questions, decisions needed, etc., without needless delay, particularly first level managers

Adopt uniform education program for all supervisors, vertical *and* horizontal, on understanding, interpreting, and applying the contract

Interpret the contract in an honest and aboveboard way

Consult employees on changes in working schedules, shifts, transfers, location, etc.

Apply a system of seniority and rotation without favoritism, e.g., assigned overtime, easy jobs, time off, vacations, best working schedules, etc.

Rate employees' performance on a uniform, systematic, and fair basis and with employees told where they stand

Coordinate and communicate effectively between department supervisors to prevent needless work by employees and cut down costs and wasted effort.

The Union Would:

Represent all employees fairly

Communicate problems, complaints, contract infractions to management

Have access to top management without runaround at lower levels

Be concerned with costs and amount of production

Insure employee has correct rating for skills he has and that he is paid for job he does, not the classification he has.

(Union had insufficient time remaining to complete this activity.)

rately, management characterized how it saw itself and then the union, and the union characterized itself and its perception of management. Significant points in each of the descriptions are shown in Box 62. The union and management then discussed these descriptions.

The discussion began with the Grid Organization Development specialist's reviewing ground rules. "It is unlikely you will agree with everything that is stated during this exchange. But let me repeat the purpose. It is to insure clarity and understanding of what is said by the other group. Later there will be ample opportunity to explore areas of disagreement. At this time, the goal is to insure that you understand how the other group thinks and feels and why they see things the way they do before challenging or disagreeing. Unless you have a need to have a particular point clarified or would like an example, I'd like to ask that you refrain from commenting on the reports as they are presented."

Discussion during this step became more subjective and emotional with accusations made from time to time. Management and the union often referred to their written descriptions of a sound relationship to give perspective to their views and discussion.

The union officers' earlier learning from Grid Seminars appeared to influence their behavior. They were able to communicate their thinking effectively with management—they talked the same language. For the most part, they avoided becoming polarized around fixed positions. This was reinforced by management's similar attempt to avoid the win-lose trap. A problem-solving attitude was adopted by the two groups during the two-day meeting and little defensiveness and much earnest listening took place during this exchange.

Management's View of Itself

Several recurring themes emerged as management presented its view of itself to the union.

Management recognized in itself a hangover from its more paternalistic days. A prevailing attitude was that the company knew what was good for employees and so could best make some kinds of decisions. The management spokesman made several points.

Box 62

Descriptions of Actual Relationships Developed by Management and the Union

Description of Management	
By Management	*By the Union*
Do not communicate adequately	Do not communicate—do not consult with employees on changes in jobs or policies —do not communicate why
Do not listen effectively—have not heard things union has tried to tell us	Are not well informed—the top management is unaware of problems because first level does not tell them
Look for political implications in everything union officers do	Do not trust intentions of officers
Have insufficient concern for union's point of view	Are sincere at top level but first level does not care
Fail to keep promises—good intentions but do not follow through	Always say, "We'll look into it," but nothing ever happens
Give inconsistent interpretations of agreements, contract, and company policies	Interpret contract differently at first level of supervision
Do not have our first level supervisors act fast enough	Are afraid to make decisions at the first level of supervision
Strive toward genuine problem solving in negotiations	———————

Box 62 continued on next page

Box 62 (cont.)

Description of Management	
By Management	*By the Union*
Study current competitive positions and the cost of living index as a basis for formulating monetary positions and employee working conditions	————————

Description of Union	
By Management	*By the Union*
Are only interested in political and personal gain	Have sincere convictions—intentions always honest
Are unaware of and unconcerned with need for company to increase productivity	Are aboveboard in dealings with management
	Are concerned with saving company money—we see much ineffective work because of poor supervision
Are willing to experiment with new and improved methods in labor-management relations	Are free agents—not run by International offices
Yield too easily to employee pressures	Represent thinking of total membership

Box 62 continued on next page

Box 62 (cont.)

Description of Union	
By Management	*By the Union*
————————	Seek interpretation of *spirit* of contract, not *letter* of contract
Make unrealistic initial demands—raise undue hopes among employees, which results in discord among employees and weakens union's executive image	Prefer to sell and persuade company rather than impose our demands—would rather problem solve
Are unaware of relationship between productivity standards and increased wages	Feel employee and company rights and obligations should be balanced
Are unaware of the company's financial position with regard to sales and profits	————————
Are unaware of competitive situation of the company	————————
Lack trust in management's commitments—you feel we do not deliver	————————

"We recognize foremost in ourselves that we have not communicated adequately with the union. We've been negligent and in many ways we'd have to admit we weren't too concerned with communication. There's been a feeling that we know best and that the union should have faith in our actions. We recognize a lot of things that we've done have been misunderstood and also that the union has done things because we have failed to communicate with them.

"For example, your real concern with the new benefits program and its delay has not been listened to. As a result, we are only now beginning to sense the problems that this created with you and the employees. The reasons for the delay have been out of our hands, but we haven't communicated this to you.

"Behind all of this is probably the fact that we have really not stopped to look at things from the point of view of the union and union officers. We've not really given the problems that you've brought to us the serious consideration that we now see that they've merited. It's probably for this reason that we have failed so frequently to keep our promises. This is not to say that we deliberately broke our promises, because they were given in good faith. But in the day-to-day effort to run the business the tendency was to give low priority to our promises to you. Our intentions were good, but we just didn't follow through on many of them. We can see now many of the difficulties that this has created for you as officers of the union and representatives of your members, to say nothing of the frustrations it has created for us."

In many ways the relationship between management and the union was attributable to the management group itself. For example, although they had realized that numerous grievances and complaints and problems with the union arose out of inconsistent interpretation and applications of agreements and company policies, upper levels of management had done little to correct the situation.

"We know this happens among our first level supervisors, who don't always act fast enough for the union. Sometimes they can't. But we haven't communicated this in those situations. But we know also that just as often the first level supervisors pass the buck rather than taking action. This is why we have said in our concept of the soundest relationship that first level supervisors should assume responsibility for resolving complaints and grievances at that level rather than sitting on them or passing them up.

"We see ourselves as running the business and making good progress even though our earnings improvement has not been particularly dramatic. We are in a strong position in the industry and we see no major obstacles in the path of the growth pattern we have projected for the company. We think you attach less significance to this achievement than it merits, because it is only in sound growth and earnings that any of us have job security."

Management's View of the Union

Management saw the union, and particularly the officers, as having little or no experience or sophistication as a union. Some of the union officers, they felt, tried to put on the external trappings of hard, tough union men. The repeated theme was that the union had little or no awareness of the industry, the company's business, or what constituted a sound basis for demanding pay and benefits for the membership.

"We blame ourselves more than the union," reported the management spokesman. "This is why in the soundest relationship we say that we should communicate far more to the union than we have in the past. As we see it, we have failed to provide the necessary education and background, particularly to you as officers of the union, but also to supervision. If we had, you and they would now have a better understanding of our whole industry—what makes it tick, what problems there are, and particularly what the problems of this company are. We feel, for example, you don't really appreciate the competitive situation we're in. If you did, we don't think that you would make some of the unrealistic demands that you have made on the company in the past."

Management felt that although some of their paternalistic attitudes had placed the union in a position of dependency, the union also contributed to and perpetuated this relationship. Union officers, for example, did not screen complaints or grievances that came to them. No matter what the complaint, union officers would carry it to management.

"I'll give you an example of that," one manager commented. "You often know that an employee doesn't have a legitimate complaint, yet you'll bring it to us and expect us to get you off the hook rather than telling the employee at the very beginning that he's got no gripe coming. You keep yourself dependent on us to bail you out.

"This also relates to our earlier comment about unrealistic demands. You accept whatever demands people come up with and then put yourself in a position of our chopping your legs off when we don't yield to them. We think this weakens your executive image as leaders of the union and makes your ineffectiveness dependent upon our inevitable reaction."

Management acknowledged that by attending this session, the union officers had demonstrated their willingness to try out new and improved methods in labor-management relations. Management summarized its view by saying, "We created the conditions jointly that we're living with today, and it's for this reason that we feel that we can jointly change them to ones we agree would be sound."

The Union's View of Itself

The items developed by the union on how they saw themselves and management were sparse. What they had developed well during their discussion in their group was a list of management violations, questions they wanted answered, and problems they wanted resolved immediately. Even during management's report one or two union members interrupted to bring up specific problems. But in each instance someone reminded the person that this was outside the ground rules. The spokesman for the union gave his comments.

"We don't have as much as management to report on. But we do have a lot of questions we want answered. We've got some things we think management better act on right now if they want to avoid trouble. But we'll save those for another time. You may be right that we don't understand the money situation of the company. But how are we supposed to know something that you've held back and protected? Maybe we haven't always been right in the past, but we have been sincere. Whatever we've done has been done in good faith. This is more than we can say for management in many instances."

Another union member commented, "We are in our positions by the will of the total membership. We're elected and therefore we have to represent our people. We have to act in their behalf because our positions aren't permanent. Management's positions, on the other hand, are permanent and you don't have to be concerned with such things."

One member of management began to object but was cut off by another.

At a later point the union spokesman said, "You ought to appreciate the kind of union you're dealing with. You'd really have problems if you had a tough union that didn't care about the company. But as far as the International goes, we're free agents. Our only concern is to represent the will of our people while keeping in mind what's good for the company. When we affiliated with the International, we did so with the clear understanding that we would operate independently in dealing with the company. If you appreciated this fact, we think you'd treat us with greater respect and try to solve problems instead of just pushing them aside.

"You never seem to realize that we are just as worried about costs as you are. In fact, when we see some of the things that management does, particularly first level supervisors, we think we're even more concerned at times than you are. What you don't know is that we could help you a lot more with costs if you'd let us.

"Here is an example. On many of our deliveries the trucks leave the warehouse at 3:30 or 4:00 in the afternoon. What has happened a lot of times is that when our trucks get to their last stops, they may have decided to close a little early without telling you or without anyone available to supervise the unloading. So the trucks have had to come all the way back and unload and the company has to pay overtime. We've tried to save the company money and have brought this up, I don't know how many times, but no one in management seems concerned enough to do anything about it. If we didn't care, we'd be glad to let our people get overtime, because they want it. But our first concern has been to do what's right and to save money where we can."

This example was followed by others where the union pointed out repeated failures on the part of management to take action where waste was being reported or where costs could have been eliminated. Management was listening well and registering obvious surprise. Their earlier comment that they had not really been listening to the union began to hit home as the dollars and cents examples emerged. Management concentrated harder as the union described its view of management.

The Union's View of Management

The gist of the union report was that they felt top management, for the most part, was sincere in its dealings with the union and concerned for its employees. They attributed a lack of interest and action to the failure of first level supervisors to communicate union requests and problems up the line. The view of the union was that all of the ills lay at the feet of indifferent and apathetic lower level supervisors.

"You have no bottom level of management," the union spokesman commented at one point. "Real management doesn't begin until you get somewhere up around the middle ranks. And since we have no direct access to higher levels of management as we used to, problems and complaints that we have just get lost, pushed aside or disregarded.

"Our thoughts for what we felt would constitute the soundest relationship between us are aimed directly at curing all the problems we see at the first level of supervision. For that reason, we would like to use our ideas of what would be the soundest relationship as a basis for talking about what we see in the current one.

"For example, why do you think we said that those responsible should exercise their authority without needless delays? This is because we never can get an answer or decision from first level supervisors. We can give you many examples, but just one that happens all the time is when an employee goes to see his boss about getting time off. But does he act like a boss? No. He passes it on and says he'll have to ask Mr. So and So about it. And that's the last the employee hears unless he goes back. And then too often it's too late, even if he gets an answer, for him to get the time that he wanted. What it boils down to is first level supervisors are scared to take responsibility. They have to go up one or even two levels to get a simple answer. And we've never had a grievance settled at the first level. The problems just get bigger and bigger until the hatch blows off.

"Next, we said there ought to be a uniform education program to acquaint all supervisors with the terms of the union contract. The reason we said this ought to be obvious. In almost every department or plant, the contract is interpreted and applied differently. Eighty percent of our problems could be eliminated if you just did that one thing."

At this juncture, one of the managers interrupted to say, "We agree. That's the same thing we said in our statement of what would be a sound relationship. But we think it ought to be a joint effort. Don't forget, your people interpret the contract differently also and create just as many problems. That's why we felt there ought to be a common understanding on both sides."

There were nods of assent among both union officers and the managers. The union spokesman continued, "Beyond that, supervisors need to interpret the contract honestly and aboveboard. Here we've got so many examples we could spend the rest of the day, but let me just give you one. No foreman is supposed to work, but they do. You always say it's an emergency or the foreman says that his boss gave him orders to do it."

"I can't understand that," the head of the largest division said. "We've been very careful in this area and except for real emergencies or on shift changes when the work can't be stopped, we've been careful to insure that our foremen don't violate this agreement. This is evidently a misunderstanding. Besides, if this were happening so frequently, why haven't you brought it to us before?"

"We've put examples of what we're talking about in our monthly meeting with the foremen every time for the past six months. And these are real violations, not ones we recognize as emergencies or necessary. You're just supporting us in what we said earlier. None of the complaints or the problems that we bring up get past the first level of supervision."

The union spokesman continued to give example after example of where first level supervisors had not been managing effectively. Although management had acknowledged the situation earlier, it was only now that they really began to grasp the full import of what the union had been saying. The scratching of pencils across their notepads signaled that the union's examples were going to be investigated back on the job.

The union went on to cite instances where indifference and lack of concern between first and second level supervisors created problems of coordination, communication, and planning between departments. Once again costly waste was revealed as the union reported inefficiency brought about by sloppy management at the bottom.

BOILING THE ISSUES DOWN TO THEIR BASIC INGREDIENTS

In the evening session of the second day and for two hours the next morning, the groups worked independently. Their task was threefold. First, they were to identify whatever had been said by the other group which needed further clarification or examples for full understanding. Second, they were to identify those areas of basic disagreement with what had been said by the other group. Finally, each group ranked the items they thought most important for improving the relationship.

Both sides hashed and rehashed what they had heard and what had been said. At first they asked for clarification of points. But as the discussion developed, participants began answering questions for themselves. Most of the clarification they initially sought was developed right within their own groups so that both issues for clarification and issues of disagreement were reduced to three or four.

When they reassembled, they quickly dealt with remaining areas needing clarification and turned attention to the one or two major issues dominant in their thinking.

Contract Negotiations

Management thought the major issue was the negotiation period they would be entering into in six months.

"We think it all important that we develop a strategy for conducting prebargaining sessions between now and when we agree to begin formal negotiations. For this reason, we would like to propose the program we outlined under our description of the soundest relationship. As we see it, if we do not take the steps to provide you with the necessary information about the industry and our competitive position, you will continue to accept and agree to any and all demands brought to you by your membership, no matter how unrealistic. If that happens, we may find ourselves faced with the same situation we faced three years ago during negotiations. With conditions as they are, this could hang us both. At the same time, we need to be apprised of your situation—the problems as you see them from your position—and to consider what bargaining issues you think most important. If these are outlined and identified early, we can give deliberate thought to them. Then we can develop realistic agenda items. If we don't do this, we see you taking untenable positions where we will have no choice but to refuse them and you will have no choice but to strike, compromise, or back down. None of these alternatives, we feel, can help you in any way. You weaken yourself in the eyes of the membership with the last two, and a strike could create conditions where it would be necessary for us to curtail operations drastically, which would mean a large layoff. We're placing our cards on the table. We think you ought to give long and serious thought to the situation as we see it."

"I wonder," said the personnel director, "if we can't consider how best to implement a plan of prebargaining and an open discussion system."

"Yes, I'd like to put that as a first item on the agenda for us to plan the next time we meet," seconded another manager.

Benefits and Insurance Programs

"We have agreed among ourselves this is important," answered one of the union officers, "but there are two other items we have to consider first."

He explained that the long delay in the company's new benefits program, which was ensnarled in government regulations and had been pending for a number of months, was causing the union officers problems. The second issue was a new company-employee participation insurance plan, which also had been pending for some time. Here the union officers were particularly disgruntled because they had gone to an insurance company and had received a proposal for a plan which they felt contained more benefits at less cost to the employee than the one being considered by management. They felt that management had not considered this alternative.

"We'll be honest with you," said the union president, "because you've been honest with us. We've got to have something to tell our people when we go back. They, and I'm not going to argue whether it's right or wrong, are going to expect us to bring back something firm from this session. We're getting a lot of pressure from our members to get action and they are becoming discouraged with us. They don't understand what's taking so long or why management hasn't acted. They are beginning to say that we are being pushed around by management, and this is making us look bad in their eyes. We have been putting them off too long. We've got to bring home the bacon if we're going to get support from the other union officers and the membership on anything that comes out of this meeting."

A STEP TOWARD PLANNING

"Let's draw up a list of agenda items that we can agree on, giving them priority, and see if a time and place can be set for working on them," suggested one manager.

"I'll suggest, then," said the union president, "that we have to put the interpretations of the benefits program and changing insurance as the first two items."

"But I don't think we have to put those as major items," said one manager. "We have already explained that these are being worked on, and there is nothing we can do. I think the most important thing we can do is to put the prebargaining item first."

"I don't agree," said the personnel director. "What the union is telling us is that as far as they and the employees are concerned, these two items are a pain in the neck. Before we can ask them to sit down and discuss these longer range issues, we need to help get rid of this source of irritation, which can be traced back to our indecisiveness. We should be just as interested as they in bringing these two items to a quick and sound resolution. I agree those two items should be first. And to aid them in giving an accurate report to their people, I think we ought to review where both of them stand at this moment. From the union's standpoint, all they can see is management taking no action when we have an advisory committee working on both of these matters. In fact, they are meeting tonight and I am scheduled to be with them since I'm part of the committee. I will be able to give more definite information tomorrow."

He went on to explain the status of each item and what was being done. The culmination of this discussion was that a joint union-management group would work to get the benefits program dislodged from whatever had been holding it up. Previously, management and the union had been in contact independently with the advisory committee. They also agreed to set up a meeting to review the insurance proposal that the union had as well as the one currently under consideration by the company so that both management and the union would be able to assess the pros and cons.

They then discussed how best to move into a system of prebargaining. It was agreed that on the following Wednesday this total management and union group would meet to plan the strategies for the next six months for conducting prebargaining and to identify key discussion areas.

"The major thing we want understood here," said one manager, "and we think it's important that your other officers and the membership understand it, is that we do not want to influence or say what ultimate positions you should take in any of the negotiable areas. Our goal should be to explore all of the information available in each area to insure that we both have the same facts and the same understanding of the total situation before we begin negotiating."

They also established a channel for continuing discussions. "I guess I was the main one pushing for this particular item," said one manager. "As I see it, one of our big problems in the past is that on our side we have not communicated things with the union so that you have been left in the dark as to why things have happened or have not happened. At the same time, whether through the fault of first level supervisors or other poor means of communication, we have not been aware of many of the problems and complaints from the union's standpoint. The result has been that these have festered and created far greater problems than we would have had if they had been brought to us immediately. Therefore, what I am suggesting is that we and the section heads and first level supervisors in the various areas get together to discuss what needs to be communicated between us and how we can do this in the fastest and most effective way. If problems can't be communicated back and forth, they can't be discussed. And if they can't be discussed, they can't be solved.

And if they're not solved, they're just going to pile up to bigger and bigger problems."

The union quickly assented and this item was added to the agenda.

It was also agreed that the personnel director and the union president as a two-man task force would prepare and distribute a summary report of all of the major discussion areas and the remaining items from the session. Once action had been initiated on these priority items, other problems could be identified and steps taken toward achieving a sounder relationship.

THE WIND-UP

The Phase 3 sessions ended here. One man and then another eventually rose and began moving out of the room. The head of the company's largest division walked around the table to the union president. "You said you could give me departments and places where we are costing ourselves a lot of unnecessary waste and overtime. Can I get those before we leave?"

"Something I've never realized before," one manager mused at the end, "is that those guys have it tougher than we do. I wouldn't want to be in their shoes."

"We get so wrapped up in the 'black and white' of things," another manager summarized, "we overlook that enormous gray area. We were going to educate the union but I've learned something myself."

In the end some of the initial concerns or doubts seemed to have substance. Most did not. They had turned out to be only superficial. Plans for the beginning of a new relationship were formed. The prognosis was "progress." Some of the significant insights gained by management and the union during the three-day confrontation are shown in Box 63. With follow-through, they constitute the building blocks for an improved union-management relationship.

From the point of view of management much understanding was achieved. A foothold for problem solving had been established but with a realistic concern—the two groups were going to try to sustain what had been achieved in this session.

The union had come into the meeting with one obvious over-riding purpose—to force management action on several immediate problems. The idea of examining and setting right

Box 63

Insights Gained from Phase 3

By Management	By the Union
Learned union officers' behavior stemmed more from basic concerns of those whom they represented than from political or ideological considerations	Achieved greater openness and respect toward management even though less than full and complete
Saw responsibility to provide union with information if the union were to take a realistic and objective approach to problems of the company	Came to see that the two specific problems of management foot dragging which were causing a deterioration in relationships with management were symptomatic of underlying causes involving attitudes which management must overcome
Came to see the depths of the problems the company had created for itself by not developing strong effective lower levels of supervision not only in its union relationships but also in the quality with which the company is operating its business activities	Recognized that management was prepared to take action to strengthen supervisory effectiveness
Saw greater concern for costs and operations by union officers than previously recognized and were embarrassed in the extent to which these concerns were not evident among supervisors	Recognized that management was genuinely concerned with problems they had been creating for the union
Came to recognize that a sound problem-solving relationship is very demanding of time and skill	Came to see longer range implications for problem solving that could emerge from Phase 3 rather than seeing the session as one for "fire-fighting"

the more fundamental relationship was only vague in their thinking. However, they departed with a longer range perspective that suggested an improved relationship with management. At the same time, there was confidence that management would act on the immediate problems which would permit them to sit across the table and resolve the more fundamental ones.

SUMMARY

This case study illustrates the kinds of barriers to intergroup effectiveness that are observed over and over again. It is difficult to reach the peak of corporate excellence when they are present. Intergroup Development is an approach to eliminating such barriers. It is designed to permit the problems present in any intergroup relationship to be identified and resolved through a diagnostic approach based on insight and involving openness of communication, with planning based on facts and evidence rather than forcing issues through win-lose power maneuvering.

Phase 3 aids groups in taking a diagnostic approach through gaining agreement on the properties of an intergroup relationship which would be present were the interaction sound and healthy. Against the perspective of this model, the strategy includes:

1. Creating conditions under which each group can understand and appreciate how the same events look when seen from the point of view of the other
2. Identifying barriers to intergroup cooperation
3. Projecting concrete programs of problem solving to provide the basis of coordination necessary to achieve corporate objectives.

The approach outlined here is not only a programmatic way of diagnosing the causes of frictions but also an explicit way of taking concrete steps to correct them. It also provides for anticipating future problems and launching action strategies to prevent them. Finally, Intergroup Development provides for identifying and making explicit for members of both sides of a cleavage the goals they must pursue through joint effort if the interests of each are to be fully realized. It thus increases the likelihood that synergistic effects will result from intergroup cooperation.

9

BUSINESS LOGIC AS THE BASIS FOR DESIGNING AN IDEAL STRATEGIC CORPORATE MODEL

An ideal strategic model is constructed in Phase 4 around six key corporate elements, as shown in Box 64. They are:

1. Definitions of minimum and optimum corporate financial objectives[1]
2. Descriptions in explicit terms of the nature and character of business activities
3. Definitions in operational terms of the scope and character of customers and markets
4. Structure for organizing and integrating business operations for synergistic results
5. Basic policies to guide business decision making, and
6. Development requirements for avoiding obsolescence and exploiting growth capacity.

Designing an ideal stategic model is an exercise in the rigorous application of business logic. Taking nothing about the operation of the business for granted, key executives apply "pure reasoning" to business actualities. Through this approach, corporate leaders can identify and evaluate the assumptions on which the corporation has been built and is operated. These assumptions are tested for validity. Those which are unacceptable are rejected and replaced with others that are sound.

Box 64

*Key Corporate Elements Are Interdependent in
Their Contribution to Corporate Strategy*

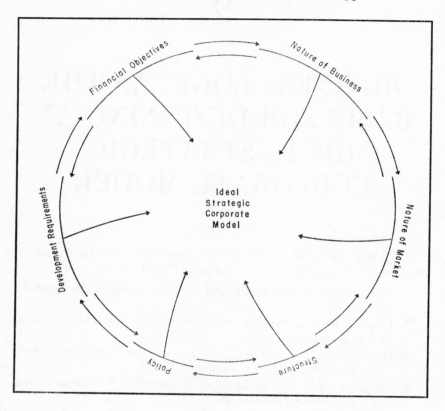

In this way, executive leadership can study the corporation, free
itself from past and present thinking, and gear the organization
for strongest possible business action.

CONSIDERATIONS UNDERLYING PHASE 4

Achieving Corporate Objectivity

The rationale of Phase 4 is based upon a widespread observation. Those who are intimately and intently concerned with

leading a business and responsible for it can be engulfed by it. Because they stand so close to it, they find it difficult to view it objectively and analytically. The very closeness and intimate acquaintance with its problems too often causes self-deception, rationalization, and other kinds of blurred focus, tunnel vision, and shortsightedness. Illustrations of illogical business thinking are shown in Box 65. The stresses and strains that seem inevitably to accompany the responsibility for leading a business cause this problem to be present in almost every company, new or old, at least in some amount and sometimes to a severe degree. In an older company there is likely to be a corporate culture containing deeply entrenched traditions, precedents, and past practices which no longer are sufficiently well geared to achieving sound financial objectives. In a newer company it is more likely that objectivity is difficult to attain because of lack of experience against which to develop convictions about corporate direction.

To achieve objectivity about the dynamic properties of a corporation, an executive must stand back and examine it from a new and different point of view. By identifying the business logic which would be applied in running an ideal business, he can get the kind of perspective which is essential for stripping away subjectivity and complacency. The objectivity gained from designing an ideal strategic model in Phase 4 makes it possible for corporate leaders not only to observe and evaluate how the corporation actually *is* being conducted but also to develop a clear picture of what it *can* and *should* become.

Replacing Business Tradition with Business Logic

Significant barriers to running a business in a businesslike way are reduced and sometimes eliminated in Phases 1 through 3. These are ones which prevent solving operational problems on the basis of fact, reason, and logic. They stem from difficulties in relationships among those who manage the corporation. Obstructed communication, faulty ways of dealing with conflict, vested interests, ignoring rather than facing up to inadequacies of individuals, organization politics, accepting mediocre standards, and tolerating low involvement of members are but a few of these.

It might be expected that once such stumbling blocks are removed, managers will make decisions according to the re-

Box 65

Comments from Top Teams Illustrate
Business Thinking Based on Business Traditions

"I believe our company thinks that its purpose is to grow at the rate possible consistent with little risk. What we seek is little more than barely enough to squeak through."

"We have never agreed on rate of return. We only look at profit margins. We are a margin conscious corporation. We aim for whatever return we can get while upping market volume."

"We put a lot of capital into protecting the backbone of one of our divisions even though the return was mediocre. We are oriented to protecting a market position or avoiding any loss of marketing position."

"We all see a quarterly report and mutter that inventory is up $10 million but this is a purely mechanical review. We decide on purchases according to availability and market prices, not by production schedules. We had a 17 weeks supply of raw materials at year end instead of the 12 needed."

"Each division is required to prepare a production plan, but the day one is issued it changes immediately. Frequent shifts are characteristic of our system of production control. Schedules change at least three times a week. My production man is constantly coming in and tearing up the schedule, saying, 'They changed their minds again.'"

"We have a centralized system of operations control. That is, both policy and administration are controlled by the key group. Every administration action, good or bad, is covered by a rule. No division head can make a change without approval of a vice president. He cannot move on salaries, hiring or firing, or pricing. You can hardly blow your nose here. We have a precedent and a rule for everything."

"We took over $500,000 out of a plant manager's budget and then it took three visits to tell him so. We had not had any consultations in advance. What consultation means to us is talk, listen, seek advice, and then do what you are going to do anyway."

quirements of business logic. This is unlikely. What is more certain is that actions continue to be based on deeply embedded business traditions and practices. Business traditions are difficult to identify and deal with. They are part of the culture's logic and language. They are its legacy of guidelines which have served in the past and which have come to have second nature power, accepted as givens and therefore operating almost as habits. Having completed Phases 1 through 3, organization members are eager to move forward. They are alert and aware of fundamental discrepancies between what *should* take place and what actually *is* occurring. Furthermore, they are prepared to take the steps essential for moving forward. Without having completed Phases 1 through 3, challenging the business traditions of a company and of the key executives who lead it is difficult. When a business is operating fairly well, either little thought is given to the question or the assumption is likely to be made that business logic already is being applied. Attempts to introduce and apply concepts of logic are likely to be met by defensiveness, with deep feelings that unfair criticism is being lodged against a management which has striven mightily to attain the results already achieved. Only after corporate executives (1) have learned to use critique for self-examination, (2) have experienced the power of thinking in terms of models, and (3) have come to grips with their own teamwork barriers, is there a sufficient degree of openness, candor, and commitment available for people to want to challenge and correct on a self-convincing basis the business logic beneath their current business performance.

Precepts of business logic are no less in the history of a company than are the behavioral practices of its culture. Dealing with behavioral practices is an important step toward excellence but an incomplete one by itself. Taking the step which results in strengthening its business logic permits a company to fuse sound behavior with valid business practice. This is the hallmark of corporate excellence. In Phase 4, business traditions and rules of thumb are challenged by the most rigorous business logic. The aim is to examine the present searchingly rather than taking it for granted. When the difficult decision to strive for a higher level of corporate excellence has been reached, all elements of business practice are subject to deliberate, detailed scrutiny. Only when existing assumptions have been tested and their soundness demonstrated is it valid to assume that limitations in thinking will have been identified and brought to an irreducible minimum. In this way, a corporation which is motivated to do so can achieve the conditions to excel.

Making Planning Effective

As shown in Chapter 1, the second most important area listed as a barrier to corporate effectiveness by managers in the United States, Great Britain, and Japan is planning. On the surface, this might seem to imply that greater effort should be applied to planning. To conclude that planning itself is a major barrier to corporate effectiveness would be the same as to attempt to solve communication problems by getting out the word.

Barriers to effective planning are much, much deeper. If corporate strategy is based on unsound business logic or if each member up and down the line is interpreting in his own way what he believes to be corporate strategy, a coherent framework for formulating operational plans is either unavailable or is not being utilized. Then planning will remain a source of difficulty no matter how much time and energy is applied to perfecting programmatic and operational aspects. When there is a widely understood strategy of the corporation based on sound business logic, difficulties of planning decrease and sometimes even disappear as barriers to organization effectiveness. Under these conditions, planning ceases to be a problem and can become the gateway to opportunity, sometimes unlimited opportunity.

THE POWER OF MODELS

A completed design for an ideal strategic model provides a corporation with objectives. It gives a framework within which sound tactical and operational decisions can be made. It can focus and concentrate the thinking, motivation, and energies of corporate members to contribute their fullest efforts to attaining corporate excellence. There is another positive effect that can be realized from a corporate model of excellence. When an ideal model of what is possible is contrasted with the existing situation, significant motivational energy is released. When Phases 1 through 3 have been completed, corporate members eagerly await leadership to acquire excellence. They are prepared to commit their efforts to moving away from the current situation. Their energies not only can be released but they also can be dedicated to corporate objectives. The conditions under which personal gratification can be attained from corporate contribution are widely present. Not only are key executives ready and capable of exercising leadership, but the base of the organization is more fully ready to receive it.

Understanding of what an ideal strategic model is, and what it is not, is essential for seeing the manner in which it can influence the strengthening of a corporation.

What the Model Is Not

An ideal strategic model is *not* (1) a projection of the future predicated upon past performance, (2) a mechanical adding up of the *status quo* segments of the company plus a "hip pocket" or emotionally charged ten or fifteen percent improvement factor, (3) a "Cloud Nine" Twenty-First Century model of a bright new world, (4) a generalized statement of the corporate virtues which persons should aspire to achieve. Nor is it a rejection of all tradition, precedent, and past practice.

What the Model Is

The ideal strategic model results from thinking systematically, creatively, and in an unfettered way. It involves freed-up thinking but contains no free-wheeling. Business logic is the criterion for developing sound formulations under the six elements of organization functioning: key financial objectives, nature of the business, nature of the market, organization structure, policy, and development requirements.

GUIDELINES THAT REMOVE CONSTRAINTS ON THINKING

The point of departure in developing the model involves achieving agreement to three general rules which demonstrate that restrictions to thinking from business tradition are removed.

1. The nature of the business should take advantage of the most recent scientific and technological knowledge. But since

what is yet to be discovered does not exist, it cannot be presumed and built into the model.

2. The nature of the business and its character cannot violate existing government or legal requirements and should anticipate trends in government regulations of business. When the ideal strategic model is being developed for a corporate component, matters over which the component has no control should be identified and accepted only when they have been demonstrated to be inevitable limitations.

3. The ultimate measure of corporate effectiveness is financial. When it fits operational realities, rate of return on assets employed is an excellent measure of corporate performance expressed in financial terms. Alternative measures for non-profit-based institutions can be designed.

If any one of these three ground rules is unacceptable, it is necessary to establish and make explicit additional or altered ground rules under which the ideal strategic model will be designed.

These specifications insure realism, because there are some limitations to corporate action on which management has little or no influence. The first two specifications are axiomatic. The matter of corporate constraints is more subtle. When an ideal strategic model is being constructed in a subordinate unit of a corporation, managers sometimes assume that there is corporate policy which creates limitations when in fact no such policy exists. Other corporate constraints may exist but be subject to change. Therefore, in the construction of the model, nothing is taken for granted but every formulation is challenged and tested for whether it contains an unchangeable limitation or a real one. The objective is to evaluate the limits of freedom under which the subordinate unit possesses the autonomy essential for self-responsible action.

Specifying a financial yardstick as the ultimate measure of business effectiveness might seem unnecessary as an explicit ground rule, particularly one so widely talked about as return on investment. But testing the soundness of business actions against the realities of financial results is more often preached than practiced. Though executives think about it, this thinking often is little more than lip-service except when corporate financial performance becomes chronically bad. Beyond these ground rules, the introduction of further limitations is avoided because no constraint to the application of business logic should be accepted as a "given" until it has been proved unchangeable.

PHASE 4 ACTIVITIES

Executive Level Designing

Those involved in Phase 4 should be the persons most responsible for the direction and character of the corporation's future. This means that Phase 4 designing, which anticipates where the company will be in the next five, ten, fifteen or more years, cannot be delegated to a planning department. Nor can it be delegated to a task force or to a person, a corporate vice president in charge of long range planning, for example. Since the top man and top team are responsible for the corporation's strategy, they have the widest overall perspective. They have the responsibility for leading the corporation, ultimate control over the resources—financial, material, and personnel—which must be committed if any goals are to be achieved. It is they who must engage themselves in Phase 4.

Design of an ideal model is separate from its implementation. Implementation activities to change the corporation from the existing to the ideal are carried out by persons and task forces from the top and echelons beneath it. For example, after an acquisition strategy as part of an ideal strategic model is formulated in Phase 4, actions which result from it could be carried out by a vice president in charge of corporate development or long range planning. Key members of executive management, therefore, engage in the study, deliberations, and decisions in this phase of Grid Organization Development. The chief executive officer and other members of executive management accountable for the conduct of the corporation must be involved. If the Grid Organization Development unit is a subordinate component of the corporation, such as a plant, those who engage in the design of an ideal strategic model include at least the corporate vice president of manufacturing, the plant manager, and key managers who report to him. If the unit is a marketing region, those who engage in this activity include the vice president of marketing, the regional marketing manager, and his key executive group. Those who engage in designing an ideal strategic model are the members of the corporation who shoulder ultimate responsibility for its results.

The Strategy of Study and Design

Completing the design of an ideal strategic model may take an extended period of time, but the initial formulation of an ideal model involves at least a week of concentrated effort. During this time, key managers free themselves from day-to-day corporate activity. As with other phases, designing an ideal strategic corporate model is an instrumented approach which employs a variety of learning strategies that aid the investigation essential for designing such a model to be carried out by executive management under self-convincing conditions. A Grid Organization Development specialist assists executive management in using these instruments, but his contribution is from supporting the learning rather than directing it.

The first step involves executives in developing convictions about the key elements of business logic which are fundamental to the operation of any corporation. Executives engage in individual study, then discuss the ideal specifications of a corporate strategy until they reach unified understanding and agreement. The objective of the background preparation is to provide all those responsible for designing the ideal strategic model with the same fundamental concepts of business logic. Several pertinent business books and articles provide the intellectual foundation for the prework of Phase 4.

The corporation as it is run becomes the next subject of examination. Against the framework of agreed upon precepts of sound business logic, actual practices can be viewed with objectivity. Having identified discrepancies between sound logic and current operations, executive management then designs the ideal strategic corporate model, which becomes a point of departure for the implementation activities of Phase 5. Much progress in completing the design of such a model is possible within a week of concentrated effort. However, additional study over weeks or months may be required before fundamental agreements can be reached to which a top team is prepared to commit itself.[2]

Lower Level Critique

Once completed by the top team, the ideal strategic model is transmitted downward in the corporation for review, evaluation, and critique, for testing its implications, and for inviting recommendations for strengthening it. The number of layers of the corporation involved in this step cannot be specified in advance. This depends on local considerations. Yet there are two specific objectives for extending the model downward. One is to achieve full communication to develop widespread understanding; the other is to insure that the best thinking within the corporation has been contributed to the final model. In this way the model is tested against the experience of those who will implement it. The contribution of lower levels, however, is through their recommendations. The decision step is a top level responsibility which in the final analysis cannot be taken by anyone but the top man. At the conclusion of Phase 4, the corporation has an ideal strategic model to guide its change, evolution, and development to acquire excellence.

KEY CORPORATE ELEMENTS

Each of the six key corporate elements has implications for the inclusive design of a corporate strategic model. These are the minimum essentials and none can be omitted. For certain situations it may be necessary to add further elements to insure completeness. Although they are separated for purposes of analysis, none can be dealt with in isolation. They are interdependent. Conclusions reached on one are determined in part by conclusions reached on others.

Key Financial Objectives

Executive management must first challenge itself to insuring the highest rate of long term return on assets employed and also place before itself, and the corporation, objectives for dollar volume that are difficult but attainable. Without such clearly stated financial criteria against which to calculate the soundness of business decisions, the possibility of achieving excellence is remote.

While many organizations express their performance in return on assets employed, relatively few use this criterion for setting objectives which influence operational decisions. Typical sharpening of financial objectives in the design of an ideal strategic model is shown in Box 66. Even though these companies expressed performance in terms of return on assets in their annual reports, not one of the three was guided significantly in its business decisions and operational activities by its financial objectives. When the operation of any company is based upon key financial objectives that are unclear and that have no minimums against which to calculate success achieved, it is likely to be operating according to a no-win policy. A test for whether return on assets employed is effectively utilized is seen when a corporation has an agreed upon minimum rate and minimum dollar volume for all segments of its operations. Temporary dips below the minimum are taken into account, but continued financial inability to realize the rate and dollar volumes in a subordinate segment having return-on-investment objectives signals an urgent need for corrective or divesting actions. Sometimes this kind of action is taken under circumstances of financial crisis. Described here is a systematic plan which insures that standards are present on a continuing basis and that review, correction, or divestment will occur according to plan. Specific and explicit statements on optimum rate of return on assets employed are also stated as well as absolute dollar magnitudes which constitute optimum objectives. These serve as goals which only can be attained through excellence of management.

When these kinds of financial objectives have pervaded an organization, its members cease justifying their actions because of being "victims of the market place" or "stuck with old equipment." These attitudes are replaced by positive, active thinking about how to overcome barriers that prevent mastery of the market place, more efficiently utilizing or replacing plant and equipment and increasing the contribution of personnel. When a corporation calculates its effectiveness by such financial objectives and is also prepared to face up to situations where its objectives are not being realized, it has a financial yardstick for measuring itself and evaluating its effectiveness.

Why is such significance placed upon designing and implementing key financial objectives expressed in terms of return

Box 66

Emphasis on and Use of Financial Objectives Changes as a Result of Designing an Ideal Strategic Model

From	*To*
Do as well as we can, with dollar volume profit improvement expected from one year to the next.	The businesses operated by this company are those which within three years can yield a 15 percent minimum and 25 percent optimum return on investment (pretax) with increases in dollar volume from the present $80 million by a compound growth factor of 15 percent. These objectives are to be reviewed on a yearly basis but not revised for at least five years.
A five percent profit margin on sales.	A minimum return on assets employed of 25 percent as a five-year objective, with a minimum, optimum and dollar volume to be set on a business-by-business basis.
Double sales and keep expense under control.	A 19.8 percent return on sales (post tax) with a five-year 20 percent compounding of dollar volume.

on investment? By using return-on-investment criteria where they can be employed, a corporation can measure its effectiveness by using the single most widely applied financial yardstick available in free enterprise business societies. It can also calculate the effectiveness with which it is applying its assets and compare itself with many other kinds of businesses. Whenever men think through to an ultimate conclusion the business logic which makes sense to them, the convictions that result become highly motivating as the basis for achieving excellence. Criteria for measuring performance that square with business logic challenge an organization to manage itself in such ways that they can be met. Only then are the personal goals of individuals as corporate members congruent with the business logic of the enterprise itself. In the game of professional football, there is only one set of ground rules by which achievement can be measured. The effectiveness of all teams is measured against these uniform standards. Return on assets employed is a set of ground rules that serves a similar purpose for the conduct of the business.

Nature of the Business

Many companies are engaged in a specific business activity, not because of deliberate intent to be in that business, but because of accident, historical circumstances, or short term opportunity. Some companies originally formulated according to business logic no longer "make sense" because of the changes resulting from developments of modern society.

When business logic is applied in the design of an ideal strategic model, the fundamental concepts underlying the nature of the business are submitted to systematic investigation to test their basic soundness. In addition, the businesses in which a corporation is engaged are thought through in terms of a company's current assets—financial, technological, and personnel. A company often has strengths and talents around which products or services can be designed to enlarge the definition and scope of the business while an underlying unity that provides the basis for synergy is retained.

During a Phase 4 activity, a publishing house clarified the nature of the business it intended to be in and was able to see its technical personnel and physical competency in designing and printing books as a core base which should be expanded into an integrated educational business. Book publishing became one step in the preparation and presentation of integrated educational systems. A construction company reformulated the concept of its business and moved away from the limitations of construction engineering to engage in several new and profitable undertakings. It added such technical client services as architectural planning and design, real estate financing and management, single and multiple housing development, and the development of industrial, institutional, and governmental complexes. In all, it expanded from one business line to sixteen profit-centered lines, of which construction continued to be the core.

These core clusters are examples of the synergistic effects that can be realized through the application of rigorous logic to the strategic design and conduct of a corporation. Usually when a decision is reached to engage in more than one business activity, not only should those business activities in which the company is engaged fit logically together, but in a well thought through business, there are many possibilities for achieving the advantages of multiplier effects. Examples from manufacturing industries include:

1. Common technology underlies the manufacture of diverse products.

2. Diversity of end products is sought where there is a high percent of interchangeability of parts, which can sometimes reach 60 to 80 percent communality.

3. The same base materials are utilized for various products, which provides the advantage of volume purchase.

4. The same equipment (sometimes with minimum alterations) can be employed in the manufacture of various products.

5. Generalist managerial skills can be applied in the supervision of diverse functions.

If a component of the business is so organized that one technical person, for example, can make the needed contributions in each of five superficially different but fundamentally similar areas, it is unnecessary to employ five persons, each of whom makes his contribution to one of the five areas. The same is true with respect to the utilization of equipment systems, of sales and distribution, and research and development. Similar combinations are possible through vertical and horizontal integration of business activities within a particular product or service area. Each of these examples suggests synergistic strategies around which a complex business operation may be built. The outcome is a return on investment advantage which might not have been realized had the business not been thought through from such a deliberately set point of view.

Several advantages can be gained from this kind of deliberate application of business logic. One is that polyglot activities that produce a discordant diversity can be eliminated and replaced by business activities which are interrelated and in harmony with these kinds of logical cores of intercorrelated possibilities. Furthermore, new business lines can be added because they "fit." Also a well thought through concept of the business provides a base line for continuous testing for technological obsolescence. When this is done, a company can grow with changes in environmental forces and not fall asleep and be overtaken by competition.

Nature of the Market

Specifying the properties of the market areas within which the corporation intends to be competitive is another key element in the design of the ideal strategic model. Properties of the nature of the market are intimately connected with the nature of the business and financial objectives. Changes in the definition of the market affect the definition of the business and financial objectives and vice versa. Yet for analytical purposes they are separated. Of particular significance in characterizing the nature of the market are those considerations that deal with both present and future: changing structure and living practices of families, population trends, changing consumer habits, the rate predicted in rise in living standards, shifting standards of health and sanitation, the rapidly increasing educational base as it applies within industrial nations, and similar emerging trends in international markets involving the developing countries. Some of these kinds of matters can be forecast and projected with a greater degree of certainty than others. But the risk entailed in making calculated judgments of future trends is undoubtedly far less than in disregarding them as impractical or visionary.

Box 67

Definition of the Market Changes as a
Result of Designing an Ideal Strategic Model

From	To
Customers served by catering service for high schools, colleges, and institutions whose menus are controlled by small personal budgets or limited institutional budgets.	Customers representing a range of eating preferences —hamburgers to caviar—a restaurant chain with a graded series of restaurants, each under its own brand name, designed to satisfy a specific segment of the consumer sector. The series of restaurants are concentrated in cities and regions to realize advantages from personnel and supervision and from centralized warehousing and distribution facilities.
Customers are those within a specified distance from a headquarters location, excluding those in specific cities where there is strong competition.	Customers are those, anywhere, whom we can service with a project team dispatched from headquarters and still meet financial criteria.
Customers who are persons needing small loans.	Customers requiring a broad based and integrated individual, industrial, and institutionalized financing service, including loans, mortgages, insurance, and other financial services.

Box 67 Continued on next page

BOX 67 (cont.)

From	*To*
Sole customers are other components of the parent served by this manufacturing subsidiary.	Customers are any buyers who can purchase the products of this manufacturing component at a profitable level.
Customers using petroleum.	Customers using energy—the fuel cell, fertilizers, gas, electricity, nuclear power.

The strategies of market analysis and definition are complex but questions about the market can be posed, such as: What is the market now, including strengths and weaknesses of maintaining it? What is the market position of competitors, including examination of their strengths and weaknesses? What is the future market potential? What are strategies, such as advertising, use of name brands and guarantees, or product servicing, for consolidating and expanding market position? What geographical boundaries, if any, should be considered as limitations that define market areas? Intelligent market strategy also can open up the possibility of gains from synergistic effects in the same manner as in other areas.

With financial objectives and the definition of the nature of the business or businesses in which the company intends to engage defined, historical or tradition-anchored concepts of the customer and extent of the market cannot be passively assumed or taken for granted. In many companies, the customer is thought of from a geographical point of view. For others, customers are defined by product lines. Both of these views and others, unless tested against the soundest business logic, can severely limit the pursuit of corporate excellence. Box 67 illustrates the increased flexibility and deepened market penetration made possible by a shift in the concept of the consumer and redefinition of the market. The companies illustrated shifted from a narrow geographical view or single product line concept to a concept not limited by locale or restricted to a limited sector of the business.

Corporate Structure

The structure of an organization divides and arranges the many activities essential for accomplishing corporate purposes. It also can provide a basis for measuring the degree to which objectives are achieved. In the design of the ideal strategic model, the underlying logic for grouping, ordering, controlling, and integrating effort is specified and made explicit. There are several matters that need to be considered in an interdependent way in the design of the corporate structure.

One is insuring that the structure of the organization reflects the logic of product and market considerations. This general statement finds application in different organizations in widely diverse forms. The kinds of issues to be thought through include (a) the degree to which common activities are segregated, and (b) coordination of interrelated but segregated activities.

Another matter in designing a sound organization structure is gearing it to reflect the financial objectives of the corporation. When the total business can be segregated into return-on-investment centers, profit centers, or cost centers, financial measurement systems can be related directly to structural components of the company. This possibility of financial measurement of component activities aids managers to relate operational decisions to the financial objectives of the company. It also makes possible soundly based merit and incentive compensation.

The third matter is conceiving organization structure in motivational as well as operational terms. This consideration, though equally as important as the others, is one often overlooked. The ideal structure should reflect factors that heighten the involvement, commitment, and effort of personnel. Achieving a sound integration of control with autonomy can bring responsible motivation to its height. When these several elements

BOX 68

Organization Structure Changes as a Result of Designing an Ideal Strategic Model

From	*To*
Centralized marketing and manufacturing facilities across product lines.	Functionally autonomous business activities with marketing and manufacturing responsibility on a product line basis. Except for minimum supervision, headquarters services as a cost center available but not imposed on decentralized operations which can either make use of them or procure comparable services on an open market basis.
A centrally located downtown loan office in each of several cities.	A series of profit-centered satellite loan offices offering financial services (i.e., loans, insurance coverage, etc.) located downtown and in suburban shopping areas with a centralized computerized service center to provide administrative and business support. Interconnection between computer centers permit transfer and servicing of accounts as customers move from city to city.

are meshed together, the ideal strategic model is likely to have a structure which has the following properties:

1. Units which are wholes are segregated (i.e., within the unit all of the parts are present which are essential for a complete operation while duplication of effort is minimized). This does not mean that all staff services have to be a part of each whole. In most cases, it does mean that access to staff services is available under local option, either from another segment of the corporation or on an open market arrangement, whichever is at lower cost.

2. Each unit's performance can be measured in terms of return on investment or an equivalent indicator of effectiveness expressed in terms of financial performance.

3. Potentials for achieving multiplier rather than additive effects are exploited.

4. Motivation stimulated by autonomy which in this context means self-control is increased through financial responsibility. The basis of supervision and control is provided through explicit financial measurement.

5. Fluidity through task forces, project teams, and the readiness for man-to-man interchanges across divisional lines provides the flexibility essential for effective integration of effort.

Major shifts in structure, which reflect the kind of thinking suggested here, often have resulted from Phase 4. Box 68 provides typical examples. They suggest how clear financial objectives and explicit statements of the nature of the business and descriptions of the customer can provide fundamental alterations in the concepts of organization structure.

Corporate Policy

Sound policy can make an outstanding contribution to the effectiveness of a corporation. Without sound policy, corporate members may have an insufficient framework for seeing the implications, alternatives, and consequences involved in key decisions in subtle and complex areas of business analysis. With such policy, a man who must cope with a complex problem has guidelines of analysis. These guidelines give him a basis of orientation to select the sounder over less sound courses of action. Without the guidance that policy can provide, the intricate implications of one approach to the solution of a problem, in contrast with others, can be quite unclear. The result is often a decision which commits action that is unsound in the light of the whole. Furthermore, in an absence of sound policy, men in different parts of the company facing essentially the same decision are likely to reach contradictory solutions or they may fail to take necessary action. The extent to which policy guidance is absent in modern corporate life is surprising. Solutions reached are likely to be tradition-founded, in that precedent acts with the power of policy. The importance attached to valid corporate policy is difficult to overestimate.

A misunderstanding that often surrounds the role of policy is that it imposes constraints which prevent managers from exercising responsibility. The thought is that if policy positions are stated in advance, they have the effect of forestalling freedom of action. Only when policies are in fact narrow and constricting in their formulation is this so. When policy is well thought through and strong, it creates the opposite effect. It provides managers a framework for confidently taking intelligent action. In this context, sound policy can aid men of ordinary competence to exercise extraordinarily sound judgment. Without strong policy, the result can be that ordinary men act with uncommonly poor judgment.

The importance of policy has long been recognized with most larger companies' having a policy manual. On closer examination, however, it is clear that many policy manuals are mixtures of policies, regulations, and rules. They cover, with varying degrees of completeness and soundness, major areas of judgment and decision that are confronted in conducting a business. Far less frequently than would be desirable, policy as expressed does not coincide with sound business logic. Furthermore, as often as not, policy as stated and the actual policy that undergirds practice are different from one another. Sometimes policy is little more than an explicit expression of traditions, precedents, and past practices. In ideal strategic model development, clear policy is systematically established when it is absent, and existing policy is tested against the most rigorous criteria of business logic and corrected if necessary. Once policy is created according to the requirements of sound business logic, it can become a vital and significant set of principles, deeply felt by those whose decisions it affects. Though the number of policy areas varies from company to company,

BOX 69

*Policy Changes as a Result of Designing an
Ideal Strategic Model*

From	*To*
Purchasing	
When available, products of the company should be used in preference to purchase of similar items from competitors.	Products of the company should be used in preference to competitors' products except where higher quality at a similar price or equal quality at a lower price items are available on the open market.
Personnel	
Persons employed by the corporation should be fully competent to perform the jobs for which they are employed with a minimum of orientation or training.	Persons employed by the corporation should be fully competent to perform the jobs for which they are employed with a minimum of orientation or training. In addition, only those persons should be employed whose potential for assuming increased responsibility in the corporation is not limited. Evaluation of personnel according to actual performance as well as for potential should be conducted no less frequently than at yearly intervals.

there are about twenty fundamental policy areas inherent in the concept of a business. They range from financial control, through pricing and product policy, to policies covering personnel selections, promotion, and development. Box 69 shows changes in policies resulting from the design of an ideal strategic model of a corporation. The two alterations in policy illustrate the shifts in thinking when policy is formulated according to an ideal model rather than in a more conventional way. In the first case, a decentralized management is authorized to make purchases based upon competitive access to the market. This policy is contrasted with one where the management is a captive customer of other parts of the organization over which it exercises no cost control. In the second case, the basis for appraising prospective employees involves far deeper and broader judgment of what a man is being employed to contribute than formerly visualized.

Thus policy can only be set after key financial objectives have been identified, the nature of the business has been systematically determined, the nature of the market has been agreed upon, and the corporate structure crystallized. Then it becomes possible to specify an intellectual framework of judgment which reflects the soundest business logic possible for any specified corporation.

Development Requirements

Development is essential to a corporation's success, survival, and growth. "Development" refers to product and market development, personnel and management development, and organization development, including business traditions and behavioral culture of the firm. It is a never ending affair and involves at least three fundamental considerations.

New knowledge becomes available in ever increasing amounts. To keep a corporation continuously up-to-date on all knowledge available for its use is one aspect of development. A second consideration is personnel obsolescence as related to the capacity to acquire and use knowledge. Obsolescence of personnel can be kept at a minimum if a learning orientation is part of the behavioral culture of an organization. A third aspect of development is in the concept of breakthrough as contrasted with lag. Lag is the distance behind knowledge frontiers. Breakthrough occurs when a company is on the leading edge and sees as one of its corporate objectives to achieve or retain breakthrough leadership in production or utilization of knowledge.

An ideal strategic model provides guidelines calculated to insure that new knowledge is utilized at a tempo which reduces lag and avoids the use of obsolescent knowledge which is costly. In some companies the goal is to run the risks involved in attempting to be on the breakthrough side rather than to run the greater risks in being on the lag and obsolescence side.

A typical shift for one company was from, "We used tried and true knowledge, letting other organizations bear the expense of costly development mistakes," to being geared to innovation as the low-risk route to profit leadership. The risks involved in the attitude that favors utilizing and producing new knowledge that can foster breakthrough or innovation are much reduced in organizations which have learned the effective use of critique under conditions of unobstructed communication. The reason is that through critique, false starts can more quickly be identified and abandoned and sound ones more quickly identified and strengthened. Furthermore, with unobstructed communication and effective critique, many of the expensive and time-consuming steps of ultra-sophisticated experimentation can be bypassed without significantly reducing the certainty on which action is based. Many alternatives can be explored with minimum effort or investment, and those exploited can be selected with the prospect of maximum payout.

SPECIAL ISSUES

Several questions arise as managers prepare to design an ideal corporate model.

Dynamic Nature of the Ideal Strategic Model

"How can you design for the future when you don't even know what it will be like? Isn't it foolhardy even to attempt it?" If operations are genuinely sound, top management is able to discern the broad concepts and outlines of the future long before it happens, take advantage of it, and anticipate when change will be required.[3] Another answer to these questions is that the ideal strategic model is not a static or unchanging blueprint but is dynamic. As unanticipated circumstances arise, the corporate model is retested and corrected if it can be improved in the light of new developments. Imperfections which are not apparent at the start are sought out and eliminated in the light of new knowledge. New concepts are continuously entered into the ideal corporate model as they emerge. Furthermore, the strategic model is subject to systematic review at designated intervals to insure its continuing soundness.

Commitment by Lower Levels

"How do others lower in the organization become committed when they don't participate in designing the model?" Commitment to the ideal corporate model by those lower in the organization can be achieved when they fully understand its implications for themselves and their work and for the future of the corporation. One way such understanding can come about is through their being provided the opportunity to recommend changes in the model before it becomes final. The ideal strategic model is not finalized until reservations, criticisms, and doubts have been analyzed, evaluated, and resolved. Furthermore, recommendations for change are submitted to a thorough investigation. Whether or not they are used, recommendations are thrashed through with those who made them. The probability is then increased that understanding and agreement with the soundness of the ideal strategic model will result in commitment to its implementation.

Spadework for Design of the Ideal Strategic Model

"If designing an ideal strategic model of the corporation is at the core of corporate effectiveness, why is it not done first?" In a few experimental Grid Organization Development projects, the design of an ideal strategic model was the first organization development activity. In no case was it possible to conclude that the experiment was a success, that it resulted in significant progress toward corporate excellence. The best explanation for lack of results from starting Grid Organization Development with the ideal strategic model is that in each instance it appeared to be impossible for the executive level of management to overcome their communication blockages. They did not first effectively eliminate barriers to communication, which included win-lose power struggles, the unwitting readiness to compromise and accommodate, and unthinking acceptance of traditions, precedents, and past practices. The ideal strategic designs that were produced lacked so much that they did not provide sound foundations for moving these corporations toward excellence. Even the limited achievement that might have been realized from an ideal strategic model designed under these circumstances was not of value. Operational managers were not prepared to act with the energy and dedication needed to move the model from the drawing board to implementation. Solving communication problems before designing an ideal strategic corporate model seems to represent the soundest order of events while running minimum risk of failure.

Ideal Strategic Model Designing Versus Management by Objectives

"Why not use the conventional management-by-objectives approach?"[5] Management by objectives may start at lower levels of management with organization members at one level thinking out and setting objectives for what would be the best accomplishment for them to achieve from their level's view. They feed the information up to the next level. In turn, that level adds to it and feeds it up a step, until it is finally assembled at the top as a "Statement of Corporate Objectives." While this type of "bottoms up" planning may increase involvement of lower levels, it often turns out that the organization model does not depart very much from the *status quo*. Departures are likely to be in degree or in making the *status quo* operation of the organization more efficient. While intimately acquainted with operations at their own levels, lower levels are without the knowledge, perspective, or responsibility for thinking and planning, which are needed for ideal strategic model development. This is somewhat like asking GI's in the field to design the grand strategy of battle.

Alternatively, some lists of broadly stated corporate objectives are set forth by top management. For purposes of participation and involvement, subordinate levels are called upon to set objectives which, when added together, will meet the broad objectives outlined by the top. This kind of organization goal setting more often than not produces commitments which look good on paper but which, in the light of business realities, may fail to materialize.

Traditional management-by-objectives approaches suffer the same limitations as a planning department approach, which involves specialists in projecting forecasts of the future. It presumes that the necessary grand strategy already is sound. The fundamental error of these approaches is that they take the existing grand strategy as a given and optimize within it. No amount of sophistication in this kind of planning can correct or eliminate deficiencies in the model.

SUMMARY

Strategies that give direction and character to corporate activities often are as much or more dictated by historical circumstances and entrenched tradition as by considerations of business logic. The possibility of achieving corporate excellence is increased to the degree that the character and functioning of a corporation is based upon business logic. Phase 4 of Grid Organization Development is designed to enable top management to formulate the broad outlines for what constitutes an ideal strategic model with its underlying premises based on sound business logic. The six key corporate elements that must be comprehensively analyzed and systematically designed in the construction of a model are interdependent. Under analysis, they form a cohesive pattern and unified whole which is the basis of the implementation activities in Phase 5.

In designing the ideal model in Phase 4 and in the implementation activities of Phase 5, key executives as well as other members of the corporation are likely to come face to face with severe and disturbing weaknesses of operations. The depth and severity of some problems sometimes makes it easier to ignore them than to confront them and find solutions for them. When this happens, executives should realize that they are placing upon the shoulders of the next management generation responsibility for problems they were unprepared to solve. For all practical purposes, such postponements usually cause even more severe and chronic difficulty for those who must eventually face them. The lack of courage implied by failure to exercise leadership in one generation is likely to create a new managerial generation with even less courage. When all of the phases of Grid Organization Development have been soundly installed and led, it becomes possible to exercise such courage, because a 9,9 system provides the strength of commitment essential for doing so.

REFERENCES

1. In the case of non-profit organizations, these may be agency service objectives as related to cost.
2. Sometimes the alterations to be made in the company in the implementation of the strategic model are so great that board-of-director consideration is essential.
3. Interesting possibilities for enriching the thinking of corporate members are contained in such models as the Delphi technique and the Monte Carlo prediction technique. See Gordon, T. J., *The Future*, Toronto: Macmillan of Canada, 1965.
4. Bowers, M. in *The Will to Manage*, New York: McGraw-Hill, 1966, presents a point of view on the strategy and structure of a company presumably brought into actuality through expert management and consultation. It is a useful study in contrast with the Grid Organization Development approach.
5. Typical examples here include: Odiorne, G. S., *Management by Objectives*, New York: Pitman, 1965; and Drucker P. F., *The Practice of Management*, New York: Harper, 1954, and *Managing for Results*, New York: Harper, 1964.

10

LAUNCHING A NEW
BUSINESS ERA

"Our organization development work during the previous year and a half has been preparing us mentally and emotionally for a major shift in the whole concept of the business. If it is to be of any value, it will have to take an indepth approach. We have to ask ourselves if we are ready to tackle this challenge in a fundamental and objective manner. Are we prepared to throw the company book out of the window and look at our investments from a fresh point of view?"

CHALLENGING THE STATUS QUO

With these words, a company president initiated the task of designing an ideal strategic corporate model. The group to whom he was speaking was the top executive committee of a company doing $300 million in annual sales. The president had been in office ten years. He is one of the outstanding business leaders in a city of close to three million persons. The company is a long established business firm and is a highly respected corporate citizen. It has four competitors. They are tough. The market is tough. The company objective of increasing market share has been realized each year over the past decade. The year-to-year gains, though modest, have been acceptable. Profits, however, have not shown a corresponding increase. It has been next to impossible to break through a stabilized plateau of earnings.

230

Grid Organization Development had been under way for a year and a half. Phases 2 and 3 had been completed throughout the corporation. Development efforts had only increased the sense of uneasiness in the top team about the leadership and direction it had been giving to the company. They shared an acute awareness that fundamental change was needed to achieve corporate excellence. Throughout the company there was a sense of anticipation that the executive group would set a new course that would move the organization off its plateau to higher earnings ground.

"When you score our past years against the hard yardstick of business reality, none of us have been satisfied to supervise the ineffective effort that we have turned in," the president continued. "I am as dissatisfied as you are. You work hard and I work hard but we have failed to produce a result that we can be proud of or gratified by in the future. This is not because of lack of effort or commitment but due to the definition of the business as it now stands.

"I don't believe we are prepared to continue in the present form. We must change the nature and scope of the business. We must create a new model which has a radically different objective. As I see it, based on the capital we have available, the objective of our business is to make the optimum rate of return on assets and maintain it for a long time. Our only purpose is to increase our profitability. We want to expand our market share but only under the condition that we are able to do so through earning a good return on assets employed."

The seven-man top team, whose membership included the president and vice president in charge of international operations, administration, manufacturing and engineering, marketing, personnel, and corporate planning, was on the threshold of designing an ideal strategic corporate model. A discussion in the Board room of two of the six key elements—establishing the financial objectives and designing the corporate structure—is presented to reflect the quality and character of thinking in this effort. The deliberations that went into the complete model ranged far beyond what is reported here. Brief summaries of portions of the discussion of these two key elements, however, show the character of thinking as well as the history of past traditions and attitudes which suggest why a profit plateau had been reached.

CLARIFYING FINANCIAL OBJECTIVES

Historically, financial objectives expressed in numerical terms had not been used as sharp, crisp, guidelines of business thought. In the company, the conventional approach was to pre-set budgets on a yearly basis with a quarterly review of deviations from the budget as a control device. The stated concern was to "get volume up," to gain a larger share of market. Percent of market had always been an important target. Organization members were comfortable when it was increasing. They were "up" when market share was up, "down" when market share was on the decline. Although profit was somewhere in the background, they felt impelled to get percent of market even higher.

The implicit faith was that with a preset budget and increased sales volume, profit would go up. When indications of a softening market appeared, additional funds were poured into advertising and promotion. As the top tried to develop explicit financial objectives, as shown in Box 70, they recognized the mental barriers of their deeply entrenched thinking.

There were two causes of the shift in thinking from a market share orientation to a return on investment concept. One was the heightened objectivity made possible by the top team's viewing the corporation from the eyes of stockholders. The argument was that in the final analysis, increases in earnings per share and a sustained improvement of the price of the stock are the ultimate tests that stockholders apply when making an investment decision. The soundness of this business logic was indisputable. Moreover, one manager pointed out that a significant number of employees were share owners. For this reason, it was maintained that these new financial objectives would be widely supported throughout the corporation.

The second argument that proved convincing was related to difficulties encountered in debt financing in the past. The management team knew that the banking community was not impressed by their financial performance and was therefore reluctant to lend money for further capital investment. If the company were to take full advantage of growth opportunities, there was no alternative except to manage the corporation in such a way as to increase banker confidence. Both of these considerations compelled members of this top team to adopt the

BOX 70

*Genuine Concern with the Organization's Earning Capacity
Results from Designing an Ideal Strategic Model*

From	*To*
Maintain or increase market share while living within a budget.	Optimal 30, minimum 20 percent pretax return on assets employed with an unlimited time horizon.
Dollar profit should improve and not fall behind last year. Return on investment computed and discussed on an after-the-fact calculation which exerted little or no influence on operational decision making.	Each business should have a specified profit improvement factor to be calculated on a business-by-business basis. The objective should be an earnings per share level which would within five years justify a price-earnings ratio of 20 to one or better.
	Share of market objectives should be established within the framework of return on assets and cash generation objectives.

position that they must shift their thinking and center their action on improving return on investment. This in turn led to the conviction that the corporation should be reorganized in ways that would permit and assist all managers to apply the same kind of financial thinking to their business decisions.

The next task was to set a minimum return on investment. The concern here was that if the minimum were to be set higher than current levels of performance, managers failing to meet it would think it unfair and arbitrary. There was also a fear that an across-the-board minimum would not reflect realities of various segments of the business. Before testing and probing, they assumed that a higher return could not be expected in some business segments and that this top-management imposed standard would result in defeatism. On the other hand, if the minimum were to be set too low, those businesses operating above it would have a tendency to feel complacent and satisfied and would have little incentive to strive for higher profitability. It also was agreed that there might be a compulsion on their part to raise the minimum at a later time. This, they were convinced, would be resisted and reacted to adversely by the rest of the management group. In spite of these difficulties, they were able to face and deal with the challenge of committing the organization to the highest possible financial objectives.

Many alternatives were considered when the values shown in Box 72 were finally set. The top team analyzed the return on investment and rate of growth of the top five percent of the 40 companies in the same broad industrial category as their own. "If other managements operating under similar conditions of product and market can accomplish these results," they reasoned, "why can't we?" This argument had overwhelming force, for it emphasized a key factor of actual difference in financial performance: managerial competence and high standards of striving.

Many opinions were voiced on the special circumstances in the company that would make these standards unfair. One by one these reservations were examined, often with the result that the team found that although many differences *did* exist, they could be eliminated by a determined management. The arguments that occurred and the conflicts they produced could be dealt with successfully because they had already developed strong convictions about 9,9 management and faced and resolved many communication barriers in their own Teamwork Development in Phase 2. The rest of the firm, furthermore, had demonstrated in Phases 1 through 3 that there was an undercurrent of eagerness for a strong indication of direction. The objectivity achieved resulted in their rejecting the convenient rationalization that "our company is different." It permitted members to acknowledge openly organization indulgences, over-staffing, unneeded headquarters services, and many examples where profit improvement could be realized if there was a strong will to achieve better results.

CHANGING THE CORPORATE STRUCTURE

Headquarters structure was the result of evolutionary changes rather than a deliberate plan for effective integration of people into the organization's objectives. Over the years, managers had been asked to expand services which had resulted in a top-heavy headquarters staff. In addition, executive dining rooms, car and chauffeur services, and a variety of other perquisites were identified. They were difficult to justify. Furthermore, though the headquarters people were hard working, they were applying attention to many nonessential activities or were overly concerned with detail. Manufacturing and marketing management in the headquarters group had been devoting a great deal of time to the most minute aspects of operational budgets and expenses. Hiring, firing, salary, pricing, market promotions—all required approval. Even a modification in a small volume product or a minor manufacturing technological innovation rallied them to protracted discussion in the Board room. Daily dealing with the minutiae of the operations was a way of life.

As the top team designed an ideal corporate structure, current arrangements thwarted them at every turn. As their thoughts crystallized, they became convinced, sometimes painfully so, of the severity of actions that would be required if the company were to be turned around. Box 71 shows this shift. Spurred on to think through an ideal model, they agreed that the company should be decentralized by product line with each product line established to permit the determination of its profit contribution as a percentage of the assets required to support it.

By structuring planning, marketing, manufacturing, product development, and support service functions in integrated components and providing measurements geared to financial objectives, managers would be able to make the same kinds of judgments in their business decisions as are made by investors in choosing between two companies. Managers would have the

BOX 71

*Need for Organization Structure Changes Becomes Obvious as
a Result of Designing an Ideal Strategic Model*

From	To
Heavy headquarters staff with regulatory and procedural control over each of nine geographical regions.	A decentralized product line organization with management and control geared to key financial objectives, with the local option to purchase from other autonomous units or on the open market. Marketing and manufacturing responsibility decentralized. Headquarters control maintained through the approval of the capital budget and setting of policy. Minimum headquarters staff.

authority and responsibility essential for the decisions that affect rate of return on investment. Several results were expected. First, they would have control over operational, personnel, and financial matters which directly and indirectly affect rate of return. They then would in effect be operating their own businesses. Reinforced by minimum and optimal rates of return on investment, motivation to organization excellence would reach its maximum height. Performance appraisal as a part of salary review and extra compensation determination would be directly correlated to measured contributions. Finally, the basis of measurement is something to which men could and would commit themselves fully because the corporate business logic squares with personal business logic. Headquarters control would be through selecting strong, effective managers, approving budget and capital appropriations, and setting clear policy.

The final formulation of what the organization structure should be did not come easily. Members unwittingly introduced unexamined assumptions into the planning discussions. This proved to be the biggest barrier. To minimize this effect, the top team listed each assumption, keeping the list before them as the various alternatives about how the business might be arranged were developed. Only in this way were they able to deal with the pressures of history and tradition.

A few members felt that they could not establish an equitable basis for appraising plant, equipment, and property across a wide range of different circumstances. Old plant and equipment on expensive downtown property, new and automated equipment in modern plant on industrial park property, property in some cases benefited by favorable tax considerations, represented some of the variables. Other members maintained that ground rules could be established which would provide a basis for just and equitable comparison across these variables for an extended period of time. Their argument was that this kind of financial engineering was difficult to accomplish and necessarily must be in a series of steps, moving from coarse to refined. The concept they decided to pursue was replacement value of plant and equipment, which eliminated most of the variables which were historical and immutable. Resistance to structuring in this manner crumbled when one executive who had had managerial experience in another company was able to describe in rich detail the way this had been accomplished and the constructive consequences that had resulted for more effective management. The conclusion was, "Since we know it has been done, the reason for reluctance must be that we don't want to face up to the comfortable rationalizations that keep us from taking action based on financial judgments. If others can do it, there's no reason why we can't. The problem is attitude and motivation."

Another question that wrenched at tradition was, "Are the many services grafted onto headquarters really essential to effective operations, or are they there only because we've become accustomed to them?" This arose when it was clear that segmented businesses were desirable as the basis for organization structure.

"How could business segments obtain genuinely essential services? Does it necessarily follow that those services are always best provided by headquarters?" The initial reaction was "Yes," because it had always been done that way. As this question was discussed, the conclusion reached was that headquarters, under a product-line, return-on-investment concept of structure, should provide only (1) those services that three or more business product segments requested and were willing to pay for as an expense under their key financial objectives; or (2) those that were deemed essential for intelligent headquarters supervision and carried out as a headquarters expense. This formulation was backed by the conviction, now firm, that genuine achievement motivation is the result when a business manager has control over his key costs and income decisions. Under this kind of formulation, it became evident that staff services retained would be streamlined and held at an essential minimum.

Another issue that had to be faced squarely if the new thinking were to be implemented was, "If a service or line of business is to be divested, this will involve far more than disposing of machines, desks, or cafeteria equipment. It means terminating long service employees—some of whom have worked for this company thirty-five years."

Personnel disruption created in major reorganization is harsh, real, and inescapable. There is no easy path around this issue. The attitude and resolution developed by this top team was that they *could* anticipate the impact from these kinds of personnel disruptions. It *could* be minimized by retraining and reassignment to existing vacancies in other parts of the business; early retirement; retirement counseling; extended advance notice; making known to employees vacancies and opportunities in other companies within the area; reemployment counseling; and just severance pay.

They saw that if these issues were not faced, it would be to the long term detriment of the profitability of the business and that of present and future employees. To insure equitability to all concerned, the top team agreed that personnel reduction decisions caused by reorganization would be made according to criteria of competence rather than present job requirements or individual skills. If the skills of those affected were not appropriate to the new organization structure, they would be offered reassignment. This would be done, where practical, by providing on-the-job development assignments and retraining. Thus separations resulting from reorganization would affect those least competent.

What does a 9,9 approach to management mean in the context of this discussion? The "9" of concern for production is a concern for achieving results in the context of business logic. The "9" of concern for people emphasizes the importance of openness and candor, confronting and resolving conflict, having strong convictions, changing one's mind in the light of new evidence. All of these are indispensable behavioral elements for achieving an integration of the corporate business logic "9" with the personal business logic "9." The concern for people "9" is a concern that involves enabling them to be effective in contributing to achieving the production objectives of the business logic "9."

FINALIZING THE IDEAL STRATEGIC CORPORATE MODEL

After completing the discussion on the other four elements, top management presented the ideal model to the next level of management for study, testing, evaluation, criticism, and recommendations for modification, revisions, extensions, and deletions. Lower levels of management were thus provided a full opportunity to contribute to matters of vital significance to them. Points of difference generating conflict were identified. In a sequence of discussions that extended over a period of several months, these points of difference were effectively resolved, some by executive management's shifting a previously held point of view and some by shifting at lower levels. Some of the issues of disagreement found effective resolution through the exploration and identification of new formulations that had not appeared in the ideal strategic model and which had been formulated by lower levels. The significant aspect of this step was that understanding and agreement based upon insight into the strategy and its implications provided the basis for the ideal model as it took operational shape.

Once the top team and the level of management immediately beneath them had discussed and agreed upon the model, it became the subject of a team action seminar throughout the corporation, with managers at all levels studying, discussing, and evaluating its subtleties and implications. This was done with the understanding that if parts of the model were found unsound, they could still be modified and changed. Thus the entire management organization was provided an opportunity to challenge the ideal model and on the basis of their own testing of its logic, to convince themselves of its soundness. The company now has an understood and agreed upon strategy to guide its long term development.

11

IMPLEMENTING THE IDEAL
STRATEGIC CORPORATE
MODEL

By the time Phase 5 is completed, the ideal strategic model has been successfully implemented. The corporation is being operated according to explicit strategic specifications established in Phase 4 rather than its traditional ways. Phase 5 involves two basic processes. One is planning, the second, implementation. Because no two companies or industries are the same, the planning and implementation must be done in a way that acknowledges the uniqueness of the situation. It is tailor-made.

What is the situation within a company when Phase 5 planning and implementation activities begin? First, many communications barriers to corporate effectiveness have been successfully eliminated. The theories of the Grid are well understood and are in daily use throughout the managerial system (Phase 1). Communication blocks in the work teams of the organization have been identified, and plans to resolve them have been implemented (Phase 2). Obstructions to effective coordination of effort between groups also have been identified, and steps have been taken to remove these (Phase 3). Finally, the top management of the corporation has designed an ideal strategic model for what the firm should become, and the model has been thought through and tested down through the organization, not only to insure its sound-

Box 72

*Implementing the Ideal Strategic Model Takes Place in a
Series of Steps*

The ideal strategic model contains business segments defined by the nature of the business and market.

Smallest independent business segments are identified—each to function as an autonomous operating unit.

Planning teams prepare designs for each business segment to be tested against varying economic conditions.

Various plans for integration of business segments are tested where similar activities are needed by several units or where dependence between units exists.

A headquarters organization is composed which contains, at a minimum, the capacity for generating investment capital and development of executive talent. Other integrating or corporate-wide staff services are added only when they are seen as essential to the health of the business and can be provided most cheaply by a headquarters service team as a contract service for the business segments themselves.

Widespread understanding of the implementation strategy in progress and as it is completed is present throughout corporate membership. This generates enthusiasm for change rather than permitting resistance to development.

---

ness but also to gain support for it and endorsement of it (Phase 4). Conditions are right for sound planning.

MOTIVATION FOR IMPLEMENTATION

The objective of Phase 5 is to utilize the intellectual and emotional energies of the entire corporation to shift from historically-based practices to ones that have been deliberately

Box 73

Attraction-Repulsion Forces Compel Action Toward
Excellence in Phase 5

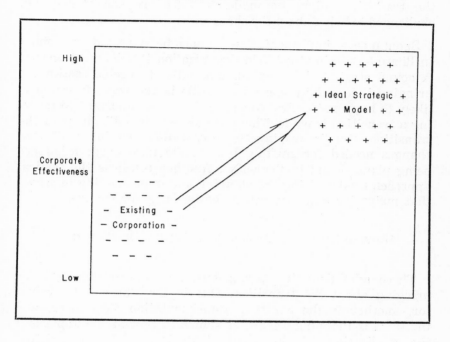

tested for soundness in the perspective of present and future conditions. Steps in implementation of the ideal strategic model are shown in Box 72. The importance of the model is difficult to overestimate. Not only is it a framework for planning change; it also provides the most challenging statement of corporate objectives that managers can confront. When members of an organization review and evaluate the properties of the ideal strategic model in comparison with what they are accustomed to, they often see a vivid contradiction between what *is* and what *should* be. When managers see this, not only are they pulled toward changing things to what they should be, but they experience a heightened repulsion with things as they are. This general situation is shown in Box 73.

The wider the gap between the ideal strategic model and the properties of the existing corporation, the greater the motivation to change, providing that all managers: 1) see the contradiction between the actual and the possible, 2) see how the transition might be made, and 3) are encouraged and challenged to bring about the change.

Spontaneous implementation cannot be expected any more in Phase 5 than in other Grid Organization Development phases. A sound strategy is essential, but without specific tactics for bringing it into daily operations, little in the way of results is likely to happen. Tactical considerations are important to insuring a transition is made. There are at least two dilemmas of the transition. One is keeping the corporation running while the changes needed for shifting toward the ideal corporation are being planned and implemented. Another concerns the tactical approach used in doing the planning and implementing in a way that maintains and strengthens enthusiasm for change.

How to Run the Corporation While Changing It

Three administrative arrangements have proved sound for bringing about the transition. One is the Phase 5 Coordinator, another is the Strategy Implementation Committee, and the third is Planning Teams, as shown in Box 74. To implement the application of the ideal strategic model, the existing business is segregated into major business areas. Other business areas may be identified which fit the ideal strategic model but which are not existing parts of the corporation. When each of these business areas is complex, it can be further divided into a number of profit, return-on-investment, or cost centers. Planning Teams are assigned to each sub-segment for design and evaluation.

Phase 5 Coordinator

Without strong and effective leadership, progress is delayed. Discouragement results when progress is less rapid than it could be. Leadership is exercised through the Phase 5 Coordinator. His responsibility is to plan and recommend tactics of

Box 74

*Administrative Arrangements for Developing
Phase 5 Plans*

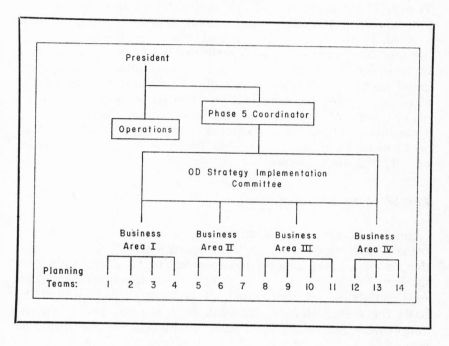

implementation to the key line executive. His function is thus
a staff function as long as he is the Phase 5 Coordinator.
Since he reports for approval to the key executive, responsibility for design of the tactics for bringing about the transition is
not simply placed upon operational management as an extra
activity nor is responsibility for approval of plans of implementation delegated. The implementation of approved plans becomes a line responsibility. The second reason for the Phase
5 Coordinator's reporting to the top of the line organization
is that when he has direct access to the top, unforeseen barriers can be removed more easily, and if indicated, the ideal
strategic model can be shifted to take into account unexpected
developments.

Strategy Implementation Committee

The Phase 5 Coordinator also heads a Strategy Implementation Committee, which gives unity and coherence to Planning Teams. The composition of this committee is of utmost importance because it designs the tactical approaches that will be utilized. It also has other responsibilities. Testing and evaluating models of simple business activities is one of them. Another is investigating combinations and integrations of the segregated units to determine the logic, feasibility, and soundness of more complex business entities. The committee is composed of members of the organization who possess both skills of systematic analysis and technical competence which need to be brought to bear on the planning and designing activities of all Planning Teams.

The Work of Planning Teams

Several special considerations are involved in planning the transition from existing to ideal operations. First, a corporation, even a small one, is too complex to be dealt with as a totality. For planning the implementation of change, its business activities are segregated. It is most desirable that the basis for segregation be financial. Cost centers, profit centers, and centers for measuring return on investment are identified according to the nature of the business as defined by the characteristics of the ideal strategic model. Next, a Planning Team is appointed for each segregable business activity. Each Planning Team is responsible for establishing how its unit's business would be organized and operated under the specifications of the ideal strategic model. The Planning Teams involve some line managers directly acquainted with each business and others who do not have a vested interest in the activity under consideration. The latter are better able to challenge ingrained assumptions that are taken for granted by those more thoroughly acquainted with the activity.

The planning of each business segment proceeds on the assumption that it functions as an autonomous operating unit. This suggests such ground rules as:

1. Cooperation with other units is unnecessary.

2. The business does not duplicate activities already being done by other businesses.

3. Wherever there are crossover points, transfer prices (including standard profit to the producing segment) or external supplies are specified.

4. External, staff, and other services may be purchased from the headquarters or contracted for from outside sources, whichever would involve the least cost.

5. Raw materials are procured on the open market or on a transfer basis, whichever is cheaper.

6. The whole process of production and distribution from purchasing and warehousing through distribution and marketing is under the control of the manager of the business component.

7. Personnel competencies essential for running the business are available.

The Strategy Implementation Committee recommends and gets approval for those who will serve on each of the Planning Teams and provides the conditions that enable each Planning Team to complete its implementation assignment. The committee is responsible for seeing that members of each Planning Team have the competence and the financial, technical, and market analysis skills essential for carrying out the kinds of concrete studies involved in the Planning Team's work. The ability for abstract reasoning is necessary but by no means sufficient. Without the indispensable management science competencies, plans drawn are likely to contain unwarranted assumptions and result in unrealistic programs. Operational precision is at a premium in the work of the Planning Teams.

Background Skills Useful in Phase 5

When a corporation contains many segregable components which can be treated as cost, profit, or return-on-investment centers, the full range of management science and technological skills is required for successful completion of Phase 5.[1] Box 75 shows some of the skills of management science and technology that have proved useful. Most of the knowledge

Box 75

*Skills of Management Science Useful in Designing
and Implementing Tactical Approaches*

Computer Simulation	Consumer Purchase Analysis
Mathematical Models to Optimize:	Product Planning Strategies
Raw Material Mix	Geo-Political Analysis
Product Mix	Operations Research
Marketing Mix	
Plant Lodgings	Regression Analysis
Distribution Channels	Human Engineering
Regional Warehouse Locations	Incentive Compensation
Purchase Price Volume	
Network Analysis	Personnel Practices Surveys
Productivity Analysis	
Industrial Engineering	Wage Surveys
Value Engineering	Cash Flow Analysis
Plant Layout and Design	Break Even Point Accounting
Materials Handling Techniques	
	Inventory Turnover Analysis
Operations Audits	
Market Research	Accounts Receivable Aging

and skills essential for tactical approaches of the kind described
are available in large organizations and constitute a reservoir of competence which can be utilized in carrying out the
studies required.

If the necessary competencies for such studies are unavailable, the choice that a corporation confronts is whether to

engage consultant assistance or to acquire skills through programs of technical training or recruiting. The latter solutions are preferable because use of these skills beyond Phase 5 is unending. If a corporation does not have significant management science skills but acquires them, it is in a much stronger position of self-reliance for continuous tactical problem solving beyond Phase 5.

THE TACTICAL APPROACH

The Strategy Implementation Committee assists the Planning Teams to do a sound job of designing the operations according to the ideal strategic model. The most exacting task is that of modeling the actual operation and conduct of each of the segregable business activities. Though demanding, this culminating step is of utmost significance, for it is at this point that the ideal design is converted to operational reality.

A Uniform Approach to Planning

Rather than each Planning Team's being commissioned to carry out this activity according to its own inclinations, it is important that a uniform tactical approach be applied. Advantages of a uniform tactical approach are several:

1. It increases the likelihood that the study will be thorough and inclusive.

2. It results in a set of conclusions about each of the models which permit direct comparison and evaluation between them.

3. A standardized analysis provides a basis for identifying the functions that headquarters should contain.

4. It tests businesses for the possibility of gaining positive synergistic effects from combinations and integrations.

5. It provides a foundation for measurement and control in conducting the redesigned businesses.

While this kind of standardized tactical approach is needed to bring a strategic model into operational reality, it is not possible, without specifying the actual business, to formulate an all inclusive model that would fit every situation. Yet certain general properties can be specified, as shown in Box 76.

BOX 76

*The Phase 5 Tactical Approach to Implementing the Ideal Strategic
Corporate Model*

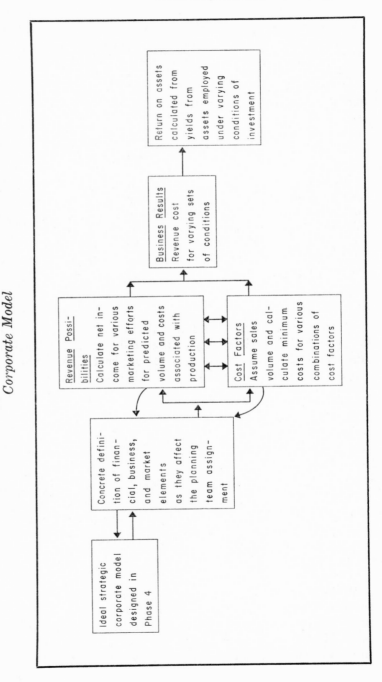

There is an interplay between income possibilities and cost factors. Each can be analyzed separately while the other is held constant. Concrete factors in either the cost or income segment are varied while other factors are fixed. In this way the contribution of each factor can be evaluated in the context of the others and interdependent influences investigated. Findings at a more advanced stage of analysis may cause a return to earlier stages to revise conditions. As with other phases, the learning of key tactical approaches is aided by instrumented study procedures which are self-administering. This makes it possible for members of the firm to learn for themselves, within team action learning designs, many of the essentials for carrying out the activities of Phase 5.

Strategy of Work

The strategy of work in Planning Teams is to examine and test the implications of a range of alternatives and a variety of working models before a recommendation for one is made. Formulating and analyzing a range of alternatives, clearly identifying the strengths and weaknesses of each, evaluating a variety of working models, indeed whenever possible simulating how the actual business would operate through test runs, mockups, computer simulations, and so on, can make a significant contribution to operational soundness of Planning Team activity. It increases the likelihood of flexible thinking, creative solutions, and of seeing the possibilities of synergistic efforts which might go unrecognized because they are not obvious on the surface. Planning Teams communicate with the line organization as well as the Strategy Implementation Committee. They present not only their final conclusions but also the alternatives that they have evaluated and reviewed and the various experimental models tested. Managers who have not engaged in the direct thinking-through process are then provided the opportunity to understand the rationale behind both the rejected alternatives and the recommended solution. This increases confidence because those who must approve the designs can comprehend why possibilities that might appear feasible to them would be unsound from a business logic point of view.

It is unnecessary for all Planning Teams to complete their work at the same time. Nor is it necessary for implementation approval and operational effort to await completion of designs by all Planning Teams. In fact, the opposite may be desirable. Once a plan is perfected, quick approval of implementation of those aspects which have no implication for the operations of other components of the business is important. Since the implementation of one set of plans may have few if any implications for other segments of the business, this is often possible. Approval of a perfected plan motivates managers to see possibilities for further progress.

Responsibility for implementation becomes a line assignment. Since line managers are directly represented on Planning Teams, however, they are continuously informed. Their participation in thinking through the implications of implementation activities results in commitment to the end product. In this way the reduction or elimination of resistances to change can occur.

Designing New Businesses

These same tactical approaches are employed in the investigation of the prospects and possibilities for getting into businesses which are not a part of existing operations. Executive management assumes responsibility for designating new business activity though it may do so on the basis of recommendations by the Strategy Implementation Committee or from others in the line organization. Thereafter, similar steps are taken to those already outlined for assessing the soundness of an action whether of expansion or acquisition.

Designing the Headquarters Organization

Once Planning Teams have made enough progress that the emerging pattern of the business has become clear, the Strategy Implementation Committee can fulfill another purpose. It designs the kind of headquarters or head office operation essential to giving direction and coordination to the component businesses designed by the Planning Teams.

BARRIERS TO PLANNING

As is true in other phases, barriers that are deeply rooted in the culture of the corporation continue to be uncovered during Phase 5 planning and implementation activities. Among those that are almost inevitable are white elephants, heirlooms, and sacred cows. Unless they are searched for and squeezed out, they can restrict efforts to reach peak effectiveness.

Disposing of White Elephants

A hindrance to implementing a plan that meets the specifications of an ideal strategic model is the necessity to find a way to deal with what is made obsolete. It is difficult to approve a plan, no matter how sound, if its implementation would produce a white elephant. An example here is an old plant built on valuable downtown, high-tax property where remodeling is unsound and expansion is not possible. A far sounder return on investment might be achieved through plant relocation. Relocating the plant creates the white elephant. When a white elephant problem arises in planning, it should be dealt with immediately. Either the Planning Team itself or others with special competence for doing so design an ideal sequence of white elephant disposal. The method is the same as that used by Planning Teams—developing a range of alternatives, testing the feasibility of each, and so on. There are several advantages to taking this step when the issue becomes a problem. One is that the feasibility of disposal of current assets can be directly tested in economic terms. Then it either becomes a reality or is introduced as a limitation. The second advantage is that once sound solutions for disposing of white elephants have been identified and their practicability demonstrated, those engaged in planning are freed of the constraints of thought which otherwise can obstruct progress.

Heirlooms and Sacred Cows

Heirlooms and sacred cows are interrelated. Though they have different underlying causes, they can have the same negative effects on constructive planning. The heirloom is a piece of the organization, physical, structural, or product, originally designed or adopted by someone held in high esteem. The thought of eliminating, replacing, or modifying it is difficult for managers who are junior in the organization. They are faced with a need to analyze the problem constructively. The same applies to sacred cows. A sacred cow is an activity or part of the organization which has been sanctified by pronouncement of a highly revered, respected, or feared executive. To challenge it is a sacrilege. The difficulty thus produced can constitute a barrier to thoughtful and sound analysis.

While both heirlooms and sacred cows exist in many corporations, once they have been analyzed both qualitatively and quantitatively, the emotions of authorship dissipate in the light of fact and evidence. Top management must be careful to maintain an environment where the problems created by white elephants, heirlooms, and sacred cows can be openly and candidly discussed.

CRITIQUE, REVIEW, AND COMMUNICATION

Monitoring Progress

A responsibility of the Strategy Implementation Committee is monitoring the progress of each Planning Team, reviewing the proposed model and alternatives, and testing assumptions in the light of the specific assignment of the Planning Team and the ideal strategic model. This kind of review and critique first insures that steps are tested for their soundness and corrected, as necessary, as each step is taken rather than after the task is completed. Second, it serves as a cross team stimulator, helping each Planning Team to take advantage of findings, insights, and analytical skills developed by the others. It insures a basic uniformity in the modeling of Planning Teams. It can quickly identify overlapping areas, duplication, and crossover points for needed integration. This constant review, critique, and consultation provides the Strategy Implementation Committee with background thinking and rationale to be used when it designs its recommended headquarters organization at a later time.

Reporting to Top Management

The Planning Teams meet with line managers and with the Strategy Implementation Committee for review, critique, and consultation. They also join the Strategy Implementation Committee to meet from time to time with key members of executive management. This is for several purposes. One is that executive management needs to be continuously involved in the plans being designed and informed about them and their implications. Another is that at certain points, planning cannot go forward until executive management has approved significant decisions that must be made. A third is that the top team members are in an excellent position to offer consultation and guidance on important planning decisions. Finally, ultimate authority for approval resides within executive management. By their very involvement, their commitment to implementation is increased.

Developing Understanding and Commitment

Communication of the progress and findings of each Planning Team should be viewed as an explicit aspect of the Phase 5 activity. Expectations of changes and their implications emerge along with progress in planning and aid anticipation of what the future is likely to be.

There are several ways to insure such communication. One is through each Planning Team's continuously reviewing its findings with the line managers most directly concerned who are not members of it. Another is by involving many line managers in technical and other analyses of specific facets of the business as one- or multi-man task forces. Their contributions are vital to the planning. A side effect is that communication is benefited. A third way is by inviting selected members of top management to attend sessions of the Planning Teams and providing them opportunities for critique of their operations. This step assists those doing the planning in increasing their effectiveness. At the same time, it provides understanding to those observing. All of these steps of direct and indirect participation not only contribute to communication and understanding but also increase the likelihood that plans meet the severest test of review and criticism.

Not all members of a corporation are capable of contributing directly to the planning in these ways. Yet their understanding is necessary to decrease resistance and earn their commitment to changes that may result from implementation. For this reason, attention should be placed upon aiding them in keeping up-to-date. This is possible through published progress reports or general conferences where objectives are defined, possibilities for achieving them identified, advantages and limitations analyzed, and reasons for the best solution explored in detail. Continually developing understanding of progress and plans is an antidote to anxiety about the unknown. It can create positive anticipation of operational improvements.

Once overall plans or their specific elements are approved, they may be studied according to the team action design originally learned in the Grid Seminar. When this has been done, it has involved providing those who will participate with pre-work study materials, multiple-choice tests, or other kinds of documents. Then in seminar-type teams, managers discuss the plans and reach a common understanding of what they entail with respect to operational segments of the company.

All of these are 9,9 ways of effectively managing change. When men have achieved the understanding which occurs as Planning Teams make progress, many problems of resistance to impending change and fear about it can be avoided. Another important aspect of communication is that as members of an organization become familiar with emerging patterns, involvement and commitment to the results are also increased. People support what they help create. They also support what is sound when it is understood. Communication strengthens the development of this kind of commitment.

These communication activities are not ended when a Planning Team's model is approved for implementation. Once such communication takes place, there is an expectation that it will be continued. Reviewing implementation progress, problems encountered, and results achieved when businesses are being operated according to their new designs, provides further opportunity to insure and increase understanding and commitment. The time required for additional communication activities is more than compensated for by the increased insight and the avoidance of resistance that results and the constructive suggestions that they can invoke.

SUMMARY

Converting the design of Phase 4 into a business reality is accomplished in Phase 5. The approach is deliberate and programmatic. It insures an orderly and coordinated conversion of the businesses of the company to bring them into line with the ideal strategic corporate model. The Phase 5 Coordinator is a key man. Reporting to the chief executive officer and leading the Strategy Implementation Committee, he captains the conversion. The business skills of management science and technology provide the tools of technical analysis required for sound implementation.

The planning made possible by Phase 5 is different from much of today's planning and superior to it. It is operational planning that can be highly effective for several reasons:

1. It takes place within a framework of business logic and corporate objectives, which has been set in Phase 4 and gives it direction and character;

2. It is led by the top team members and therefore has the maximum likelihood of approval by virtue of their background understanding and commitment to change and progress;

3. Other frequently encountered obstructions to sound planning that are rooted in communication difficulties have been much reduced with the completion of Phases 1 through 3 and sometimes altogether eliminated; and

4. Team action skills, learned in Phase 1 and strengthened in Phase 2, also add significantly to the capacity of an organization's membership in bringing about the kind of conversion that Phase 5 entails.

Phases 4 and 5, considered as two phases of a planning unity and coming after the earlier phases designed to increase the behavioral effectiveness of the firm, are quite different in character than what is commonly understood by the term, "management by objectives." The operational plans formulated and implemented in Phase 5 are not limited or determined by outmoded traditions, precedents, and past practices or by faulty or limited corporate business logic. Both of these barriers to sound business action have already been brought under organization correction and control.

Finally, behavioral science approaches that contribute to increasing the soundness of the firm's behavioral culture serve as a foundation and framework within which management science techniques of analysis and problem solving can find their fullest utilization.

REFERENCES

1. Background sources for Phase 5 activities include: Ansoff, H. I. *Corporate Strategy.* New York: McGraw-Hill, 1966; Beranek, W. *Analysis of Financial Decisions.* Homewood, Ill.: Irwin, 1963; Chandler, A. D., Jr. *Strategy and Structure.* Cambridge, Mass.: The M. I. T. Press, 1962; Churchman, C. W. Ackoff, R. L. & Arnoff, E. L. *Introduction to Operations Research.* New York: Wiley, 1937; Cyert, R. M. & March, J. G. *A Behavioral Theory of the Firm.* Englewood Cliffs, N. J.: Prentice-Hall, 1963; Nadler, G. *Work Design.* Homewood, Ill.: Irwin, 1963; Stanford Research Institute. Reports on the Long Range Planning Service. Menlo Park, Calif.: Steiner, G. A. *Managerial Long-Range Planning,* New York: McGraw-Hill, 1963; Williams, J. D. *The Compleat Strategyst.* New York: McGraw-Hill, 1954.

12

GETTING OPERATIONAL ABOUT IMPLEMENTATION

This chapter continues the organization development story of the company described in Chapter 10. The experiences of one Planning Team are described as its members redesigned a product-line segment of the business to meet the specifications set forth in the ideal strategic corporate model.

FORMING THE PHASE 5 IMPLEMENTATION COMMITTEE

As a first step of Phase 5, a Strategy Implementation Committee had been selected to be responsible for coordinating Phase 5 activities. The committee designed a tactical approach to be applied by each business segment and appointed Planning Teams for each business segment. Planning Team *A* was one of these.

The leader for Planning Team *A* was a man with management science training. His responsibility was to provide the direction, continuity, drive, and strength essential for the successful completion of the endeavor. The head of the engineering department was selected, partly because of his technical engineering skills, partly because of his financial acumen, and partly because of his leadership strength. The other six managers from various segments of the company provided additional skills and knowledge. A marketing manager, a manufacturing manager, an accountant, a personnel manager, an industrial engineer, and a systems analyst made up Planning Team A. The objective was to insure that the team contained the widest diversity of experience for comprehensive analysis of their particular business segment. The same considerations went into the selection of members for the other Planning Teams which were working in parallel to design other segments of the business.

PROBLEMS AND BARRIERS AS SEEN BY PLANNING TEAM A

For analytical purposes, the company's operations had been segmented into the smallest identifiable business segments. Planning Team A was assigned an autonomous profit-centered business. It was to be designed as a complete entity, that is, without provision of staff services which formerly had been supplied by headquarters. No capital or other restrictions were placed on the business except that it was required to operate in a manner consistent with the six ideal elements contained in the strategic model as formulated by the top team. Team A was to test, evaluate, and recommend how its business would be operated to achieve the specified financial objectives. To do this, team members would provide a definitive proposal for the design of the operations of the business, including sales and marketing strategies, manufacturing requirements, location, operational policy formulation, staffing and manning considerations, and all of the other essentials for the operation of a profitable business.

To insure that no part of business thinking would be omitted and that alternative proposals would receive thorough consideration, Team A spent four months testing alternatives against the many variables that needed to be considered. During that time, they met regularly but not on a full time basis. As the work got under way, they found the process of disassembling the business and assembling it again from the ground up to be a far different matter than simply analyzing the existing operation and looking for improvements in it. Box 77 shows some of the concerns, reservations, and pressures operating on Planning Team A as its members worked on their proposal.

Members quickly discovered how little they really knew about the existing business. Fact finding and data gathering

Box 77

Difficulties Encountered by a Phase 5 Planning Team

Task grew more complex as the work progressed.

More information was needed on the current business than was available in readily useable form; much of the needed data had to be dug out.

There were reservations about to what degree the top team would be prepared to accept certain solutions which appeared commercially sound but radical in terms of corporate history.

Retaining objectivity when vested interests of members were involved was difficult.

Would the top team be as committed and receptive to change at the end of the Planning Team's work as they were at the beginning?

Would there be enough commitment in line management to carry the recommended proposal through to definitive implementation?

---

took several weeks before they could even begin to set out the dimensions of the design. Starting from elaborate budgeting information, they soon found that the character of knowledge required was far deeper than had been supposed. Once the necessary facts had been obtained, they were struck by a simple conclusion: with these facts alone, potential for improving profitability had become obvious.

These newly acquired facts stimulated another concern. Were they competent to carry out the work? The task as they saw it loomed far more complex than they had originally thought. Company members had become accustomed to depending on rules of thumb, on precedent-based assumptions about the business, and on internal or outside experts to recommend solutions for specialized problems. They were often tempted, therefore, to make convenient assumptions or seek expert advice when the going got rough. Each time they resisted, however, and it soon became a matter of pride to develop their own competencies.

Over the years, the company had offered a variety of courses to its employees to provide them with skills in the use of different management science techniques. Much valuable learning had taken place which was applicable to this new situation. However, the need for even more knowledge and new skills among the members of Planning Team A became evident in Phase 5. They actively took steps to acquire additional skills to do a more effective job. Among the more significant categories were computer operations, advanced developments in automation, network analysis, operations research, value engineering and analysis, the economics of real estate, and plant location. Some members already had an indepth appreciation of the many facets and potential usefulness of industrial design from plant layout and design to work simplification and the technologies of market research. While these specialties also provided an indispensable contribution, the proficiency already was there and did not need to be developed further.

The real significance of how the effect of tradition can obscure possibilities for improvement came home to the Planning Team members. They found it necessary to specify every assumption made in their work and to test its validity and implications. This proved one of their more formidable tasks. As one manager expressed it, "After all, we don't recognize tradition even when it's staring us in the face. We've floundered many times because we let ourselves stay tied to the past. Seeing new opportunities and possibilities didn't come readily. Each time we had to dislodge our thinking from convention."

Other issues prevented their work from going smoothly. As the proposal took shape and its full complexity was understood, they wondered if they could communicate effectively to their line managers who would implement the plan. Would it be understood and would it stand an operational test under fire? All were concerns that Planning Team A had to wrestle with as the work moved forward. The result was a toughening up, a conviction that the design for this segment could and would prove sound.

THE TOP TEAM REVIEWS THE FINAL PRODUCT

Some time later, the full proposal was presented to the top team. They had maintained liaison and had communicated information on their work as it progressed. Now the final proposal was to be reviewed for approval. The Planning Team members did not feel confident that the top team would recognize the depth and thoroughness to which they had probed in designing the proposed business model. They also suspected that there might have been some loss of enthusiasm for change among members of the top team. The *A* Team had all the strength of conviction and commitment that results from hard, joint effort and the sharp conflicts which had been successfully worked through to produce the product they were ready to present.

Contrary to the concerns of Planning Team *A*, the top team stood solidly behind all but one of the recommendations. During the first presentation, they differed sharply with the Planning Team members, who felt that great efficiency could be gained from an increased use of interchangeability of parts across the product-line component of the business. The top team felt that each variation of the product line should stand fairly well on its own without consideration for combining parts between them. The top man entered the discussion by saying that he would have it no other way because, as he said, he would "prefer a plan where the expense of parts was calculated without considerations of redesign of parts." Members of Planning Team *A* felt defeated on this point and were crestfallen because they felt their approach was better. They also felt the president had involved himself in technical detail, the implications of which he was not in a position to grasp readily. They sensed in him a "business as usual" attitude.

The president recognized their reaction, realized he had jumped too hurriedly into an area of technical detail, and reconvened the session the next day. He reopened the issue at that time and his doubts and reservations were dealt with in a satisfactory manner. The approach was thoroughly discussed to a successful conclusion, which was essentially the same as that recommended initially by the Planning Team. This action gave Planning Team *A* a shot in the arm. One member com-

Box 78

Reactions of Top Team to the Work of the Planning Team

Convinced of the prospects of long range health for the company

Confident that the thinking and activities under way were not only essential but mandatory to the financial growth of the business

Took reassurance from the solid business logic built into the proposal

"Most realistic long range planning ever undertaken in this company"

Box 79

Gains in Managerial Effectiveness from Phase 5 Participation

Came to recognize and appreciate complexities involved in business logic and strategy

Learned how to approach the business in a scientific way, to analyze and evaluate variables selectively

Grew to take corporate perspective as opposed to previous functional or departmental view

Looked at existing business more critically, grew more and more displeased with current efforts

Gained a new perspective of the role of planning in effective management

Focused on results expected by using return on assets as the basis for business decisions in comparison with conventional profit and loss and share of market thinking

---

Box 79 continued on next page

Box 79 (Cont.)

Acquired a broader respect for and understanding of the contribution to operating a profitable business of management science techniques

Grasped deeper implications of effective teamwork for increasing the soundness of an implementation plan

Developed more basic insight into the dynamics of resistance to change

mented, "A year ago, he (the president) never would have done that. Things are looking up."

The top team also looked to the future with confidence. Box 78 shows some of the general attitudes that were evident at this time.

The members of the Planning Team concluded that as a result of their work they had also achieved indirect gains beyond their initial specific objectives. These are shown in Box 79.

Clearly they had a new perspective on corporate performance. Their roles as managers had taken on a different dimension. How they looked at the company and gauged its effectiveness was far more crisp, systematic, and objective. In thinking through the planning for the company's future they had better equipped themselves for that future.

13

SYSTEMATIC CRITIQUE

Critique is a way of examining progress—measuring and evaluating its direction, quantity, quality, and rate. Systematic critique, the final phase of Grid Organization Development, involves a review of progress and consolidation of gain. It also provides the basis for taking the first step beyond Grid Organization Development since it permits planning of further development activities. (See Appendix V, "The Scientific Method Model of Learning.")

The role of critique in bringing about change has been described. The degree of importance that should be attached to it as a fundamental strategy for strengthening problem solving cannot be overestimated.

At the beginning of Grid Organization Development, the most significant barriers reported by managers as major obstacles to corporate excellence are communication and planning. Critique is further down the list. When organization members re-examine corporate barriers in preparation for Teamwork Development, critique has shifted upward in significance to first place. This means that managers have learned and now recognize that critique is a critical factor in achieving corporate excellence. The importance that attaches to the more effective use of critique increases even further after Teamwork Development is completed. The same is true for Phases 3, 4, and 5. Phase 6 is the culminating step in Grid Organization Development. The primary activity is that of critique.

CRITIQUE AS A METHOD FOR ORGANIZATION STUDY

Critique is a highly important source of insight into present problems and their causes and is the basis for strengthening the direction, quality, and rate of progress. The fact that its importance is not fully appreciated by corporate members before formal Grid study stands out as a number-one blind spot. They do not see its prime significance until after having learned to use it. Once the power of critique has been demonstrated through results obtained in getting at the real issues of organization life, this blind spot is removed. Its use brings insight to bear on understanding the causes of problems of communication and planning. Phase 6 makes use of critique in an all inclusive way as a method of measuring and reviewing progress from the inception of Grid Organization Development onward. It also serves as the basis for planning further development necessary in the period ahead.

Many advantages arise from the sound and effective use of critique as a method of individual, team, and organization study:

1. It permits investigation of problems and their underlying causes in a climate in which something constructive can be done to resolve them.

2. It contributes to replacing subjectivity and self-deception with an objective assessment of problems and their causes.

3. By measuring progress, those involved gain a more accurate basis for seeing where they are and what they must do to make further progress toward excellence.

4. It provides a basis for drawing conclusions during and at the end of an activity and for generalizing in such a way as to anticipate and avoid problems in future undertakings.

5. It makes available possibilities that otherwise might not be recognized, examined, and made explicit.

6. It increases involvement of all those who have some responsibility for solving a problem.

7. By identifying causes of problems, it aids corporate members in developing their diagnostic skills and finding ways to develop operational skills which increase their competence.

8. It provides a basis for seeing operational activities in the perspective of the whole, with the result that problems are not dealt with in isolation but can be worked on in a planned and organized manner.

APPROACHES TO CRITIQUE

There are at least three approaches to critique embedded throughout Grid Organization Development.

Formal Critique Periods

Learning how to use critique is one of the objectives of a Grid Seminar. Periods of formal critique are scheduled into the Grid Seminar sequence throughout the week. The same is true for each of the activities in Phases 2 through 5. These are face-to-face situations of critique where team members try to identify problems and the progress made in reducing them and to formulate strategies for increasing the effectiveness of effort.

Spontaneous Critique

Not only does critique apply to all phases of Grid Organization Development, but its most important place of application is on the job. The interruption of a problem-solving or decision-making activity with spontaneous critique is an effective way of dealing with problems that are being encountered.

Systematic Critique

The introduction of systematic measurement and evaluation procedures can be made deliberately to identify problems and solutions to them, to learn through generalization, and to formulate next steps of development.

In Phase 6, each of these three approaches to critique is used but greatest emphasis is placed upon the systematic approach. The conclusions developed in Phase 6 are valid because benchmarks are established from data systematically gathered from the organization during Phase 1. Steps of formal measurement are taken during and after each succeeding phase. These measures provide a basis for tracking progress from the inception to the culmination of Grid Organization Development and beyond.

Strategies of Systematic Critique

There are many different ways of gathering data for Phase 6 activities.

1. *Quantitative Measurement.* This approach involves the use of organization indexes of performance from return on investment and other financial measures through an endless variety of operational indicators to the use of instruments that assess behavior, knowledge, and attitudes. The measurements taken and used to assess Grid Organization Development progress are identified and agreed upon in advance. They are systematically gathered or administered at intervals throughout the total effort.

2. *Evaluation Teams.* A number of evaluation teams can be established to assess and interpret change by the use of these indicators. A typical evaluation team is one which assesses changes in financial indexes and causes to which such changes are attributable. Its purpose is to monitor rate of return, amount, and market share, to assess what causes or interplay of causes are responsible for any changes observed. Another evaluation team might be responsible for assessing the problem-solving character of union-management relations. Additional ones might be concerned with organization structure, line-staff relations, and a myriad of others.

3. *Independent Panels.* A panel can be composed of several persons without a vested interest in the outcome who, on a planned schedule, are provided a body of facts and data without information as to the source or the conditions under which the data were gathered. It is the task of the panel to independently evaluate the data and develop the appropriate interpretations.

4. *Other Approaches.* These are the three prime strategies of systematic critique but there are other ways to measure

progress. Records maintained by the Organization Development Coordinator can be useful. Discussions by teams given task paragraphs who meet at designated intervals provide a means to assess the reactions of a representative sample of organization members to progress being made and problems encountered. Contract research undertaken by persons outside the organization, such as a university research group, is still another approach.

5. *Phase 6 Instruments*. Phase 6, like other phases of Grid Organization Development, includes use of instruments to measure various organization matters. The Phase 6 instrument, which is completed by all levels, consists of approximately one hundred questions which are organized into five categories (which vary somewhat with the business being studied). One is "Individual Behavior." Such issues as managerial approaches, participation, involvement, commitment, organization identification, and sense of personal stake in corporate effectiveness are included. Another is "Teamwork." It includes questions on the quality of coordination, the character of conflict management, the extent to which time is used effectively, the degree of candor, the character and effectiveness of planning, implementation, and followup, the quality of communication, and the use of critique. A third category is centered upon intergroup problem solving and cooperation between major divisions, departments, sections, and units. The objective is the identification of ways by which intergroup effectiveness might be increased. The fourth category deals with "Corporate Strategy." These questions are designed to detect and identify the assumptions of corporate strategy, particularly those used in Phase 4, in contrast with post Phase 5 implementation activities. It evaluates the extent to which planning is seen to be sound, vital, and significant and the extent to which progress is seen as being made at the maximum rate possible. The fifth category, "Organization Culture," deals with questions designed to permit examination and identification of the extent to which managerial performance is based upon tradition, precedent, and past practices, as contrasted with the degree to which the culture is seen to be supporting and rewarding problem-solving achievement.

These questions are answered in three different time perspectives. First, they are answered to indicate how members of the organization recall the *past*—the circumstances that existed before the Grid Organization Development effort. By contrast, the questions also are answered to indicate how the *present* situation is seen. Finally, they are answered with respect to how the corporation might be expected to be operating at a specific *future* time, in one or two years, for example. These questionnaires can be used at intervals during Grid Organization Development if an extensive intermediary analysis is required. The data are analyzed and interpreted to show the extent of perceived change accomplished from the beginning to the present and those areas in which change is needed between the present and the future. Even when pre-Phase 1 data have not been collected, this instrument provides a basis for a "backward" look.

Each person appraises his own scores in comparison with norms. Each work team examines the manner in which its members view the situation. The data can be analyzed by division, department, section, unit, by job level, or by age. Management can also use them to identify new areas within which accomplishment is possible or existing areas where further progress is needed for excellence to be reached. Findings can be made widely available throughout the organization. This way of summing up accomplishment and identifying directions in Phase 6 for future development is both an ending and a new beginning.

SUMMARY

Whatever the approach or combinations of them, an important step in the use of these data is that they be made widely available throughout the organization so that after they are studied and interpreted, generalizations can be drawn and recommendations made for next steps of development. This step can be taken either through work teams or through organizational diagonal slice teams. Maximum gains take place when the activity is an organized one with each critique team reporting in summary form its findings, conclusions, and recommendations. These are integrated in a final document by the

Organization Development Coordinator, which provides a basis for planning next steps of post Phase 6 development. There is a final benefit from the use of systematic critique. The strategies of measurement employed provide a way of assessing achievements and attitudes throughout the corporation. This self-confronting method, which permits identification of the current situation and comparison of it with what would truly be sound, is in itself sound management.

With completion of Phase 6, one sequence of developmental activities has been brought to a conclusion. Organization development is by no means ended. Development is an endless process. In some organizations, because of personnel changes or promotions or for other reasons, phases have been repeated after the completion of the first Grid Organization Development cycle. It is desirable and essential, however, that it be viewed, not simply as a way of life that should involve everyone continuously, but rather as a whole with a definite beginning and ending time. There should be an understanding, however, that the end of one total cycle of development effort may also represent the beginning of a new sequence.

14

THE PYRAMID THEORY
FOR ACHIEVING
CORPORATE EXCELLENCE

The idea that a systems approach to developing a corporation can be deliberately applied has been evolving and becoming clearer for a long time. Systematic insight into the problems involved and the conditions essential for corporate excellence has come primarily from major experiments in organization development since World War II. The cornerstone concept which has proved to be at the base of effective corporate behavior and performance is corporate culture. Concentration on the development of individuals, even of teams, without awareness of the impact on their behavior of the culture in which they are operating, produces disappointing results.

To a very large extent, corporate members who do learn about ways that might increase effectiveness find themselves frustrated in their attempts to bring about change against the massive weight of corporate culture, which says in effect, "Do as you have done in the past." Thus, individual development has proved to be a far too limited definition of the problem of development. It is only with recognition that corporate culture is the key to individual action that change begins to occur. Corporate culture, including the intertwining threads of behavior, business logic, and management science, is a massive fabric.

Any attempt to change the texture of the fabric by changing one thread is wasteful and ineffective. The real problem of corporate excellence is that of unraveling the old cultural fabric and reweaving it according to new designs. Insight into the nature of corporate culture is beneath the theory, strategy, tactics, and techniques of Grid Organization Development.

Once the concept of corporate culture was recognized, more rapid progress in learning how to perfect it was made. Then it became possible to develop understanding of how an organization might free itself from its webs of conventional thoughts and attitudes, of outmoded traditions, precedents, and past practices. For many corporations, culturally ingrained influences included poor teamwork, inappropriate use of authority, destructive intergroup relations, and lack of direction or sense of corporate purpose as well as faulty business logic and the handling of specific business problems on the basis of trial and error, hunch and intuition, or dogma and edict. Corporate members recognized that such characteristics of culture brought about a variety of problems, which they labeled problems of communication and problems of planning. Experiments in organization development demonstrated that the way to achieve excellence was not to treat these symptoms but to change the corporate culture itself where the causes of the symptoms resided.

Solving corporate problems by changing the culture requires a different approach than treating symptoms. First, the approach is an educational one in which members of the organization learn basic concepts for increasing effectiveness, acquire skills in their application, and develop that intense degree of motivation which spurs striving and propels the changing of what *is* to what *should be*. Phases of implementation make possible the introduction of change and development through situations involving diagnosis and discovery, treatment and correction, and prevention through planning. Knowledge rooted in several disciplines is learned and applied to the conduct of the business. Then old problems can be recognized and, in the light of new knowledge, ways found for solving them. Grid Organization Development provides a framework of concepts and methods of application through which such changes can be brought about.

This chapter has three objectives. One is to identify the cultural conditions essential for corporate effectiveness. Another is to recapitulate the six-phase sequence of educational and application activities encompassed in Grid Organization Development. The final objective is to evaluate implications of the Grid approach for achieving corporate excellence in the unfolding of industrial society, not only in more advanced nations but also in developing countries.

THE PYRAMID THEORY OF CORPORATE EXCELLENCE

The systems of a corporation can be described with a model of a pyramid. This is shown in Box 80. At the pinnacle of the pyramid, the significant components of corporate culture essential for full organization competence come together as the point of excellence. Each of the four sides represents a body of knowledge, understanding, and skills which must be present and utilized throughout the corporation. If any side is missing or weak, the corporation is unable to achieve excellence. The pyramid is tipped away from an upright position of excellence. It veers in one direction or another to some degree. With sides of full strength, the corporation can achieve and sustain excellence in its performance. Starting at the front and moving counterclockwise around the pyramid, Side 1 represents knowledge of behavioral science, Side 2, the skills to apply it; Side 3 identifies fundamental precepts of business logic and the fourth side constitutes the skills of applying management science to operations.

The Behavioral Culture of a Corporation

As members of an organization pursue business objectives, they must and do interact with one another. The quality and character of interaction shapes the organization's behavioral culture. If communication is clear and unobstructed and problem solving is approached in the light of the firm's objectives, one kind of culture is present. If communication is closed, hidden, defensive, and circumspect, and if problem solving is approached in the light of personal gain or vested interests, another kind of culture prevails. Still another kind of culture is present when interactions are tentative, political, or opportunistic, when organization members are prepared to go part way, to accept a half loaf as better than none, or salute the

Box 80

The Pyramid Theory of Corporate Excellence

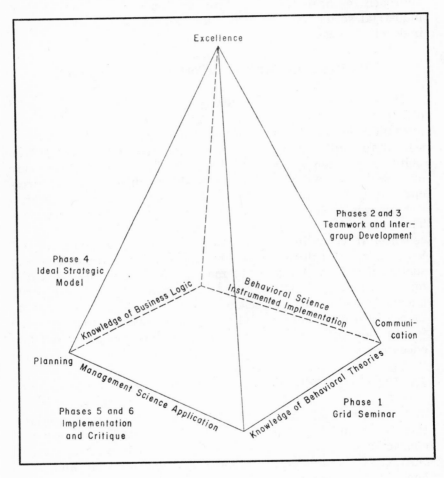

tenets of bureaucracy. Corporate excellence can only be achieved when:

1. A culture is created within which organization members are motivated to become involved in corporate problems and committed to solving them;

2. Teamwork characterized by a genuine sense of participation produces synergistic results;

3. Conflicts are brought out into the open for analysis and resolution; and

4. Solutions that fall short of soundness are rejected for ones that actually solve problems.

The behavioral culture is most likely to be improved by changing the underlying thinking and attitudes which influence managerial actions.

Bringing about a sound behavioral culture requires two steps. The first is learning theories of the Grid. This provides organization members a sound basis for thinking and analysis, and for defining and evaluating problems. It supplies an intellectual foundation from which planning for change becomes possible. The second part is application. It involves use of Grid theories for examination of the behavioral culture of an organization— how authority is exercised, how teamwork occurs, the quality of coordination and cooperation between interacting groups. Learning comes first, application, afterward. Learning theory without going forward to apply it is unlikely to affect the behavioral culture of the organization. Trying to change the behavioral culture without using theory is also unlikely to improve it.

Side 1 of the pyramid, learning behavioral science theories, is Phase 1 of Grid Organization Development. All members of the firm participate in a Grid Seminar on a diagonal slice basis, learning the Grid theories in an action-based, educational approach. The learning is conceptual and systematic on the one hand, involving learning principles of behavior that apply in the general case. On the other hand, it is specific and concrete since each corporate member is able to evaluate the quality and character of his thinking in the light of the principles acquired.

Side 2 of the pyramid represents the use of behavioral science techniques, applying the behavioral concepts and principles learned to the problem-solving operations of the firm. This is done through Phases 2 and 3 of Grid Organization Development. Phase 2 involves all the teams in the organization, starting at the top and proceeding downward. By comparing how the team actually works with what would constitute sound teamwork, members of each team are able to study, evaluate, and change their hidden and silent culture—team-based traditions, precedents, and past practices. The objective of Phase 2 is to create conditions under which each of the natural units of the organization can evaluate its culture and design strategies for changing it to achieve excellence of performance.

The other major point of application, Phase 3, is intergroup relations. It involves an examination of the behavioral cultures of units of the corporation that must coordinate efforts and cooperate to achieve their corporate objectives. It also involves use of the Grid to evaluate what the quality of the interaction *is* as contrasted to what it *should be* to be truly sound. Plans for change, when implemented among interacting groups where cooperation and coordination are essential, result in a strong and effective intergroup behavior culture.

The Business Culture of a Corporation

No organization can take for granted that it has at its core sound and rigorous business logic. Yet the achievement of corporate excellence makes it mandatory that the business logic of the firm be in line with the tenets of success in a free enterprise society. Side 3 of the pyramid indicates that the business logic under which the firm operates is sound and valid.

One of the major barriers to corporate excellence is that a corporation develops its own culture of business traditions, precedents, and past practices, just as it develops its own behavior culture. To the extent that its business traditions are out of line with business logic, limitations are present which impede excellence. Furthermore, the unjustified assumption is too often made that when a person is designated as an executive or manager, he is presumed to have insight into the subtleties of thinking and the conceptual properties of business logic.

Phase 4 is designed to provide a firm with the soundest of business logic as the basis for integrating operational effort. The strategy involves evaluating present business thinking against the thinking that would be required under sound free enterprise business logic. With the completion of Phase 4, the leadership of the company has reached agreements about the nature of the business, its short and long term financial objectives, its markets, what would constitute sound structure and policy, and development requirements for strong growth. With an explicit statement of the logic it intends to pursue, the organization is prepared to move on to the next phase.

Side 4 of the pyramid converts the operation of the firm from its present business traditions, precedents, and past practices into a system predicated upon the business logic formulated in Phase 4. This takes place in Phase 5, an implementation phase. Members throughout the organization use management science techniques not only to evaluate the operation of the existing business but also to specify necessary changes in operations to meet the requirements of business logic identified in the Phase 4 ideal strategic model. A wide range of management science techniques is called into use, from computer simulation of alternative operational models to systematic study of plant layout and design as well as manufacturing and marketing methods.

But nothing is static. Businesses change. The tendency toward backsliding is always present and even in the strongest behavioral and business cultures standards of excellence will be eroded. Phase 6, which is also part of the fourth side of the pyramid, provides for continual corporate self-examination insuring that new actions brought about during the earlier phases do not become precedents, no longer suited to emerging requirements. It insures that practices initiated in response to one set of circumstances do not become today's sacred cows, no longer valid but blindly accepted. Phase 6 involves the use of techniques of critique which have been employed throughout the first five phases of Grid Organization Development.

The pinnacle of corporate excellence is supported on each side and reached through a corporate culture of behavioral theory and behavioral science technique, and business logic and management science technique. Any approach which concentrates upon only one or two of the sides of the pyramid, that is, one subsystem or another, and disregards the others is unlikely to result in a corporation which can achieve excellence within the demands and challenges of a free enterprise society.

IMPLICATIONS

Many societies already have evolved to a relatively advanced capacity to utilize scientifically-based concepts and techniques of business action. A climate of readiness to progress to a higher plane of corporate effectiveness is present. The next step of development, it appears, will be in a shift away from business cultures which utilize their human resources with less than full effectiveness and toward a corporate life where maximum synergistic results can be achieved through competent, resourceful, committed men and unlimited technological possibilities. Such a situation might well bring about an explosive leap forward. Then what appears to be "advanced management" today will be seen a decade from now as merely a base on which it was possible to build further dramatic progress in development. This suggests that standards of managerial and organizational competence by which men and corporations will be judged in coming decades will become ever more demanding and ever more difficult to achieve. It also means that genuine reward and personal gratification will result from their acquiring and applying the concepts and skills essential for meeting these new standards of excellence.

Appendix I

CONSIDERATIONS IN THE DESIGN AND EXECUTION OF INCOMPANY GRID SEMINARS

Once the decision to pursue excellence through Grid Organization Development has been made, the first major step is to conduct Grid Seminars within the company. The incompany seminar is identical to the pilot seminar. Additional considerations arise, however, because the organization-wide involvement of managers in this educational step is more complex than in the pilot seminar test run. The kinds of questions dealt with are, "Who conducts the seminars? Who attends them? When and where are they held?"

The strongest conditions yet found for bringing about change in connection with Grid Organization Development are described here. Actual situations may contain limitations that make it necessary to modify the model in varying degrees.

GRID SEMINAR INSTRUCTION

The Grid Seminar is in itself a series of experiments, typically like those in physics or chemistry or in behavioral science laboratories in colleges and universities. Persons act to solve

Box 81

Learning Activities in a Grid Seminar Involve Self-Learning
Rather than Instructor Teaching

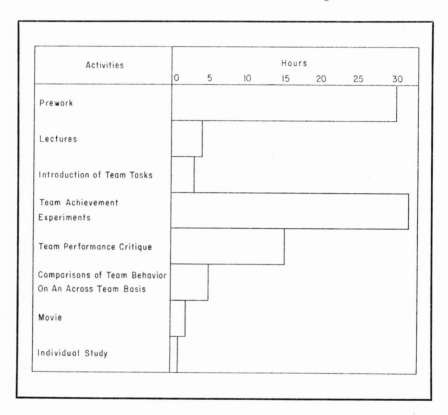

problems. They solve them in ways that produce data. The data
are evaluated and interpreted. Organizationally relevant learning comes from using the Grid as a framework for thinking
through and interpreting the behavior and performance data
produced in these achievement experiments. It is *action* learning, as shown in Box 81.

A seminar starts with a brief explanation of its activities. An
experiment is undertaken and completed. Then come periods
of summary and interpretation from which participants may

Box 82

*Instructor Activities in a Grid Seminar Involve Guiding
Participants in Completing the Achievement Experiments
and Learning from Them*

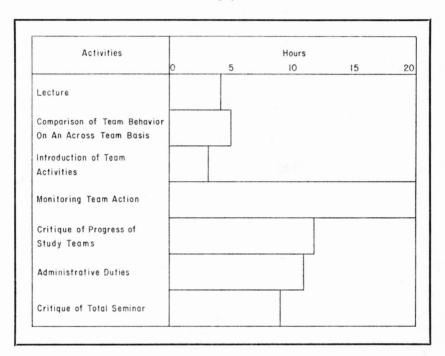

draw generalizations. Neither the brief explanations, the summaries, or the generalization periods demand professional lecturing skills. They do require of the instructor a sound understanding of the experiments and a systematic understanding of the implications to be drawn from them, as shown in Box 82.

Who Instructs?

Because of the character of the educational approach, Grid Seminars are conducted by line managers. First, what are the alternatives for instruction? Who besides the line managers might carry the instructional responsibility?

Applied Behavioral Scientists. In many behavioral science courses that take place within a company, the responsibility for instruction is taken by outside, professional personnel—usually behavioral scientists from universities and consulting firms. These are men who have spent most of their lives investigating behavior and seeking to understand it, either through "pure" experiments or through field studies undertaken within the framework of corporate activity. Because of this experience, university education, and professional competence in teaching, managements in many organizations prefer to use them as instructors when human behavior is the subject matter rather than "risking" it to insiders. The line of reasoning is, "We're neophytes at this game of teaching about behavior. Let's not play amateur psychologists. Let's get the real pro's to do it for us." However, the behavioral learning in a Grid Seminar is directly related to behavior on the job—of supervisors and subordinates—and those with the most direct experience are usually line managers themselves.

The contribution to learning by behavioral scientists in the context of Grid Organization Development is through the theory, the design of the Grid Seminar experiments, and the instruments used to interpret them, and to the five phases of application that follow. Direct face-to-face contributions are also made by Grid Organization Development specialists at key points throughout the six-phase sequence. One kind of contribution is through installation support. A Grid Organization Development specialist is available to consult with managers as they go about conducting the pilot Grid Seminar. They also provide installation assistance in the first application of Teamwork Development in Phase 2. They do the same in the first Phase 3 Intergroup Development. They can be highly valuable in assisting the top team in developing the ideal corporate model at the start of Phase 4 and when they engage in the first step of implementation of the model in Phase 5. The Grid Organization Development specialists' contribution, though important, is limited. It is most valuable at key points along the way where a new activity is about to be initiated, but its value is in supporting the line manager's responsibility rather than substituting for it.

Company Training Staff. Another alternative is to use the company training staff rather than line managers for Grid

Seminar instructors. Managements often logically argue, "We have qualified men right in the firm to do the instructing. Why should we spend time preparing line managers to do what our training people already can do as well or even better than line people ever will be able to do? Looked at from another way, would it not be a waste of the training staff's time for them *not* to instruct when, quite obviously, this is a situation where they can make a contribution?" These are genuine considerations. The fundamental weakness in them, however, is that if the training staff discharges these kinds of responsibilities, the possibility of strong line involvement and commitment to achieving results is reduced. Furthermore, there are important ways in which training department skills can be brought to bear on the effort.

Why Line Manager Instructors?

The professional behavioral scientist probably has focused a lifetime of intellectual effort on understanding behavior, and a training staff's instructional competence may even exceed that of the behavioral scientist. Line manager instruction is far better, however, for several reasons.

Responsibility for Results. A major reason for having line managers as instructors is that when outside behavioral scientists or training staff members are used, the responsibility for organization change tends to rest upon them. It is *they,* not the *line managers,* who are the advocates of change. Yet they carry no responsibility for operational results. When line managers serve as instructors, the responsibility for change rests upon the shoulders of those who *are* responsible for results. When the line managers themselves become convinced that systematic concepts of behavior are important to successful management and that they can be learned, the result is a kind of commitment that goes far toward achieving an extra personal investment so essential for insuring results. Furthermore, their commitment to successful followup produces an antidote to fadeout. Quite often this commitment is extremely strong. It has sometimes even made the difference between giving up and going forward into later phases of Grid Organization Development. Line manager commitment makes the difference between going through the motions of just another training course and using training as a means to the end of actually increasing the organization's productivity and profit.

On-the-Job Experience. The technical language and the background of deep systematic study of behavior of the behavioral scientist does not necessarily qualify him to evaluate a concrete corporate behavior situation. Perhaps far better qualified to do so is a line manager who may have spent as much as twenty years in trying to understand the reactions of those he manages. There is no evidence that behavorial scientists have greater insight than do line managers into behavior in operational problem-solving situations, particularly those who have not been responsible for the supervision of work under profit-motivated conditions.

Line Manager Development. The matter of "development" is another reason for line managers to serve as instructors in preference to applied behavioral scientists or training staff members. The intellectual properties of the Grid are not complex, esoteric, or difficult to learn by men with a few years of managerial experience. The opportunity to monitor study teams and observe the problems that people experience in trying to increase their capacities for achievement is sobering. Many line managers are impressed by the depth and severity of organization problems associated with ineffective behavior. Awareness of this fact is in itself an important source of development.

Training Department Support. A reason to prefer line managers over training staff members for instruction is that this places the line and training staff in a fundamentally sound relationship with one another. The training staff makes its contribution by consulting and supporting line instructors, by helping them to do the best possible job. This kind of support of line by staff is highly desirable.

The training department's responsibility is line manager "development." Much of management and supervision in corporations today is little more than good instruction, so the difference between instructing as a formal Grid Seminar leader and daily instruction on the job as a line activity is only one of degree.

How Are Manager-Instructors Selected?

Not everyone makes an ideal instructor. Considerations that should enter into selection of line managers for instructors include the criteria discussed in the section on good "seeds."

Top Men as Instructors. The top man of an organization is in many ways its best instructor, the number-two man is next best, and so on when all other things are equal. When the top man takes positive leadership, applies his time, and gives his personal attention to organization development, he in effect tells all in the organization something positive about his own convictions which words, no matter how well chosen, cannot convey. His actions communicate. They express his commitment. The character of this commitment can be demonstrated in no better way than for the top manager to instruct, and the same applies for other key executives.

Availability. In most organizations, a few men are seen as indispensable to operations. The natural tendency is to select as instructors those who are *not* among the most indispensable. It is important that the most indispensable line managers be represented among those who engage in instruction. The more indispensable a man is to the effective operation of the corporation, the more indispensable he is as an instructor. The reasons are that it signifies to the corporation that the Grid Seminar is a significant activity and also gives the "indispensable" man the opportunity for personal development.

High Potential Men as Instructors. If all other qualifications are equal in the choice between two candidates, the one selected should be the man with the greater long range potential for progressing in the organization. Asking a person to accept instructor responsibility is asking him to accept a development assignment. Because of the gain through personal development, those of high potential should have the opportunity of development of potential for long term actual use.

Long Range Implications. Time and time again it has been observed that instruction in a Grid Seminar increases a man's commitment to apply what he has learned, as Box 83 illustrates.[1]

Box 83

Managers Who Instruct in Grid Seminars Show the Greatest
Gain in Their Effectiveness as Bosses

Percent of Ex-Instructors Rated as Least
and Most Improved by their Subordinates

Least Improved	Neither Least Nor Most Improved	Most Improved
4	23	73

All managers were rated for degree of improvement and those
nominated as most improved were studied to discover the reasons for their improvement. These data show that having served
as an instructor was an important factor in bringing about improvement.

Instruction also aids a person in gaining greater insight into
issues of organization effectiveness because of the study required
in preparation for instruction. Those who instruct should be in
key positions to *further* the total organization development effort
in later phases. As an example, top men who have instructed
often have a most effective Phase 2 experience in Teamwork Development. When men lead departments and are responsible for
reducing interdivisional or interdepartmental rivalries, they are
among the most eager to gain the benefits from achieving intergroup coordination in Phase 3. The same is true in the ideal
strategic model planning of Phase 4 and beyond.

How Can Competence of Line Instructors Be Strengthened?

Granted that there is an advantage in having line managers
as instructors, how can their competence be brought to a high
level? What does this assignment require?

As a first step the line manager attends a regular Grid Seminar, either a public or an incompany seminar. Afterward,

though not necessarily immediately, he attends one for another week for instructor preparation where two other line managers are teaching the seminar. After completing the instructor development program, he becomes a junior instructor, joining another man who has previously been a junior instructor and who now takes the lead instructor responsibility. Finally, he moves from junior instructor to senior instructor and in turn is joined by another manager who has completed the instructor development program and is prepared to be a junior instructor. The line manager has then completed his instructional activities.

After his attendance at a Grid Seminar, therefore, it takes three more weeks to complete the entire sequence. They need not be successive weeks. A line manager can spend a week in an instructor development program and then return to his job, serve later for a week as a junior instructor, returning to his job until the time when he serves as a senior instructor. No line manager needs to be away from his regular assignment for more than three weeks as far as the instructional aspect is concerned, or for more than a week at a time. This insures a continuation of work without any serious interruptions. Furthermore, no line manager needs to be asked to instruct more than two seminars, one time as a junior and one as a senior instructor. This arrangement has two advantages. One is that a line manager is not asked to instruct beyond the point where diminishing returns in his own learning have set in. The other is that many more line managers have the opportunity to engage in Grid Seminar instruction. Benefits from learning and the personal commitment to later efforts that comes with instruction in this way are spread as widely as possible through the organization.

When wage personnel participate in Grid Seminars it is sound for a management member and a union officer to team together as the two instructors. When Grid Organization Development takes place in foreign subsidiaries, where some of the personnel are from the country where the headquarters is located and others are resident nationals, the arrangement of members to serve together as instructor teams that has been found sound involves pairs made up of a foreign manager and a resident national. When a headquarters and region and plant simultaneously are participating in Grid Seminars, instructor teams may be composed of pairs, one from headquarters and one from the region or plant.

Line managers themselves attach importance to the process of learning to instruct. Many companies, once into Grid Organization Development, have doubled the number of managers attending instructor development programs. Members of these organizations are convinced that learning to instruct is as valuable as the actual execution of instruction.

What Takes Place in an Instructor Development Seminar?

In the instructor development program the seminar design is learned thoroughly and the rationale for it explored in depth.

Instructor development participants observe Grid study teams as they engage in experiments. The instructor-to-be aids in critiqueing the seminar activities. He prepares outlines for lectures, which provides him with concrete materials for later use in guiding the progress of the seminar as an instructor. He is enabled to relate Phase 1 to the total Grid Organization Development effort and gain an overview of the complete Grid approach to organization development.

As managers in the instructor development program monitor study teams, their observations of two or more teams struggling with the same problem but with differing degrees of success provide a basis for understanding differences between effective and ineffective behavior and their causes. As they see the kinds of action that bring about positive results or failures, their own leadership skills are strengthened. Although the seminar is designed to be self-administering, sometimes a study team reaches a point of impasse where intervention can contribute to resolving the difficulty and moving the learning forward. Then it may be useful for the manager-instructor to intervene to aid the study team in grasping more clearly the problems that are barriers to effectiveness and in learning from this experience how to cope with and overcome such problems, as shown in Box 84. When and how to intervene is also studied in the instructor development program.

While only a few hours are devoted to formal presentations during Grid Seminars, these are significant. The line manager learns to organize a presentation and think about how he would deliver it. Line managers who have engaged in instructor development have said that besides learning how to conduct a Grid Seminar, they also gained confidence and learned to make the

Box 84

*The Need for Intervention in Grid Seminar Study Teams
Is Not Common*

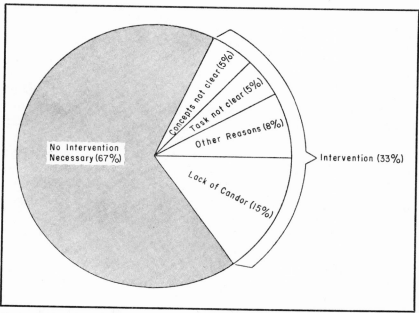

Data are for 61 teams

kind of formal presentation that made them more effective managers.

Contributions of the Training Organization

Once a decision has been made to conduct Grid Seminars for the company, the training organization can provide excellent staff support to instructors. By attending an instructor development program themselves, training staff members can not only evaluate how line instruction is done but also develop their own instructor-of-instructor skills. During an incompany seminar they can help those line managers attending the instructor development program to pretest their presentations and become more effective by dry running and debriefing the various instructional trial runs.

Further assistance is given through support on matters of administration—distributing prework, insuring that training materials are on time and in place and in the right amounts, for example. The training department can free line managers from these administrative responsibilities so that they can concentrate fully on the quality of learning by participants.

GRID SEMINAR PARTICIPATION

Who Participates in an Incompany Grid Seminar?

The maximum impact is possible when those who participate in Grid Organization Development are all those employed by the corporation. Included are persons who manage others, technical and staff professionals who are individual contributors not having supervisory responsibility, and secretarial, clerical, and wage personnel. This is not to say that Grid activity is always begun with the total corporate membership. Many companies begin by extending organization development to managerial, technical, and supervisory personnel. Experiments are continuously providing data showing the usefulness of extending Grid Organization Development to wage levels. However, participation by wage and hourly personnel is not essential to the initiation of a Grid Organization Development effort but is better as an extension of development activities. The decision on extending Grid learning to other than managerial levels can be made at a later time.

How Should a Seminar Be Composed?

Although one hundred percent of a firm's members may be engaged in Grid Organization Development, all cannot participate in Grid Seminars at one and the same time. Three ways by which members of a firm can be selected to participate in a particular Grid study team are by a *vertical, horizontal,* or *diagonal* slice, as shown in Box 85.

The Vertical Slice. When a vertical slice is used, those participating in the study team are from the same department or function. The participants represent hierarchy, with bosses included with their subordinates. The advantage of the vertical slice is that bosses and subordinates together learn about such matters as how to face up to conflict. This should make it pos-

Box 85

Diagonal Slice Team Composition Is Used in a Grid Seminar

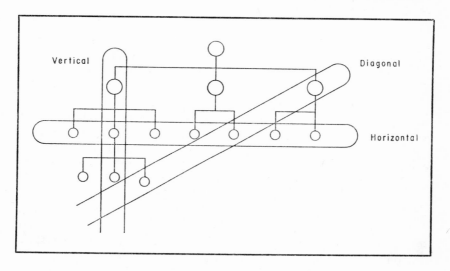

sible for them to apply what they learn to improve the quality of their own relationships on the job. This, of course, is the key objective of Teamwork Development of Phase 2. But this kind of arrangement has a significant disadvantage for Grid Seminar study team composition. It is that the very presence of hierarchy makes the learning situation more difficult. If boss-subordinate problems already exist, the persons involved are naturally reluctant to face these problems. They tend to hold back rather than to engage themselves in the open and spontaneous interchange that is essential to sound learning. This does not provide a good learning situation. With the lack of a foundation of learning, existing relationship problems are barriers to problem solving, so the vertical slice study team is not good for problem solving either. Another disadvantage of the vertical slice is that students have little opportunity for cross-fertilization of ideas with persons representing other parts of the organization. Members of one part study with those they work with day in and day out and do not have chances to exchange views with others. There is little basis for a person to gain a deeper sense of identification with the corporation as a whole. The disadvantages of the vertical slice outweigh its advantages and it is not recommended. Furthermore, all of the advantages of the vertical slice are gained from Teamwork Development when the vertical slice in actual organization work teams is the study unit.

The Horizontal Slice. Through use of the horizontal slice, members are selected from many functions of the organization, but all represent the same general level within its hierarchy. The advantage is that it completely eliminates the kind of hierarchical relationships which can increase the difficulty of learning or even stifle it. When participants come from different divisions and functions, they can also exchange views about the company and better comprehend the whole, although even this exchange of views is not fully effective. Persons from the same level of hierarchy often have such similar views of the organization that they are seeing with tunnel vision, not panoramic. Bringing them together can in effect reinforce built-in assumptions. The horizontal slice denies them the opportunity of coming in contact with representatives of other levels. For these reasons, the horizontal slice is not recommended either.

The Diagonal Slice. When the diagonal slice is used, several functions of the organization as well as levels of hierarchy are represented in the same study team. The composition is a replica of the company. The diagonal slice makes possible an exchange of perspective not only among persons from different functions but among those from different levels as well. A boss and a subordinate may be present in the same seminar in the diagonal arrangement but unlike the situation in the vertical arrangement, they do not engage in learning in the same study team.

Level of Jobs and Education. In a diagonal slice Grid team, line and staff managers, technical and professional men, and supervisors study together. The same is true for personnel of different ages and organization functions. The only basis for grouping is that insofar as possible, each Grid team should be composed to be a miniature of the organization.

When a Grid Seminar is formed, the question almost always raised is whether "lower level" members are able to participate effectively with "higher level" ones. The implication is that lower level members, because they are more likely to be men with practical experience, may not be able to learn as fast as men with college backgrounds, particularly those holding degrees. The lower level men often have a depth of practical experience as rich as that of technical personnel. When men who have risen from the ranks have opportunities to study and learn with college educated managers, they gain a better understanding of the technical man's thinking—how he goes about analyzing a problem, formulating alternatives, and weighing advantages and disadvantages. For a man from the ranks, this in itself can be an education. On the other hand, men from the ranks also are more likely to understand behavior in concrete terms and be able to provide insight otherwise not readily available to those whose approach to life is more likely to be conceptual and analytical than behavioral and subjective.

Another related question is, "What is the minimum education a man needs to be able to benefit from Grid Seminar participation?" The level of formal education is far less important than a man's ability to comprehend concepts. Many persons with little formal education have effectively educated themselves. There are limits. If a man has a reading comprehension equivalent to the sixth grade public school level, whether or not he actually completed the sixth grade, he usually has essential skills for learning in a Grid Seminar.

The one disadvantage of diagonal slice selection stems more from the final choice of the participants than from the method itself. It is related to level and indirectly to education. It is that when levels are too far apart within the hierarchy—vice president and front line supervisor in a large company, for example, participants find it difficult to interact in an easy and understanding way. While the diagonal slice method is the most desirable of the three, a sound selection of levels should probably be limited to three or four levels.

Truncated diagonals offer a solution to this problem, as shown in Box 86. Several levels study together, but not all are represented in a study team. For example, a team might start with managers from a high level and include those several levels below. Another team might have several levels but start somewhat lower from the top. In this way, higher level managers study with one another and lower levels also study with one another, but the distance from the highest to the lowest man

Box 86

*Truncated Diagonal Slice Study Teams Include Managers
from Several Sequential Levels*

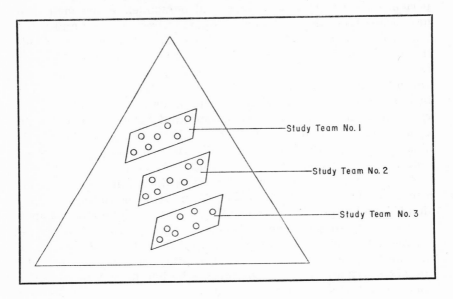

in the study team is more limited than is true for the total company.

Non-supervisory personnel are usually included in Grid Organization Development as an extension. This means that those who engage together in study teams are lower level managers and wage and hourly personnel. This is particularly desirable. Participants are permitted to gain insight into the emotions surrounding the cleavage between the management organization and operating levels. Observers have often pointed to this as one of the important contributors to strengthening the effectiveness of lower level supervisors and the identification of wage and hourly personnel with corporate objectives of excellence in performance.

Should Women Managers Participate?

There is no reason to make a distinction between men and women attending a Grid Seminar. Participation is based on a person's being a corporate member, and not because of any other selection criteria. When several women are in the same seminar, it has been found better to include more than one on the same study team rather than arranging for one per study team. The women in the same Grid study team can then exchange views on the learning experience. They are better able to decide whether treatment received is based upon their activities and attitudes as corporate members or whether it seems related to their being women. If there is only one woman on a team, it is more difficult to make this kind of appraisal. This kind of clarification has proved important to aiding women in thinking through some of the considerations involved in being corporate members.

Should Those Near Retirement Participate?

When a man is nearing retirement, he may not see value in increasing his further involvement with the organization within the short time remaining to him. On the other hand, many managers near retirement find gratifying personal reward in the learning itself and in the opportunity to be in a learning situation with others. For these reasons, men preparing to retire certainly should be invited to participate.

How Many Should Participate in One Seminar?

There is no hard and fast answer to this question, but there are some ground rules. Achieving speed in organization learning must be balanced against insuring that organization performance does not falter because too many people are absent from work at the same time. Company after company has found that under the diagonal slice concept of seminar composition, about ten percent of the working organization can be away from the work site without undesirable effects on organization performance. Use of this proportion as a guideline also produces a minimum of disruption of working teams. The diagonal slice approach insures that no work unit is seriously depleted.

While ten percent is effective for an organization of 100, 250, or even 500 managers, a limitation of automatic use of the figure arises in organizations with more than 500. The limitation stems from the seminar learning point of view. The question is, "How many people in a seminar is too many?" The maximum number

Box 87

*Team Performance Is Unrelated to Number of Team
Members from 5 to 10*

Number of Team Members	5	6	7	8	9	10
Percent Improvement in Team Average Effectiveness in Excess of Typical Individual Scores	35.7	28.4	26.3	32.8	42.4	35.5

Team performances vary widely because of the effectiveness of members in integrating their information and efforts. The size of the team (from 5 to 10 members) appears not to be significant. Team size, therefore, can be selected according to other considerations related to work, such as how many men can be released, etc. Data are from 120 teams, 20 for each team size.

is around 75 for two instructors for an incompany seminar. Companies with more than 600 managers may decrease the percent of people away at any one time, or two seminars (of 40 to 60 participants) might be conducted simultaneously but independently.

How Large Are Study Teams?

Five is the minimum number of members for a study team. This permits variety in points of view. With less than five in a study team, there are so few points of view that problems of pooling individual resources cannot be thoroughly enough studied for maximum learning. A study team of more than ten is too large to permit the degree of interaction and spontaneity of conversation that is desirable. Box 87 shows that there is no consistent relation between team scores on effectiveness measures and number of members on the team within the range of from five to ten.

Both number and size of study teams in each seminar may vary. At least two study teams are essential because of the learning provided by one study team's comparing its performance with that of another. With three study teams, there is the added advantage that each can be ranked along with the other two. This increases motivation to learn. At the opposite extreme, however, there can be so many study teams that it becomes difficult to make meaningful comparisons. When the number of teams is as many as nine or ten, so much time may be devoted to reporting back by study teams that the seminar becomes unwieldy.

The number of persons to be placed together in a study team also depends on the size of the seminar. If the seminar has 49 participants, seven-man study teams are appropriate. The fewer the persons in a seminar, the smaller the teams. If there were to be 24 in a seminar, for example, four study teams of six each would be preferable to three study teams of eight each. Three teams of eight would make better learning units than two of twelve.

ADMINISTRATIVE CONSIDERATIONS

There are many administrative matters which are important for creating conditions under which effective learning can take place. These are a few of the more important ones.

Where Should a Grid Seminar Be Conducted?

The question usually is whether a company facility should be used as the site of the seminars or an outside location that is far enough away that participants are removed from the work situation and for all practical purposes free of it. A residential training site permits participants to stay together and gain the advantages of informal discussions during meals and after the study day is completed.

Many organizations have their own onsite training facilities which are ideal for Grid Seminars. Use of them reduces living and travel expenses. Yet it also means that those engaged in study are easily accessible to others back on the job for consultation on routine business matters and operations. Those on the job are tempted to call those in a Grid Seminar for guidance on problems that arise.

The "Thousand Mile" Rule. These difficulties are not insurmountable. Non-participants in a particular seminar can be asked to live by the "thousand mile" rule. It is that organization members *not* attending a Grid Seminar are asked *not* to call upon a seminar participant unless they would do so if the man were on a business trip a thousand miles or more away. If a problem is so urgent that a man would be called even though on an extended trip, he should be called during the seminar. On the other hand, if one would not think of calling him at such a distance, he should not be reached during the seminar. Similarly, those in the seminar are asked to check back only if they would do so while one thousand miles away on a trip. In many companies, the thousand mile rule has been used effectively. It has enabled companies to take advantage of their organizations' onsite training facilities without negative effects on the seminar learning.

The Close-to-Home Participant. Some participants live near enough to the training site that they can work through the evening and not have long trips home. Should they live at home or be requested to stay at the training site? Does living at home detract from the learning? Use of a company training facility has economic advantages when most participants live near enough to it since living expenses associated with learning are more than 50 percent of the cost of the training expense. It has been found to result in little inconvenience or learning loss.

Why Is the Schedule So Concentrated?

The Grid Seminar is a five-day activity. It starts on Sunday night and continues through Friday. This means one week off the job. And the five days are five days of full work. Learning activities take place morning, afternoon, and evening. No provision is made for an afternoon off, nor is there any other way of making it "easier" for participants, by giving them a night off mid-week, for example. This period of time has been proved an irreducible minimum. Further reduction makes the learning shallow for too many. The time needed in fact amounts to more than five days since each person is involved in home study before attending the seminar. The homework, or "prework," takes between twenty and fifty hours depending upon a man's reading rate and the thoroughness of his preparation. The learning can be considered of two weeks' duration, with the first learning under home study conditions and the second learning under school conditions.

There are valid reasons for this approach to learning. For example, organization members realize that time spent in learning does not contribute immediately to their effectiveness in solving work problems although its whole purpose is to contribute to future performance. It becomes apparent that when a company is prepared to commit the time and energies of its members to a learning process and to meet the expenses associated with it as well, it should be able to expect in return full utilization of the time available for learning.

A Grid Seminar is also an intrinsically interesting learning experience. Corporate members generally find that the intensity of the work is stimulating. In many organizations, because of an outstanding problem which calls for immediate attention and can be handled appropriately after a Grid Seminar, the learning activity has been extended by one, two, or more days. Participants have completed the five-day Grid Seminar and then continued to study in depth the particular organization problem demanding their close attention and understanding.

Should Seminars Be Conducted Back-to-Back or Spaced Out Over a Longer Time Period?

Managers often weigh the advantages and disadvantages of conducting seminars week after week or spreading them out to one a month or even one a quarter. A back-to-back versus a spaced schedule is shown in Box 88. An advantage is gained through back-to-back seminars. The seminar phase of learning can be concluded rapidly and the organization can move quickly into Teamwork Development. Teamwork Development is the beginning of real payout and the quicker organization members see results, the more motivated they are to try for more. As more and more persons complete the learning, there is more

Box 88

Back-To-Back Versus Once-A-Month Grid Seminars in Two 300-Manager Companies

	Jan	Feb	March	April	May	June	July	Aug	Sept	Oct	Nov	Dec
Company A Back-To-Back	///	///	///									
Company B Spaced	///	///	///	///	///				///	///	///	///

and more understanding of the concepts and of Grid language. It finds daily use in job situations. Moving the whole organization through Grid Seminars as quickly as possible also avoids the problem of the "haves" and "have nots"—those who have the knowledge because they have attended a Grid Seminar, and the others. When seminars are spaced widely apart, on-the-job reinforcement through daily use takes place much more slowly.

What Steps Contribute to Involvement?

Personal involvement and individual commitment comprise bases for learning and applying what has been learned to on-the-job problem solving. The initial challenge is in finding a way to arouse individual interest in becoming involved and committed to this learning and application. Besides seeding and pilot seminars, a well handled orientation to the seminar and the prework itself can increase interest and readiness to participate fully in the learning.

Orientation. Those who are to participate in a Grid Seminar convene about a month before its start for an hour or two of orientation—a history of the project and what it is intended to accomplish. What a Grid Seminar is like, who will be participating, the criteria for composing Grid study teams, and the thousand mile rule are described. Points of inquiry are answered and points of misunderstanding clarified. Such pre-seminar orientation increases understanding and arouses interest among participants. They are stimulated by the program's possibilities and look forward with greater enthusiasm to the learning activities. This step also provides a good illustration of the readiness to communicate and to base action upon understanding as contrasted with simply telling people what will be expected of them.

Prework. Prework serves two purposes. It aids understanding of underlying Grid concepts and is a valuable contributor to involvement. Participants read *The Managerial Grid* book. They use their Grid learning to describe their own concepts of managing. This learning is in itself rewarding. The result is that the prework is not a burden but rather provides a strong and constructive reinforcement of attitudes toward the learning. This enables participants to make better use of the learning situation when they attend the Grid Seminar. Involvement is increased because they are clear about what they are undertaking. Nothing is accepted on faith. Nothing is hidden from view. There are no gimmicks.

What Use Is Made of Scores?

During the Grid Seminar sessions, participants complete many measurement instruments which show how each manager describes himself and his company. Copies of the completed instruments are not—under any circumstances—to be placed in a man's individual personnel file.

The data generated in a Grid Seminar are not useful for personnel or administrative judgments. Such information has no place in the appraisal of managerial competence. The data form no valid basis for reward. Were they to be used in these ways, the foundations and objectives of Grid Organization Development would be disregarded. This would constitute a violation of the very trust and confidence on which the learning situation is based. Organizations should and must evaluate their members and they need to do so as objectively as possible. But this should be a regular activity of management. It has no place in connection with an activity intended for learning purposes only.

These data are very useful for learning purposes. They can be used for summarizing and establishing organizational trends which can help a company to see itself as a problem-solving and production system or to see its strengths and weaknesses. When they are used in these ways, there is no issue of violation of confidence. Each person's data contribute only to a statistical analysis and to the establishment of trends. When these data are not in the personnel files, participants who have this concern can be given unqualified assurances that there is no risk in completing the measurement instruments accurately and with sincerity.

SUMMARY

In this section, considerations of design and execution of incompany Grid Seminars have been presented. Points of rationale have been explored to make understandable the strongest way yet known for moving effectively into Grid Organization Development. To the degree that these conditions can be met, the likelihood of success is increased. Many details which might be regarded as unimportant may, in fact, have significant effects on the outcome. This is particularly so because the Grid Seminar is both the first phase and the foundation for the development effort. With a well laid foundation, the next phases can be entered into with increased prospects of success.

REFERENCES

1. See also Blake, R. R., Mouton, J. S., Barnes, L. B. & Greiner, L. E. Breakthrough in Organization Development. *Harvard Business Review,* 1964, *42,* 152.

Appendix II

THE OD COORDINATOR'S JOB

In Grid Organization Development as in any organized activity, one person is needed to take the responsibility for coordination during the program's execution. This is the overall job of the OD Coordinator from the beginning of Phase 1 through Phase 6.

Through his active participation in it, the top man gives the effort its character, direction, and force. Since Grid Organization Development is an activity which involves responsibility for everyone in the organization, leadership of programmatic aspects of the effort is of a different character than is true for either a line or staff responsibility. The OD Coordinator's job is not like that of a top man or a person who has ultimate authority to make decisions. It is rather a job of maintaining continuity of the effort, of catalyzing activity, and of keeping track of the various parts of it. The aim is to insure coordination of effort where such coordination would produce better results than would independent action. His activities can be more specifically identified with each of the phases. In each, he provides the focus for insuring that the effort is sound and effective and is achieving the results for which it is intended.

PHASE 1: GRID SEMINARS

The OD Coordinator's many and varied activities in the Grid Seminar phase generally relate to seeing that the sessions are soundly conducted. He is not responsible for instructing them.

This is a line management responsibility. By engaging in several activities, he maintains contact with the participants and instructors.

Instruction

Serving as Instructor. The OD Coordinator is usually responsible for instruction in at least one Grid Seminar, probably one of the earlier ones in the series and ideally in the pilot seminar. This gives him firsthand knowledge of the problems of instructing a seminar and the skills required to do it.

Selecting Other Instructors. The OD Coordinator participates in selecting seminar instructors. His contribution to such decisions concerns the caliber of managers to be selected for instructors and the timing of their participation in instruction efforts.

Monitoring the Instruction. He stays in close touch with each Grid Seminar as it is being conducted. He visits from time to time to sample the quality of instruction and to participate in instructor critique sessions. In these sessions, members conducting a seminar evaluate the results being achieved. When engaging in this kind of activity, the OD Coordinator can contribute knowledge from his own experience of problems that others have confronted and help the instructors critique their own activities more thoroughly. He also attends the sessions on diagnosing organization culture. He does this to keep himself as fully informed as possible on barriers to organization effectiveness which will be subject to improvement efforts in later phases. Top managers also find it rewarding to attend these culture diagnosis sessions as they often provide insight into some of the organization's problems.

Planning

Scheduling Participants. Scheduling of participants in Grid Seminar sessions requires many decisions related to the availability of participants in terms of their regular work assignments as well as personal considerations. The OD Coordinator

is responsible for arranging for organization members to attend
each seminar. Beyond this, he must oversee the distribution and
collection of their prework materials and the correlation of
the prework data with the computer equipment if statistical
analyses are desired.

Composing Study Teams. The goal in composing study teams
is twofold. It is to insure that different levels of the organization's membership are represented but that direct work colleagues, and bosses and subordinates, are not included on the
same team. Mechanical methods have often been used effectively
to compose the study teams. Someone, however, must take the
responsibility of reviewing the study teams to insure that their
composition is sound. This also is one of the responsibilities of
the OD Coordinator.

Handling the Mechanics. Mechanical and physical details surrounding the location, facilities, timing, equipment, and instructional materials for conducting the Grid Seminar must be supervised. He arranges for installation support of the pilot Grid
Seminar by a Grid Organization Development specialist. These
considerations also fall within the realm of his activities.

Reports and Research

Collating and Summarizing Organization Diagnosis Reports.
Each seminar provides for concentrated study and diagnostic
examination of the organization's problems. Information of
value for the design of later organization development activities
is available from findings of these organization diagnosis sessions.
For them to be most useful as the basis for future planning, the
various organization diagnosis reports are collated and summarized under his supervision.

Evaluating Participant Reactions. For basic soundness of the
Grid Organization Development effort, the reactions of participants should be continually evaluated. Then needed changes to
increase seminar effectiveness can be made as required. The
OD Coordinator is responsible for this kind of gauging of participant reaction.

Progress Report to Line Management. He reviews general trends and reports progress to line management. He does not report anything that involves evaluation on an individual basis of those attending the seminars.

Research Liaison and Data Maintenance. Much of the data made available in statistical form through Grid Seminars provide valuable insight into characteristics of the organization. These data often contribute to critique, research, and evaluation efforts being made by the organization to study its development progress. The OD Coordinator arranges for data summaries that are useful in research analyses. If the company designs and executes a strong systematic critique of the sort described in Phase 6, his job is somewhat different, and he may call on a Grid Organization Development specialist for assistance. In this case he creates the design for systematic critique, sometimes working with computer specialists, preparing for the analysis and treatment of data, arranging a schedule for data gathering at key time intervals in the Grid Organization Development effort. When it is possible, he arranges for collection and comparison of data from the development unit with data from a control or comparison location.

Public Relations. Grid Organization Development projects often stimulate interest from persons outside the development unit. Visits help them to become acquainted firsthand with the strategies and tactics of the effort. He is the logical person to provide for the briefing of these visitors.

PHASE 2: TEAMWORK DEVELOPMENT

Many critical contributions are needed to insure the success of Teamwork Development. It represents the first step of application beyond the individual manager himself to the corporate situation. With Teamwork Development well organized, supported from the top, and moving down through the organization, the development effort is almost insured of success. The role of the OD Coordinator in Phase 2 activities is in aiding line managers to conduct Teamwork Development.

Organizing Phase 2 Activities

Planning and Critique. One aspect of his role is to project in general terms key considerations of organizing and administering the activities. He reviews the activities of Teamwork Development with the top team as an orientation step for their own participation. After the top team has completed their sessions, he helps them develop a schedule of Teamwork Development for lower levels. This pattern of orientation, critique, and scheduling for successive Teamwork Development sessions is carried out at each level of the company.

Work Team Composition. There are many organization problems that could be solved through good team action. There are many that are not solved very effectively. This may be because concepts of team action are poorly developed. It also may be because there is a lack of clear identification of the organization's groupings of members whose activities are interdependent in that each contributes to the solution of overriding problems. It also may be because various groups of persons who have joint responsibility for solving problems fail to recognize the team requirements involved. The OD Coordinator's responsibility is to aid in the identification of teams. It is the exception rather than the rule that teams are known and easily identified simply by reference to the organization chart. Rather he focuses on the issue of how teams should be defined for development purposes in order to pose the problem of team definition clearly. (See Appendix III)

Schedules. There are wide variations between corporations in the number of teams participating in team development. With very few exceptions, each man is a member of two teams, the one in which he is a subordinate reporting to a boss, and the one in which he is a boss with subordinates reporting to him. When it is recognized that it takes four or more days to gain the full advantages of Teamwork Development, it is clear that careful analysis, planning, scheduling, and organization of Phase 2 sessions is needed to keep the company operating while releasing teams for development purposes.

Design Administration

Phase 2 is an organized programmatic approach to Teamwork Development which utilizes learning instruments, its own time schedule, and other systematic properties which can be specified in advance. Responsibility for the success of any Teamwork Development session rests on the boss of that team. However, the OD Coordinator may be called upon to assist Teamwork Development activities either directly himself or to arrange for others who have served as instructors to sit in with a work team during its development sessions.

Appropriate Support Persons for Teams. When a team requests such assistance, it is essential that the support person working with the team be a member of another department. In the organizational hierarchy, he should also be at least on the same level as the boss of the team with which he will work.

Instructional Materials. The OD Coordinator arranges for the Phase 2 instructional materials to be available for the use of the teams. As in Phase 1, he collates the data and summarizes results of teams' progress and checks with teams on a followup basis to insure that critique activities are taking place.

Insuring a Successful Top Team Development Experience

While it is important that all organization members achieve a successful Teamwork Development effort, it is particularly critical that the top team do so first. All subordinate members of the top team are bosses one step down. If they have been through an effective and rewarding Phase 2 experience in their first effort, they are more highly motivated to insure similar success in teams for whom they are the bosses. The OD Coordinator arranges for a Grid Organization Development specialist to assist in this first effort.

After the top team has completed its Teamwork Development, it is in an excellent position to critique the experience before the next step is taken. The OD Coordinator arranges for this critique activity to occur. Thereafter, he continues to monitor progress and aids in the critique of the program.

Assessing Progress

Research and Review. Another of his activities is to continue
to assess development progress in Phase 2. As in Phase 1 this
may involve research assessment and monitoring the activities
to evaluate directly the progress being achieved. It may include
taking a Phase 6 approach to systematic critique. This involves
more extensive data gathering, analysis, and interpretation. Regardless of method, the assessment of the program's effectiveness
on a continuing basis is important. It is only good management
to have a clear comprehension of the extent to which the identified organizational goals are being achieved. Corrective steps
can then be introduced to insure that progress toward them is
sound. If it is not, management is prepared to revise goals so
that they may be more realistic or to rectify problems preventing their attainment.

Continuing Critique. The OD Coordinator may schedule meetings with other organization members assisting in the Phase 2
effort for three purposes: (1) to assess progress, (2) to identify
problems and barriers, and (3) to introduce corrective steps.
Such progress reviews constitute an excellent occasion for bringing a Grid Organization Development specialist into the situation. An outside point of view can then be applied in measuring
progress and in considering ways of deepening and strengthening Phase 2 that may not occur to insiders.

PHASE 3: INTERGROUP DEVELOPMENT

Initiating Intergroup Contact

Once points of intergroup contact are identified in Phase 1
and in Phase 2, the organization members responsible for coordination of intergroup effort are more than anxious to dig into
the causes of any problems and iron out the difficulties behind
them. They often turn to the OD Coordinator as the responsible
person in the organization to bring about Phase 3 Intergroup
Development activities. He works directly with the members of
each of the groups. He proposes schedules, helps decide who
should participate, aids in preparation of the task paragraphs
that specify the existence of the problem, arranges for meeting
places, and assists with many other tasks.

Depending on the severity of the intergroup problem and the level in the organization at which it exists, the OD Coordinator may himself serve as a neutral person to supervise the evolution of the steps needed to bring the problem to resolution. If the groups that face an intergroup problem are much higher in rank than he is, however, or if the problem is one of undue complexity, or the first Intergroup Development activity to take place, he may arrange for the participation of a Grid Organization Development specialist. In this event, he would share with him the responsibility for carrying out the intergroup confrontation. As a next step, he would again take responsibility by projecting and arranging followup steps and would assist in their implementation.

Maintaining Records of Intergroup Problem Solving

A final kind of activity of the OD Coordinator is to summarize the kinds of intergroup problems that have been resolved and those that remain at the end of Phase 3 and develop generalizations about them. As he did at the end of Phases 1 and 2, he would arrange for the key executives to review the Phase 3 effort for progress realized and problems remaining.

PHASE 4: DESIGNING AN IDEAL STRATEGIC MODEL

The OD Coordinator makes several contributions to the top team's design of an ideal strategic corporate model. One is in his reviewing the design of Phase 4 and making the administrative arrangements necessary to carry it through. Second, he arranges participation of a Grid Organization Development specialist to assist. Third, he may or may not attend the top team's Phase 4 sessions as an observer. The advantage is that it puts him in a stronger position as a member of the Strategy Implementation Committee of Phase 5 to communicate intentions that the top team built into the model and to clarify any ambiguities that the written version of the ideal model may contain.

PHASE 5: IMPLEMENTATION

The role of the OD Coordinator shifts significantly in Phase 5 from what it has been in Phases 1 through 4. The reason is that a person other than the OD Coordinator is appointed and serves as a Phase 5 Coordinator. The activities of Phase 5 which entail a wide range of analytical approaches for implementing the strategic model are best led by a manager of senior rank with outstanding analytical and technical skills. The Coordinator in Phase 5 needs technical skills not needed by an OD Coordinator. The OD Coordinator serves as a member of the Strategy Implementation Committee and continues his other developmental responsibilities.

APPLICATION PROJECTS

The OD Coordinator assists in the solution of specific company problems through developing and spurring application projects in that he:

1. Encourages members to write task paragraphs that define a problem without specifying preferred solutions

2. Aids in the design of team action materials for problems that resist solution because of knowledge deficiencies, and

3. Assists line management in thinking through who might best be assigned to problem-solving task forces.

The application projects are described more fully in Appendix IV. They entail efforts which are designed to solve ongoing problems of the organization as they are recognized and as organization personnel see the possibilities of solving them. These application projects may get under way shortly after Phase 1.

PHASE 6: SYSTEMATIC CRITIQUE

The OD Coordinator's job in Phase 6 is that of insuring a systematic critique of the development effort along longitudinal lines and making it widely available throughout the organization as the basis for review, consolidation, and replanning. His activities through the earlier phases—collating and summarizing data, keeping a log of developmental activities and application projects, administering systematic instruments at various times —all contribute to a wealth of information that is useful for critique activities.

SELECTING THE OD COORDINATOR

The OD Coordinator exercises significant leadership when a Grid Organization Development project is successful. He is the key person in initiating, organizing, programming, and auditing activities. In many other ways, he sees to it that the effort does not bog down. His success is based upon enthusiasm and personal desire to increase effectiveness. Careful selection of someone suitable for the role of the OD Coordinator cannot be over-emphasized.

Grid Organization Development in important ways is related to the improvement of personnel. Therefore, a person with wide employee relations or personnel department background might be expected to make an excellent OD Coordinator. In many successful projects to date, however, men with line background experience have proved more successful as OD Coordinators. It is most important that this project be sharply set off from other kinds of personnel and developmental approaches. Since it is a line activity from beginning to end, it is consistent with the character of the whole venture for the OD Coordinator to be a line manager. It can be supported in many ways by an effective employee relations staff, but experience suggests that the responsibility for initiating Grid Organization Development, conducting it, and evaluating it should rest in the line organization to the fullest degree possible.

Other considerations of selection, such as competence and level, are similar to those involved in instructor selection. However, another factor is the man's long range potential. If the activity is seen as a development opportunity for the man, then it stands to reason that a person of high caliber and long range potential is more likely to be benefited by having the OD Coordinator opportunity.

Strategies of Grid Organization Development are based upon effective interaction, involvement, participation, and increasing the degree to which individual line managers sense and act according to organization objectives. Therefore, the OD Coordinator should be a man who works naturally in this way. As an OD Coordinator, he is in fact operating without direct authority and must accomplish his objectives by arousing understanding, agreement, and commitment. Therefore, the ability to work in a 9,9 way is also a significant factor in selecting the OD Coordinator.

HOW THE OD COORDINATOR WORKS WITH THE GRID
ORGANIZATION DEVELOPMENT SPECIALIST

The OD Coordinator provides an essential link for funneling knowledge available from outside the corporation into the development effort. The whole of Grid Organization Development is designed and implemented through instruments and organized activities. The result is that knowledge and consultation from outside the organization are relied upon only at key developmental points: installation of the pilot seminar, completion of the top team's Teamwork Development activity, introduction of the first Intergroup Development sequence, initiating work on the design of the Ideal Strategic Corporate Model, getting the Strategy Implementation Committee and Planning Teams started, and in certain activities of overall summary and critique. The aim is to limit this kind of outside support to contributions which can genuinely strengthen the effort. The OD Coordinator arranges for having these key contributions available at the particular time in the development effort that they are needed. He also maintains continuing liaison with the Grid Organization Development specialist in order to be able to review and critique present activities and next steps with a knowledgeable person who, many times, can suggest alternative possibilities and provide necessary perspective for seeing the whole. Because of their wide experiences in many companies, Grid Organization Development specialists are in an excellent position to provide the consultation and installation support essential for maintaining direction, continuity, and strength in the development effort.

ADMINISTRATIVE CONSIDERATIONS IN THE DESIGN AND EXECUTION OF TEAMWORK DEVELOPMENT

Teamwork Development takes place, team by team, down through an organization. Several administrative matters should be considered in its execution.

TEAM COMPOSITION

Identifying teams in an organization is often surprisingly complicated. All persons who report to one man usually constitute a team. There are, however, four circumstances which present special issues.

What Makes It Complicated to Define the Team?

Sometimes several persons have the same boss but are assembled under him for administrative purposes only. They are not a "team" in the problem-solving or operational sense. None of the persons who report to the boss receive his direct supervision. Neither do they work with the others who also report to him. Members do not have an interdependence that compels joint effort to achieve superordinate goals. While it may be a tidy administrative unit, it is not a work team within the team concept.

A second special circumstance occurs when several persons constitute a team yet do not have one boss. An organizational situation or problem may have brought them together. When they convene, they contribute to the solution of the particular problem without a formal boss in the organization hierarchy. They *do* constitute a team in the true meaning of the word because their unity is dictated by the nature of the problem which can only be successfully handled through their effective interdependence. The ability of organization members to make and break teams in this manner is a hallmark of organization flexibility.

A third circumstance which produces a dilemma for defining a team is more common than the other two. The structure of the organization and the relationships within it may be an unexamined part of the organization's culture. Its members fit into the structure and occupy their particular positions, not because this is the best way to get work done, but because management has compromised on issues where conflict or strong personal feelings could be stirred up, has smoothed them over, or accommodated to them. Under these circumstances, when management begins to define teams, many contradictions in structure and relationships stand out in bold relief.

A fourth situation contributing complexity to defining teams arises when a genuine team effort is required within a formal team for certain kinds of problems. On other problems, solo efforts are most effective. The solution here is to ferret out the kinds of actions best handled in a one-alone way, those best handled on a one-to-one basis, and those most soundly handled on a one-to-all or total team basis.

In the most meaningful sense of the term, a team consists of those corporate members who shoulder a common responsibility. Only through genuine interdependence can it be properly discharged. Such interdependence calls for clear goals and objectives, close coordination, communication of information and perspective, mutual support and backup assistance, and clear planning and anticipation among members of what each is intending to do. Teamwork does *not* mean that everyone on the team works together all the time. An invalid assumption is presuming that teamwork means meetings. Meetings *per se* may or may not have anything to do with teamwork. Many organizations have excellent teams in which each member is able to carry out his own activities and anticipate the actions of others simultaneously, even though they only rarely meet for discussion, communication, and planning. Members may not even be located in the same geographical area. Teamwork is a direct result of the agreed-upon strategy of working together. Each person is a team member, and each is carrying out a piece of the team's responsibility which contributes to the whole even though all may be working alone. Isolation is more apparent than real. Boxes 89A, B, C, and D demonstrate some of the structural arrangements that may or may not be defined as "teams" for Teamwork Development.

To How Many Teams Can One Man Belong?

Except for the top man in the organization (president, regional vice president, plant manager, and so on) and those at the bottom of the pyramid, each man participates in Teamwork Development at least twice—first as a subordinate and then in the team of which he is the boss. This would suggest that except for the top and bottom of the organizational pyramid, each man participates in only two Teamwork Development activities. This may or may not be so. In many companies, it has been found, a person may hold a key assignment in three or more teams which are quasi-permanent. The man in this situation should participate in as many Teamwork Development sessions as he holds significant team memberships.

How Many Should Engage in a Phase 2 Session?

All persons who belong to a team should actually participate in its Teamwork Development. The largest size work team yet observed is 25. The smallest number possible for a work team is two, the situation of a one-over-one working relationship, or

BOX 89A
POSSIBLE TEAM FORMATION 1

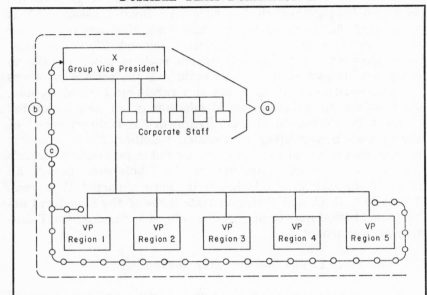

All Regional Vice Presidents report to the Group Vice President (X). They rarely meet as a group, but the Group Vice President and others on his staff visit each Region frequently. What is his work team?

a. X + his corporate staff? ─────────

b. X + his corporate staff + Regional VP's? - - - - -

c. X + Regional VP's? o-o-o-o-o

of a one-with-one relationship, such as two colleagues, neither of whom is boss of the other, but both of whom shoulder responsibility for an outcome. When there are as many as 25 members, it is quite unlikely that, under critical examination, the team will prove to be a sound grouping of persons around common objectives. A two-man team may prove sound under such examination, but often it too is found to be an ill designed arrangement for achieving high quality results.

Box 89B
POSSIBLE TEAM FORMATION 2

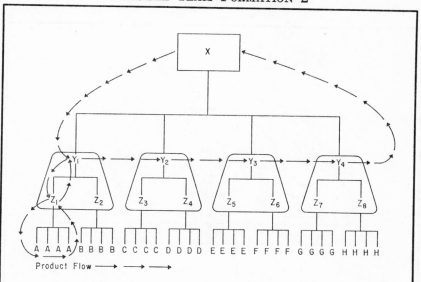

Y Managers (who report to X) have responsibility for functional components of a manufacturing process operation. Each Z manager has a close knit interdependent relationship with those who report to him. The Z managers and their subordinates clearly are a work team. The product flow is from Y_1 to Y_2 to Y_3 to Y_4. Thus X and those who report to him are a work team. Each Y manager works more or less independently with his Z managers. Do the Y-Z-Z level clusters constitute teams for development purposes?

How Many Levels of Hierarchy Should Be Involved in Teamwork Development?

This is a difficult question to answer in general terms. Ordinarily Phase 2 does not include more levels than a boss and those subordinates who report directly to him. In organizations in which the boss has an assistant who is regarded as being at an intermediate level, all three levels would obviously be involved.

Box 89C
POSSIBLE TEAM FORMATION 3

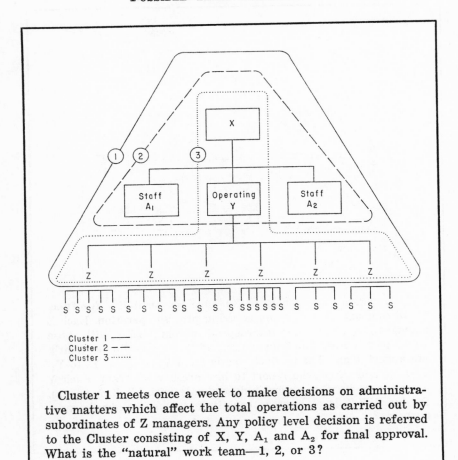

Cluster 1 ——
Cluster 2 – –
Cluster 3 ······

Cluster 1 meets once a week to make decisions on administrative matters which affect the total operations as carried out by subordinates of Z managers. Any policy level decision is referred to the Cluster consisting of X, Y, A_1 and A_2 for final approval. What is the "natural" work team—1, 2, or 3?

Am I Part of a Team?

Sometimes team members do not recognize that they are part of a team. In many situations persons act as individuals when they should operate as members of a team. This contradiction may be readily apparent to an outside observer who can see the necessity for coordination of efforts. The people in this kind

Box 89D

POSSIBLE TEAM FORMATION 4

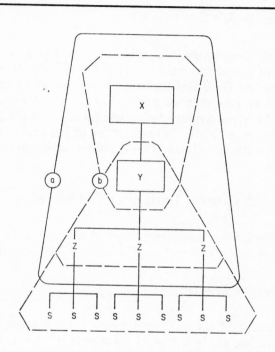

Y is subordinate to X. All Z's report to Y and Y reports to X who is responsible for the operation. The managerial level teams in this situation are:

a. Just one comprised of X, Y, and Z's ———————

b. Two teams, X and Y, and Y and the Z managers - - - - -

of situation can analyze and evaluate the issue of whether there should be interdependence among them. This involves their studying the pros and cons of increasing their team integration. If a conclusion that they are a team is reached, then they need to develop a sense of "teamness" before Teamwork Development can be engaged in. If members have never worked together or planned jointly or held critiques of their efforts, the issue is one of deciding whether there are areas for team action which, if exploited, would contribute to corporate effectiveness.

Where Does Phase 2 Start?

Teamwork Development should start at the top of the Grid Organization Development unit. If seeding and attendance at a pilot incompany Grid Seminar has involved *all* members of the top team, it can be started at the top of an organization while Phase 1 Grid Seminars are being conducted at middle and lower levels. In this way the top is leading the organization in strengthening team culture. Those whose voices carry greatest weight set the pace.

TEAMWORK DEVELOPMENT LEADERSHIP

Responsibility for achieving Phase 2 objectives rests with line management as in Phase 1, but with one important difference.

Why the Boss as Leader?

The boss is the "natural" leader of the work team in its operational activities. He is the most vital part of the work team and needs, along with other members, to participate in the investigation of team performance. Yet, while taking part as a participating member, he also serves his own work team as "instructor." In the final analysis, it is his responsibility to insure that the development objectives of the team's activities are realized. It is the boss's job, therefore, to be both boss and the instructor of the activities.

Who Leads the Top Team?

Teamwork Development starts with the top team. Still, no member of the organization has had a direct Phase 2 experience. To make its contribution to the development effort, it must be successful. The top team is probably the most important team in the organization. If top management is not successful in its own Phase 2, it is hardly to be expected that others will exert as much effort as if their top team had truly come to grips with barriers preventing increased effectiveness and opportunities for it. How to provide assistance to the top team in Phase 2 is a special issue.

The strategy for aiding the top team to be successful in achieving Phase 2 objectives is for a Grid Organization Development specialist to provide installation support for the top team. In a way, he is the one who assists the top man to install Teamwork Development within his own team—but this is with the top team only.

An outsider is preferable in this instance even to an insider from the training staff who has the competence, skill, and know-how to be fully qualified to assist in this activity. Put in this position, an insider often feels ill at ease in "listening" to problems discussed by the top team because he is of lower rank than the top man and probably lower than most of the members of the top team. The top team is likely to sense the impropriety of talking candidly about their problems or significant problems of the organization before an insider of lower rank.

After the top team has successfully completed its own Phase 2, each member (except the top man) repeats the activity with his subordinates. Ordinarily the second application requires no outside assistance, as each boss has engaged in Teamwork Development and is well prepared to lead the work team for which he is the boss.

ADMINISTRATIVE CONSIDERATIONS

How Much Time Is Needed to Complete Teamwork Development?

It requires about five days for the organized activities, as shown in Box 90. Then several months of intermittent activity are required for full implementation of the plans that are set in the initial period. The organized activities take place morning and afternoon, usually without late evening work. They can be completed on the job. An exception is the top team's activity. Because of the significance of this team, and since it is the first to have a Teamwork Development experience, it has been found desirable to create an off-the-job, live-in arrangement for that team.

Box 90

Teamwork Development Activities Are Undertaken Independently by Each Team from the Top Team Down Through the Entire Organization

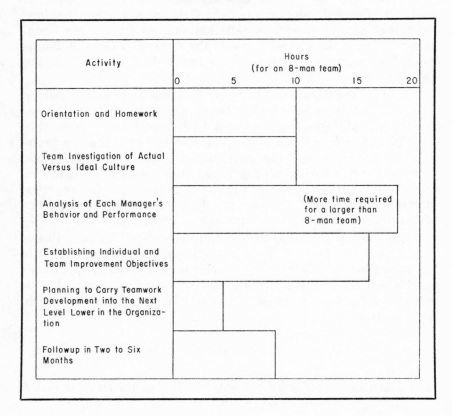

During the period of organized activities, the team sets objectives which it strives to achieve during ensuing months. Setting of individual and team objectives is designed to become a way of life as Teamwork Development moves toward achieving a sound system of work based on management by objectives. Management by objectives continues long after the formal aspects of Phase 2 have been completed. Because Phase 2 involves teams with operational responsibilities, it is often not practical to

take four or five consecutive days off the job. To do so can leave
a hole in the organization under circumstances where delegation
is not a realistic possibility. Therefore, it may be spaced out over
alternate days over a two-week period, for example, or so that
it takes place every afternoon over a two-week period, or one
day a week for five weeks.

Orientation to Teamwork Development

The content of Phase 2 is sometimes a source of concern to
managers. Personal matters which are of vital significance not
only for operational effectiveness but also for career development are discussed since Teamwork Development is aimed at
the very core of organization—team and personal effectiveness.

There are several ways to help team members recognize the
importance of the contribution that Phase 2 can provide and to
reduce or eliminate groundless worries. One is to achieve sound
and full prior understanding of the content of the activities.
When managers who are about to engage in Teamwork Development understand fully its purposes and anticipated outcomes,
they find little difficulty in recognizing the validity of the activities and its importance, not only to the organization but
also for themselves. A part of this orientation is for the team
to "walk through" the study materials. This aids them in seeing
what is entailed and what is not included. It permits reemphasis
of the fact that matters of individual behavior which are to be
discussed in Teamwork Development are limited to work-related
performance, behavior, and attitudes which should be reviewed
with every team member. The intent is to avoid discussion of
personal matters which do not have direct relevance to work.

Sometimes, of course, there are situations involving personal
incompetence. These cannot be ignored. A firm cannot achieve
excellence while winking at conditions that prevent excellence.
Once the members of an organization have completed Phase 1,
clarifying their personal objectives, and in Phase 2 have made
a searching examination of team culture, it is relatively rare
that personal incompetence is a problem of major proportions.
Thus, anxiety and concern about this problem often evaporates
when a studied effort is applied to understanding what really
lies beneath the situation that is less than fully effective.

Why Start Grid Organization Development with a Diagonal
Slice in Phase 1 If the Goal Is Application to the Team?

A question sometimes raised is, "Why not start with team development if that's where you're headed?" One of the best conditions for learning is a "neutral" atmosphere. Students are then free to experiment with various ways of achieving effectiveness. The diagonal slice study team, where neither his boss nor his colleagues are present, provides conditions under which a person can be open and candid, expressing himself directly without worrying about whether his boss will understand. If through Phase 1 he has learned theories of the Grid and the use of critique of personal performance, a man is prepared for Phase 2. He can engage in the same kind of study in the team with his boss and colleagues present. He has a background of confidence and skills acquired in the diagonal slice team. This double approach markedly increases the possibility that persons will learn what they *need* to learn in the Grid Seminar and thereafter be able to apply the learning effectively within their teams.

The key to effective Teamwork Development is in achieving the unobstructed, valid discussion of those matters of individual and team behavior and performance which must necessarily be talked through and resolved if corporate effectiveness is to be achieved. Organization members in Phase 2 learn to discuss the very problems which are barriers and obstructions to achieving that effectiveness. The objective of Teamwork Development is to identify, diagnose, and place into operation actual plans for correcting the stultifying problems of communication.

What Are the Major Barriers to Candor?

One of the primary barriers to candor is a person's concern about being open with his boss. This is all too often based upon an invalid fear of reprisal. Such fear for the most part is an unfounded anxiety. A far greater danger to a man's career lies in obstructed communication. This constitutes a built-in limitation to genuine mutual understanding and to his own capacity for growth and development. In the long run, it can be expected to do him more disservice than the remote risks involved in the candid and unobstructed communication called for as the condition for a constructive Phase 2 activity. His very anxiety can be a major barrier to candid communication. Rarely have bosses been found to feel anything but rewarded from hearing from subordinates ways in which they may increase their effectiveness. Vindictiveness is feared, but vindictiveness is unlikely to result if the communication is genuine. Obstructed communication is what undermines respect for authority. Openness and candor are perhaps the only genuine foundations for respect for authority. This is particularly true when organization advancement is on a merit basis. If such is not the case, perhaps one of the major routes through which a merit basis for advancement can be achieved is through increasing the candor and objectivity of assessments of behavior and performance.

Another barrier is a person's concern about revealing what he perceives as limitations among his colleagues. The basis for this concern also is likely to be exaggerated. The purpose of Phase 2 is to identify problems in such a manner as to discover solutions to them rather than simply being critical or pointing a finger at others. Many of the limitations and deficiencies of individual performance which come under discussion in Phase 2 already are well known. They have been talked about informally time after time. They have been bandied about in gripe sessions. But seldom have they been pointed out to the only man to whom the information could be of assistance in causing behavior to change. In instances where a person's behavior has been discussed directly, it is most likely to have been approached in such a disguised way that he did not recognize what was being said. What is already known has not been subjected to open communication directly with the person involved. The great advantage of Phase 2 is that these matters are brought into the open. Then something can be done about them.

SUMMARY

The sound handling of administrative and technical problems that arise in the implementation of Teamwork Development is important to the success of this phase of Grid Organization Development. The formation of Phase 2 study teams compels an organization to think through how its activities are organized and arranged. It also results in detailed examination of the effectiveness with which organization members apply their efforts in the pursuit of organization objectives. In the process of completing Teamwork Development, important barriers to corporate effectiveness come under study and correction.

SOLVING OPERATIONAL PROBLEMS THROUGH ORGANIZATION DEVELOPMENT APPLICATION PROJECTS

At the completion of a Grid Seminar there is high energy and commitment to solve concrete organizational problems. Corporate members are enthusiastically ready to accept challenges placed before them. They are motivated to dig into operational problems in a team-action way.

BARRIERS TO ACHIEVING RESULTS

As an organization progresses through the various phases of Grid Organization Development, problems that are widely known many times are seen in a new light. People feel a sense of urgency for solving them. What is it that needs to be done to focus this available energy? There are at least two critical steps. One is to define problems in explicit terms. The second is to set steps in motion which will bring to bear efforts needed to solve these problems. If initiative is not taken to bring into focus the issue of operational problem solving and to insure understanding of the need for it, people may fail to see the results they anticipate. Often they say to themselves, "Perhaps it would be better to wait until a particular phase of Grid Organization Development is reached. Then problems in this category will come under scrutiny and resolution." The tendency to wait may be reinforced by the fact that many corporate problems have been around for so long that the corporation's members have been accustomed to them. The thought that action might be needed to overcome this inertia simply does not occur to anyone. A general proposition can provide a guideline for sound action. It is that whenever an old problem is seen in a new light, a new problem is identified, motivation and commitment to solve a problem is present, and skills of team action are available to cope with it, then immediate efforts toward its solution should be applied. It is in the interest of sound business management to solve a problem at the moment that the potential for doing so exists rather than waiting to do so at a later phase of development. This line of reasoning has resulted in special kinds of application projects within the organized framework of Grid Organization Development. Sometimes these have been referred to as Phase 1*A*, 2*A*, or 3*A* application projects.

A 1*A* project represents either an individual or team effort to bring Grid learning to bear on the solution of operational problems after the Grid Seminar of Phase 1. A 2*A* project is the same kind of activity during or after completion of Teamwork Development activities of Phase 2. A 3*A* project is stimulated by a Phase 3 Intergroup Development activity.

Many corporations find themselves faced with a contradiction. It is that problems exist that are barriers to effectiveness and need to be solved. Knowledge essential for solving them is available within the organization but is not applied. The gap in skill which often prevents needed knowledge from being applied to the solution of important problems is in teamwork. Grid Seminars provide this skill to the degree essential for bringing available knowledge to bear on the solution of problems. Various application task force strategies are for the purpose of deliberate identification of such problems and use of team action to bring available organization knowledge to bear upon its solution.

An example of an application project will illustrate an organization's putting Grid Seminar learning to work upon completion of Phase 1. It took place in a plant where the manufacturing process consumes large quantities of water, steam, electricity, and gas. An earlier engineering study had indicated that without significant capital expenditures, better management of the utilities could result in a major reduction of production expenses. Though the technical study had been available for several months, little had happened.

After Phase 1 had been completed but before Phase 2 was under way, management decided to concentrate energy on achieving reduction in the utilities expense through team action methods. First a study was made of why little or no action had resulted from the technical report which was available. The cause could not be found in the technical competence of the engineers who could influence the expense of utilities. They had the intellectual and technical understanding of utilities engineering. The root of the problem was sought elsewhere. It was finally concluded that the matter of reducing utilities costs was partly an attitude problem, partly a knowledge problem.

The source of the barriers from faulty attitudes toward utilities engineering was seen to be caused by top management. The plant manager had released the report. He had encouraged those managers who were responsible to initiate action. He had then turned his attentions elsewhere. Several months later he was disappointed that results had not been achieved. Lower levels of management were acting consistent with the attention they observed in top management. Top management had really not demonstrated its convictions. Therefore little force was felt from their delegation of responsibility for action to lower levels. The knowledge aspect of the problem was that while many managers knew about the technical study, few had read it in depth and with enough understanding to comprehend its implications for cost reduction.

The 1A application project was in several steps. First, the technical study was redistributed. A true-false test accompanied it to be completed as prework. Team discussion of the contents of the document and the test was completed by the top management group. Members demonstrated to one another that they had achieved full and indepth understanding of the technicalities and of the yield that could result from corrective action. Their enthusiasm resulted in a decision that about 320 engineers would repeat the same team-action type study as they had completed. The engineers' study of the document lasted a half day. The other half day was devoted to planning by the engineers, who were composed into discussion units of ten men each, of concrete steps that they might take to bring about the necessary improvements. Within six months, a large utilities cost reduction had occurred.

This example identifies typical barriers to getting results. The technical study clearly indicated the potential gain from better utilities management, but *attitudes* were widely present which said, "This is not important." Therefore engineers had not used the report to *understand in depth* the degree to which they might bring about the necessary actions. Both the attitude and knowledge aspects had to be dealt with as the basis for concentrating the necessary energy on the solution of this problem.

There are countless opportunities for solving this kind of problem through application projects after Phase 1 and during succeeding phases.

DEFINING PROBLEMS AND IDENTIFYING THEIR CAUSES

The advantages for defining and solving application projects are:

1. Benefits to the company are immediately realized. Managers do not have to wait until later phases to see results of their own efforts.
2. Success in bringing about solutions to such problems motivates managers to search for more opportunities. Such success produces a "can do" attitude which is self-reinforcing.

Identifying the reasons behind unsolved problems is the first step. The search for the problems that exist, some of which have been around so long that they have become chronic, has not often been given the attention it merits. Failure to have solved these problems may be attributable to any one of three causes or a combination of them.

One cause may be *attitudes*. Either the problem is not seen as important, people have given up trying, or others are seen as more appealing. Problems often persist because the *knowledge* essential for coping with them is insufficient even though the facts may be available. Sometimes problems persist because of *lack of skill*, either technical or in teamwork, for seeing how to get at the problem. After Phase 1 Grid Seminars have been completed, it is likely that teamwork skills sufficient to solve many kinds of problems are more than sufficient. Thus the great majority of problems that persist are likely to be either knowledge or attitude problems. A key to getting started on application projects is for the OD Coordinator to take responsibility for initiating action on the first effort.

Problems Caused by Insufficient Knowledge

No matter how hard the organization tries to solve them, organization problems often persist and resist solution because the people who need to take definitive action do not have enough facts. Without enough knowledge, commitment to experiment and to find solutions is likely to be low. The problem is likely to be ignored rather than faced.

Better Communication to Solve Problems. Managers usually view problems caused by insufficient knowledge as problems of poor communication. Attempts to solve them through communication programs often fail. Communication techniques as conventionally applied do not bring about the knowledge required for the solution. Commitment to the idea that a solution can be found may be lacking. An implicit assumption is likely to be that if the message is simple, clear, and direct, the issues will be understood. When they are not, it is likely that knowledge is insufficient even though facts may be available. When the problem is a knowledge problem, a team action design can be employed very effectively. Involving organization members in discussing, debating, and testing the facts available to them increases their knowledge.

An Example of a Knowledge Problem. In one organization, actions of lower level supervisors often were reversed by higher management during the grievance procedure. The grievances were usually settled in the union's favor. It seemed clear that lower level supervisors were not interpreting the contract properly. The conventional solution to this problem was to give copies of the union-management agreement to all supervisors for them to read. Management followed up this action by scheduling a meeting so that everyone responsible for administering the contract could raise questions about its intentions or implications. While this strategy had been applied, the problems of contract interpretation persisted.

After Phase 1, ways to achieve genuine organization-wide understanding of the union-management contract became the focus of an application project. A strategy of participation was adopted whereby the contract interpretation problem was viewed as stemming from insufficient knowledge. The contract was made the basis of a team action design. A multiple choice test of its contents was produced. After all supervisors had received the contract, the multiple choice test was distributed. Supervisors completed the test. They were then assembled in ten-man diagonal slice teams, similar in composition to the Grid Seminar study teams. The task of each team was to come to agreement on the answer to each test item. This challenge forced the examination of issues of interpretation and differences of points of view about the meaning of the contract. It enabled each supervisor to discover subjects where he had thought he had complete knowledge but in fact did not. At the end of the team discussion, the team answer was scored. Items which were still misunderstood were discussed until there was essentially 100 percent understanding of the facts of the union contract.

The next step under this strategy was a discussion. The instructions were, "Given our present understanding of the union contract, where have we been misinterpreting it in the past, where has the union been misinterpreting it, and what implications does our present knowledge have for our everyday actions?" The supervisory force moved into an excellent position to develop standards for their own actions in administering the contract. The latter step deals with the attitude aspects of the issue. This approach to the communications problem is an example of the way in which knowledge can be assured. It was not merely assumed that because material was distributed or persons were told, they understood the implications of the contract. The strategy of employing the team action design, as shown in this example, is the basis for solving the knowledge problem and begins directly with assuring understanding of the background information relevant to the specific issues. The basic educational model lends itself to a variety of applications. It has been used for study of such diverse topics as company policy, union-management relations, job description content, safety, organization traditions, quality control, salary administration, or profit improvement. Under this 9,9 approach, understanding as the basis for action is not presumed but insured.

Problems Related to Attitudes

Another category of organization problems includes those often seen by management as motivation problems. On more thorough inquiry, many times these are found to be problems of attitudes. The approach to an attitude problem is different from the approach to a knowledge problem.

Personal Attitudes Anchored to Organization Norms. Attitudes are rooted in the mores and standards of conduct of the various membership groups throughout the organization. An attitude is often shared by many persons who do not routinely interact on a day-by-day basis but who are a significant group who deliberately and unwittingly set standards of conduct. A professional, scientific, or engineering group is an example. In these instances attitudes, therefore, cannot be changed by working with individuals on a one-by-one or even a team basis. The difficulty of grappling with attitude issues in conventional forms is shown in an example.

An Example of an Attitude Problem. One organization faced a severe and chronic problem of employees' leaving work early. Higher levels of management had cracked down on numerous occasions. For short periods the problem would seem to be corrected only to reappear later. Treating it as a motivation issue, management had sought to punish these front line foremen who were not discharging their supervisory responsibilities.

Treating it as an attitude problem, management dealt with the difficulty in an entirely different manner. As the first step, they selected twelve foremen from a total of seventy. (Two were chosen from each of six areas, each area supervised by about twelve men.) The representative group convened to discuss the task paragraph questions, "What are the causes of the early quitting problem? What steps can be taken to correct it?" After discussing the problem, they returned to their areas and discussed it again with the group from which they had been selected.

They then reported their area discussions back to the representative group and continued the cycle until the problem had been clearly defined and steps toward its correction outlined and implemented. The twelve foremen in the representative group became the supervising task force to insure that the implementation for correcting the problem was effectively applied and that the negative condition would not recur.

As the foremen initially discussed the problem, they had felt that its source was lack of motivation among wage employees and that it was not a problem of supervision. They listed numerous possible causes. Poor supervision was one possibility. They discussed it at length and finally concluded that poor supervision was the primary cause because no supervisor wanted to be tough and exert responsible control over his men when other foremen were not doing the same thing. The difficulty lay in the fact that each foreman did not want to break from the group and crack down on early quitting. Lax supervision had become accepted practice. The solution was seen in attaining agreement among all foremen that they would deal with the problem together. Then if a foreman were not to take steps which were consistent with his responsibilities, he would be seen as going against the accepted standard.

To take the step of changing the attitudes about behavior, each representative went to his work group to talk through the problem of shifting behavior away from early quitting. Each work team achieved agreement that every foreman would take steps to insure that early quitting did not occur. The representatives met again and an agreed upon plan of action was determined. Rather than installing a crash program, they outlined a sequence of steps. The representatives returned to their work groups to talk through the steps of action and get understanding of them. The early quitting problem was resolved. The supervisors felt better since they were exercising responsible supervision. With the enforcement of the rules, wage men reported that they had greater respect for the supervisors and that this had cleared up an area of uncertainty for them.

Problems Combining Attitude and Lack of Knowledge

Many improvement opportunities are neither knowledge nor attitude problems but are combinations of problem-solving difficulties related to both deficiency in knowledge and wrong kinds of attitudes. The following is an example of a problem that came from a mixture of negative attitudes and lack of knowledge in a large organization.

One subsidiary's wage rate structure had resulted in pay rates twenty percent higher than those of the highest competitor in the area and in the industry. This company is in an industry that pays the highest nationwide rates, as shown in industry-by-industry comparisons. Because the company had let its wage rates get so far out of line, it was finding it harder and harder to maintain a competitive position. Action to bring the rates into line was imperative. To maintain its favorable community reputation, the company was prepared to maintain a wage rate which would be as high as the average of the three highest competitors within a 200 mile radius in a highly industrial area. The company's strategy was not to reverse past decisions or reduce rates but to avoid meeting the general wage increases of the industry until its rates matched the average of the three highest competitors. This objective had been clearly defined over an extended period of time. However, in practice, each time that a general wage increase pattern formed in the industry, the company's leaders felt such pressures that they matched it. Rates continued to rise, moving the company to an even more untenable situation for maintaining a competitive position in the industry.

After all managers had completed a Grid Seminar, correcting the wage structure was identified as an application project. This time the strategy of solution involved an effort to achieve understanding and agreement on *not needing the wage round* rather than digging in heels and forcing acceptance of *not receiving it* on a win-lose basis. As the problem was evaluated it became clear that one difficulty was lack of knowledge and understanding among lower level supervisors and wage personnel about how much wage rates were reducing the company's ability to meet competition. Another difficulty, however, was in attitudes. Supervisors at lower levels believed that the subsidiary should meet whatever rate demands were made on an industry-wide basis because the parent corporation was doing so well.

A team action design was built around an extensive and impartial study of the rate structure of the industry and the geo-

graphic area, plus a multiple choice test based on the content
of the wage study. The study was used as the basis for producing comprehension. It was made widely available for reading.
Thereafter, the multiple choice test was completed by each supervisor. As another step, all management members convened in
study teams on a diagonal slice basis and discussed to the point
of team agreement what the best answer was for each of the
multiple choice test items. This enabled supervisors to exchange
information on their understanding of the issues. Most important, those who had misunderstandings of the problem recognized alternative ways of viewing the issues. Following team
agreement on the multiple choice test, scoring was completed as
is typical in a team effectiveness design. As a next step, all items
that had been incorrectly answered were further discussed until
widespread understanding had been obtained.

In the discussions that took place, each study team spent approximately twelve hours on the problem. It became apparent
among team members that the attitude that the local plant should
participate in periodic increases because the parent company
was doing so well was unjustified. They based this conclusion
on the recognized fact that the unit under discussion was a profit
center with its future based upon how well it could do competi-
tively and not a cost center with its fate dependent upon the
performance of its parent company.

Through these discussions, knowledge of the real rate structure problem was significantly increased. Attitudes toward correcting the problem were dramatically reversed. They shifted
to a positive direction of getting the problem solved. After completion of this knowledge training and attitude development,
line managers were able to communicate effectively with wage
personnel and the union. Nor was it difficult to achieve agreement on the desirability of foregoing general wage increases
until such time as the organization's wage rates had moved into
a sound competitive position.

Understanding and Conviction as the Basis for Action

From a conventional management point of view, this problem
would appear as simply a problem of communication and motivation. Reexamination of it after the development project showed

that it was resolved through understanding and conviction. It was a matter of aiding organization members to acquire the knowledge needed to understand the situation. Furthermore, they developed commitment to attitudes which would legitimately reflect their concern for retaining the competitiveness so essential to the long range growth and development of the organization. After knowledge and attitudes of members of the management force had been dealt with, problems of communication skill and motivation to discuss real issues with wage personnel no longer needed attention. Each management member continually worked at aiding others in understanding the situation as he did.

ADMINISTRATION OF APPLICATION PROJECTS

The objective of application efforts in a Grid Organization Development project is to identify specific barriers to corporate effectiveness and develop action steps for eliminating them during Phases 1 through 2. These are beyond the specific projects that take place as part of Teamwork or Intergroup Development activities. Administrative requirements for maintaining the direction and continuity of problem-solving efforts in these phases can be taken care of by the OD Coordinator (See Appendix II). Occasional monitoring and review by a Grid Organization Development specialist can many times result in his aiding members in seeing additional opportunities that might otherwise be missed. While problems of maintaining direction and continuity of an organization development effort can be easily handled in a 500 manager organization by an OD Coordinator, an organization of 1,500 managers requires a more complex administrative arrangement. The primary question is whether the arrangements are being made to aid the organization to maintain the direction and continuity of the Grid Organization Development effort or to aid it in developing solutions for problems. For maintaining direction and continuity, *structural* arrangements are appropriate. For solving problems, *functional* arrangements are sound. A useful structural arrangement for keeping the organization development effort on course is the steering committee. There may be corporate OD Steering Committees or division OD Steering Committees. For each, there are helpful guidelines concerning number of members, their selection, and action expected of them.

The Corporate OD Steering Committee

Many Grid Organization Development opportunities cut across department lines and constitute major undertakings. They compete with other activities for the time and energy of the organization's membership. Assignment of priority, therefore, and other coordination activities are needed at a high level to insure sound and orderly application of limited resources. The basic responsibility of the corporate OD Steering Committee is to see that those needs are fulfilled. Since membership on the committee cuts across department lines, if necessary, they can authorize the initiation of major projects. Most important, they set priorities for each project on the basis of evaluation of the size and importance of all application projects.

Who Are Its Members?

The corporate OD Steering Committee is composed of high ranking organization members. They represent all major components of the organization at the corporate level. The committee usually includes the executive vice president and executives from the major divisions, departments, regions, or functions of the organization. Since one development objective is to insure that the program is executed by line managers, each member of the corporate OD Steering Committee should have management responsibility as opposed to being an individual contributor from a staff department. The OD Coordinator, however, is a regular member.

How Often Does the Committee Meet?

The answer to this question depends on the seriousness of the problems being considered, the intensity of effort being applied, and the size of the organization. Larger organizations usually have more projects under way and therefore a greater need for coordination. After initial strategies have been set in motion, a two- or three-hour meeting twice a month is usually enough to maintain direction and momentum.

What Does the Committee Do?

The corporate OD Steering Committee maintains direction and continuity of the effort in several ways:

1. *Projects.* It is responsible for selecting them.

2. *Priorities.* It sets priorities when not enough members of the organization are available for two projects to be carried on simultaneously.

3. *Personnel.* It recommends organization members to serve on task forces, backup committees, and other special groups. When application projects cut across department lines, it becomes the responsibility of this committee to appoint members to each problem-solving group. It does so, however, on the basis of suggestions from the departments needing representation in the group in question.

4. *Project Definition and Review.* The committee may prepare statements of the definition of the project or review those already formulated at a lower level. It is responsible for insuring the thorough definition of the problem needing solution and for reviewing progress and results. It also monitors progress by systematically reviewing results of task forces, backup committees, or other special groups.

5. *Recommendations.* The committee prepares summaries of results, alternatives produced, ideas generated, or recommendations of working groups for solutions to their problems. This committee is not responsible for execution of change, as this should receive top management approval and authorization.

In summary, the corporate OD Steering Committee remains at the helm of the organization's development effort and coordinates action and recommends further activities.

DIVISIONAL OD STEERING COMMITTEES

Large organizations with many functional components have found it useful in their Grid Organization Development efforts to have each major division form its own divisional OD Steering Committee. These committees perform the same functions for the divisions as the corporate OD Steering Committee performs for projects that have corporate-wide implications. The divisional committee is also an important information source for the corporate committee on views of lower echelon members toward problems that need attention and can only be solved at the corporate level. In the case of the large organization, a division may have its own OD Coordinator. Composition of the committee, frequency of meetings, and committee activities for the divisional OD Steering Committee are comparable to those of the corporate OD Steering Committee.

In summary, these two bodies, the corporate OD Steering Committee and the divisional OD Steering Committee, guide the overall effort regardless of the content of the specific problems or projects which are dealt with by their members. Their purpose is coordination, not problem solving.

TASK FORCES OR PROJECT TEAMS

A task force or project team is a useful approach for solving several different kinds of problems.

Correlation of Information. When a solution to a problem is being developed, facts from various sources must be collected and correlated. In one large company, its mechanical unit used a task force to study the kinds of lubrication seals for repairing mechanical devices of various sizes. Members of the organization possessed a wealth of experience with many kinds of seals. Maintaining an inventory of so many different kinds was costly. The problem needed a solution that would standardize these seals for uniform application. A basis for composition of the task force was experience in the use of different kinds of equipment. The widest possible range of knowledge and experience was sought in choosing representatives for the task force who would correlate, evaluate, and use this information as a basis for drawing up uniform specifications.

Everybody's Problem Is Nobody's Problem. Sometimes a problem affects everyone but no one is specifically responsible for its solution. One organization experienced such a problem in the need to correct important deficiencies in its performance evaluation system. A task force was set up to identify causes for important complaints about the administration of the wage and salary system. Its members concluded that the problem lay not in the wage and salary structure or the performance evaluation methods used but rather in an insufficient understanding of the rationale and methods of implementing the system soundly. It was an "everybody's business is nobody's business" type difficulty until defined with causes identified and solutions proposed. Once a solution had been proposed, a team action seminar was used which provided the whole organization with the information needed about the rationale on which the system was based and the manner in which management intended that it be administered.

This is a good example of a line management task force engaged in the kind of study usually made by a staff organization or an employee relations department. In this case, the line management task force assumed the responsibility for diagnosing the causes of the very problems being experienced by line managers in their attempts to carry out the performance evaluation system. They developed the strategies for a solution to the problem. Involvement and effective participation were achieved along with sharp reduction in complaints about the system.

The task force deals with one problem only. Its goal is to find and recommend or implement a solution as rapidly as possible and disband. A task force is not a problem-solving group or committee. It can be one man, or it can be two or more competent and well informed organization members whose purpose is to find a sound definition of a problem and to diagnose its causes and make recommendations as to its solution. Recommendations of a variety of approaches to the solution are expected. For all practical purposes, task force work is staff work carried out by line managers. Beyond the management development implications of task force assignment are many other advantages from the organization's point of view, such as development of solutions that are likely to be acceptable by line managers and therefore increase the likelihood of their commitment to act upon the solutions. In organizations that have developed the task force strategy in depth, a side result has been a shrinking staff organization. Furthermore, line managers who engage in task force types of staff work seem not only to be doing a better line management job but also to be gaining an important developmental advantage that is denied them when this kind of work is limited to the staff organization.

SUMMARY

Many kinds of organization problems are combination problems, produced partly by lack of knowledge, partly by attitudes that are inconsistent with legitimate organization purposes. When knowledge problems and attitude problems are dealt with through development activities, many issues thought to be ones of communication, motivation, and planning rapidly come under control.

The tendency of management to miscalculate the cause of a problem and therefore treat the wrong cause can appear in still a different way. Many issues of behavior and performance are seen as matters of technique and skill. Far more often, presumed deficiencies of technique or skill are only symptoms of deeperlying problems of attitude and conviction on the one hand and knowledge and understanding on the other. When there is commitment, there is often enough skill to achieve the desired level of performance.

Appendix V

THE SCIENTIFIC METHOD
MODEL OF LEARNING

Human learning is essential to the improvements in corporate performance made possible through Grid Organization Development. The strategy of learning that undergirds Grid Organization Development can be described here. In many significant ways it parallels strategies of scientific inquiry as acquired in the physical sciences and therefore is referred to as the "scientific method of learning."

STEPS IN THE SCIENTIFIC METHOD LEARNING CYCLE

The scientific method as applied to organization learning can be described as a five-step circular process. The steps include theory, action, critique, generalization, and application, as shown in Box 91. Completion of all steps in one cycle provides the basis for a new cycle since the final step of application is the source of further insight and provides new theories for initiating the next.[1]

Theory

Theory is more than intuition and hunch as the basis for guiding action. It is neither random, trial and error, nor is it free association. A person can explain clearly to himself, and

Box 91

Scientific Method Model of Learning

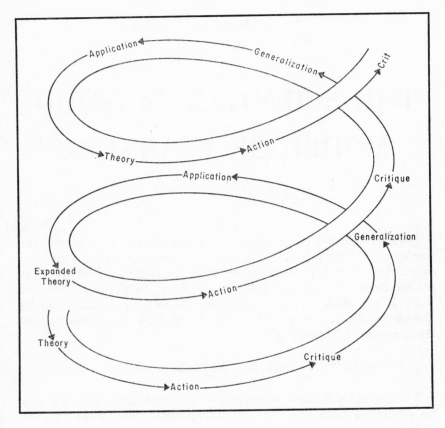

so to others as well, the logic and reasoning behind his actions. As used here, theory may range from a simple map of common sense explanation, through attitudes, beliefs, and convictions, through a deliberate plan of action to be taken, to a sophisticated, logical statement of systematic hypotheses that specify results expected in quantifiable terms. The closer the theory is to the right end of the spectrum shown in Box 92, the greater the likelihood that it can serve as a sound basis for learning. But no matter how crude the theory, its formulation is an essential first step in the scientific method model of learning. In

Box 92

The Theory Spectrum

Non-Theoretical Basis for Action		Theoretical Basis for Action			
Trial and error	Hunch and intuition	Common sense explanation	Attitudes, beliefs, and convictions	Plans and planning	Theory expressed in the form of explicit hypotheses that can be tested

situations where there is little theory available for selecting an action, there is no alternative but to start with a crude theory. The objective of learning is to replace crude theory with sophisticated theory as rapidly as possible.

Action

The second step is applying effort to achieve a result. Action. Sometimes it is physical effort. Energy is applied directly to causing something to happen. It may be a mental action—taking a thought step. Whether physical or mental, the action reveals a theory lying beneath it whether the person taking the action realizes it or not. Sometimes a person can provide clearly and precisely a valid description for the theory basis of his actions. Sometimes the description he provides for the theoretical basis of action is clear and concise but entirely invalid without his recognizing it. Whether the theory is valid or not, the action step is necessary if the possibility of learning is to occur.

Critique

Learning does not result from the action itself. Critique, the third step, is study of the relationships between theory and action. Critique questions are: Did the action produce the expected results? To what degree? Were there unanticipated results or side effects? Are there other explanations that account for the results obtained? Critique is a way of investigating how well the person understands the theory that has guided his action and how well the theory accounts for the results obtained. Critique makes possible testing the theory. Without it, learning does not occur as there is neither a basis for clarifying the theory or determining to what degree it was right or wrong.

Critique takes several forms. In social learning, one aspect of critique is personal feedback. Observers of a person's action report what they interpret to have been the theory basis of his action and how his actions affected them. This enables him to compare his own explanation of his action with their observations and his inferences about his action's effects with their subjective reports. Critique may also be used for judging performance and achievement. Evaluation of operational results in terms of the theory of the action makes it possible to identify and eliminate barriers to achievement, whether caused by poor theory or inappropriate action. In Grid Organization Development, critique is applied extensively for these purposes.

Whether it involves personal feedback or the evaluation of achievement, critique can be made a more powerful source of learning through the design of second steps of action that are systematic and include planned variations. When systematic and planned variations of actions are possible, it becomes practical to compare them. Comparison provides the basis for identifying similarities and differences in actions and in results stemming from different actions with several important advantages. One is that each action can be described more accurately when compared with others. The second is that such comparison aids in clarifying the theory which was applied when results of the action are evaluated and interpreted. A third is that it provides a clear basis for connections of cause and effect.

The exercise of critique in and of itself does not lead to full learning. While critique contributes importantly to learning from experience, something else is needed for genuine insight.

Generalization

Generalization is the step of summarizing and drawing conclusions from the first three steps. When critique findings show that the theory-based action has produced the expected results, that there is no other explanation of why the action was sound, and that there were no unanticipated side effects, the generalization is that the theory was sound. It is accepted with confidence because it has a high degree of validity. Alternatively it may be concluded that the theory was wrong and should be replaced with a sounder one or that the theory is sound in some respects but unsound in others and should be revised in order to serve as a valid source of guidance for new action.

Application

In organization life the proof of the theory is in its utility as demonstrated through operational results. Learning that has no impact on organization achievement, though it may be interesting, has little usefulness. The final test of the learning model, therefore, is in application of the newly learned theory to operating the business. When more effective organization performance occurs, learning has surely taken place. Not only is the theory understood, but also the action taken has produced the desired result.

CONTRIBUTION TO ORGANIZATION EFFECTIVENESS

These are the five steps in the scientific method model of learning. Its use can contribute to organization effectiveness in several ways:

1. By leading to more deliberate examination of theory, it can result in a valid conceptual map for predicting the consequences of various actions.

2. By emphasizing action, it can lead to the development of skills essential for achieving effective results.

3. By focusing on critique, it makes it possible for any action, whether interpersonal or operational, to become a subject of study and learning. This is the key to increased effectiveness and reduced self-deception as well, particularly when a person is aided in evaluating his action and experience by others who have observed it and are prepared to provide an unbiased assessment of what they have observed.

4. By emphasizing generalization, which in turn contributes to the development and refinement of theory, it provides a basis for the fullest use of intelligence as the foundation for action.

5. By emphasizing application, the learning cycle becomes not only personal and vital but specific and relevant as the main resource for the solution of significant individual and organizational problems.

No step in the scientific method model of learning is more important than another. All are critical and must be taken if learning is to result. This five-step model is presented as if learning takes place in slow motion, but the most complex mental activity can occur in a flash. Unless mental activity is slowed down and made deliberate, however, it is likely that one step or another will be bypassed. This is particularly true with respect to the first, third, and fourth steps—theory, critique, and generalization. Actions are often taken without thought for what action should be taken. Frequently insufficient effort is applied to critique. Summarizing the cycle of activity by drawing generalizations from what has been learned generally is not considered important.

True scientific inquiry requires the most deliberate application of this learning model. Great effort is applied to formulating the theory to be tested and designing the actions to be applied in testing it. Great care is taken to create conditions for applying these actions in a way to insure that unwanted influences do not intrude to contaminate results. Data are gathered and often subjected to the most thorough statistical tests. Findings are summarized and conclusions reached which verify the theory or lead to its rejection or modification. The gain from this highly deliberate application of the scientific method model of learning in the physical sciences suggests that similar gains are possible even when the situation to which it is applied cannot be so rigorously controlled. This model is equally useful whether the activity to which it is applied is for discovery, education, correction, or prevention, all of which are important in Grid Organization Development.

USES OF THE SCIENTIFIC METHOD OF LEARNING IN GRID
ORGANIZATION DEVELOPMENT

This five-step learning model is employed in an endless variety of ways in the six phases of Grid Organization Development. Examples of its use will aid in the understanding of this concept of learning.

Grid Seminars

The first major application of the scientific method model of learning is at the level of the individual in Phase 1. The Grid describes major theories utilized in corporate behavior. The experiments in the Grid Seminar result in actions of varying degrees of effectiveness. Critique periods permit participants to evaluate how the actions fit the theories and generalize about the validity of each theory as the basis for achieving effective results. By the end of a Grid Seminar, the participant not only has learned which of the several thories is most characteristic of his own approach, but also has learned alternative possibilities for strengthening personal effectiveness.

Teamwork Development

After managers have learned the theories of the Grid in this highly personal way, the learning model is deepened in Phase 2. Members of each actual team in the organization convene to critique their performance in the light of theory, to generalize from it, and to plan ways of shifting the team's action to bring it in tune with theories of behavior that have been shown to increase operational effectiveness.

Intergroup Development

The same cycle of application takes place in Phase 3. The organization problems to which the learning model is applied are in the relationships between groups. The objective is to develop more effective coordination and cooperation between these groups.

Designing an Ideal Strategic Corporate Model

In Phase 4, the effort shifts from concentrating on increasing the effectiveness of the company's behavioral culture to strengthening its business logic. An organization's self-deception about the validity of its business logic is no less important than a person's self-deception about his behavior. The theory of business logic that would be employed in an excellent company is made explicit in Phase 4. The business actions that would flow from this ideal logic are compared with the organization's actual business decision-making precepts. Critique is used to discover similarities and differences between ideal and actual business logic. Conclusions are drawn and generalizations reached on what the ideal strategic corporate business logic should consist of for future application.

Implementing the Ideal Strategic Corporate Model

In Phase 5, the organization investigates how each of its major activities should be operated under the ideal strategic corporate model, which is the organization's business theory. A range of alternative ways for operating the business are identified. Through mock-ups, simulation, trial runs, and similar tactics of testing, critique permits selection of those ways of operating the business that are most likely to meet the requirements of sound business logic. The conclusions reached in the form of generalizations become the basis for actual change in the conduct of the business.

Critique

Phase 6 is designed for a review and survey of the entire Grid Organization Development effort. It answers the question of whether the behavior culture of the firm is sound and consistent in the light of behavioral science theories and from the standpoint of effective utilization of personnel. It also permits a survey of the extent to which the business logic employed is valid and where improvement, correction, or further development can increase effectiveness.

SUMMARY

The subjects for application of the learning model in each phase provide an orderly build-up from the simple to the complex. Problems of communication between team members and between groups provide a natural build-up in that after difficulties at the individual level have been identified, problems can be confronted in teams. When team problems have been reduced, intergroup problems can be brought into focus and resolved. Removal of barriers to effectiveness at these three levels provides a foundation for moving to the next higher level of complexity, which involves fundamental issues of planning. In this phase, the application of the learning model in designing an ideal strategic corporate model of business logic is the most challenging and difficult of all. But it is unlikely that fundamental solutions to problems of planning can be implemented in Phase 5 unless the behavioral culture of the company has already reached a level of true excellence. The final step is critique to find the basis for generalization about further steps toward corporate excellence.

REFERENCES

1. Blake, R. R. Mouton, J. S. University Training in Human Relations Skills. *Group Psychotherapy*, 1961, *14*, 3 & 4. This article included the first published description of the scientific method model of learning. The model described here represents an expansion and refinement of that described in 1961 in the light of field experiments in organization development completed since that time.

Index

Italicized numbers specify Grid styles as differentiated from page numbers.

—Grid theories in, 52

— *See also* Grid Seminar

Phase 2: critique for problem solving in, 115

—motivation through objective setting in, 111

—team communication in, 106

—team culture in, 102

—team objectivity in, 100

—team standards of excellence in, 107

—teamwork skills in, 113

Behavior: knowledge of by line managers, 286

management of, *xi*, 5-6, 24-25

manager objection to criticism of in *Phase 2* Case Study II, 137

measurement of in *Phase 6*, 270

patterns of, 92

shifts in example of attitude problem, 338

systems of supervising, 28

top team, 71

work-oriented discussed in *Phase 2*, 327, 329

Behavior elements, 50, 102

Behavior theory: use of, 5-6

Behavioral science: and the learning process, 347-354

application of to business operations, *xi*, 277-278

change methods, 78

experiments in, 282-283, 328

formulations of as applied to management, 28

future developments and, 279-280

testing management actions with, 15-16

theories of learned in *Phase 1*, 14, 66

Behavioral scientists: in Grid OD, 83, 284, 325

literature by, 78, 90-91

vs. line manager instructors, 284

Benchmarks through critique: *Phase 1 vs. Phase 6*, 268

Benefits, 195

Benevolent Authoritative system of behavior, 28

Benevolent autocrat or *9,5*, 25

Benne, K. D., 91

Bennis, W. G., 91

Beranek, W., 258

Bias *vs.* fact in listening, 55

Blake, R. R., 29, 33, 66, 90, 91, 174, 305, 355

Board of directors and stategic model, 229

Boss as "natural" leader, 324

Boss-subordinate relationship: and vertical slice, 292

communication difficulties in, 5

warmth of, 19

Bowers, M., 229

Bradford, L. P., 91

Breakthrough: an aspect of development in *Phase 4*, 224-225

Budgets in *Phase 4* Case Study, 232

Business: areas of in *Phase 5* Implementation, 243-244

culture of in pyramid theory, 278

nature of, 7, 201

—*See also* Nature of the business

pace of changed, 1

redefinition of through *Phase 4*, 214

segments of in *Phase 5*, 246-247

traditional thinking by top teams, 204

Business logic: *x*, 6-10, 202, 210-228, 353

and financial objectives, 214, 233

and market analysis, 218-219

and nature of the business, 214

and scientific method model of learning, 353-354

in *Phase 4*, 203, 218-219, 279

in *Phase 4* Case Study, 239

lack of, 6-7, 203, 274

use of, 9-10, 201, 210

C

Candor: before and after Grid Seminar, 38, 56

in communication, 54-55

in *Phase 2*, 42, 103, 120

Case method *vs.* the Grid Seminar approach, 37

Chandler, A. D., Jr., 258

Change: behavioral, 53, 92

cultural, 274

induction of, 78

management of by *9,9* methods in *Phase 5*, 256

measurement of in *Phase 6*, 271

need for recognized, 93, 231

resistance to, 256

responsibility for organization, 285

Chaplain, industrial, 26